LEABHARLANNA CHONTAE FHINE GALL
FINGAL COUNTY LIBRARIES

Items should be returned on or before the last date shown below. Items may be renewed by personal application, writing, telephone or by accessing the online Catalogue Service on Fingal Libraries' website. To renew give date due, borrower ticket number and PIN number if using onlinc catalogue. Fines are charged on overdue items and will include postage incurred in recovery. Damage to, or loss of items will be charged to the borrower.

QUINNTESSENTIAL BAKING

Frances Quinn

QUINNTESSENTIAL BAKING

BLOOMSBURY

LONDON · OXFORD · NEW YORK · NEW DELHI · SYDNEY

INTRODUCTION

This is not simply a baking book that will help you turn out an abundance of delicious cakes and biscuits (though, of course, that's a very important part of it!). This is also a book about the imagination – my imagination initially, but also, I hope, yours.

I am a designer just as much as I am a baker, and ideas are as important to me as ingredients. I would no more be without a pencil and paper in my kitchen than I would a spoon or a whisk. People often ask me which I'd rather do: bake or design. But for me, the two are absolutely inseparable. Every bake I create begins life as an idea, which I sketch out with the help of a collection of inspiring images and ingredients. The mood board eventually leads to the cake board.

Just as a potter can use clay to make lots of different pots, so a baker can shape biscuit dough or meringue in a multitude of ways. I see ingredients as yet another medium I can design with, looking for similarities in shape, colour and texture between non-edible and edible things: the way the papery skin on a flower bulb looks like filo pastry, for instance, or the similarity between a rose petal and a dried slice of beetroot. From the beginning I wanted this book to be a witty and wonderful visual feast, as well as a smorgasbord of delicious bakes.

I was born in the same year that my parents opened a bookshop, so was surrounded by the work of illustrators such as Quentin Blake, Judith Kerr and the Ahlbergs from a young age. From Bruce Bogtrotter's chocolate cake in *Matilda* to the impressive eating of *The Tiger Who Came to Tea*, food and fiction inspired me to study art, and I dreamt of becoming an illustrator myself. However, while doing an art foundation course, I fell in love with textiles: studying them enabled me to combine my love of drawing, colour and texture in a particularly bold and graphic way. I find that creating bakes and biscuits does the same thing.

A love of food always ran in parallel with my passion for art and design. I grew up in a big, busy family, the youngest of five. The kitchen was a space in which I felt completely comfortable: somewhere to play and explore as well as eat.

I have always believed that ideas breed ideas. To quote one of my heroes, designer Paul Smith: 'There is inspiration in everything.' Once you let your imagination run free, and start thinking outside the box (or the bowl), you'll discover how true this is. Food should be fun, and I love wordplay just as much as I like visual puns within my designs – that's why you'll find a fluffy llama on one of my banana cakes (who can resist the word 'banana-llama'?!) and why I re-imagined millionaire's shortbread as millionaire's shortchange. Ideas come to me at random times, and one theme, key ingredient or word can help to trigger a thought process that might eventually lead me on to a finished design.

As with all baking, it's important to measure ingredients accurately and follow baking times with care. But when it comes to decorating and adorning your bakes, anything goes! My edible designs are bold, light-hearted and graphic, rather than pretty and twee. Although I respect the art of sugarcraft, I have never felt very comfortable within the established tradition of conventional cake-decorating: fondant flowers and delicately piped swirls of icing are not for me.

I love to take a simple concept – something as mundane as a brick wall (see p.92) – and devise a way to represent it that creates that spark of recognition when people see it, as well as the desire to devour it! And I'm compelled by the challenge of reproducing everyday items with baking ingredients. There's a unique kind of satisfaction that comes from making uncannily life-like baked beans using caramel sauce and nuts (p.43) or creating white chocolate candles that look exactly like the real thing – complete with charred wicks and dripping wax (p.299). With very few exceptions, every item within each of my edible designs is just that – edible! It's important to me that these bakes taste as good as they look.

Because you can't make a great edible design without great building blocks, this book is structured around fifteen essential recipes, from a light vanilla sponge to a billowy meringue. All of these basic recipes are good enough to enjoy with almost no adornment, decorated very simply with a coating of cream or a trickle of melted chocolate (you'll find my finishing suggestions at the end of every basic recipe). But each cake and biscuit can also be used as the basis for countless edible designs, as the ensuing recipes demonstrate. In order to give you the maximum opportunity for exploring your own creativity, I've included information on scaling mixtures up or down, so you can bake cakes and biscuits in a range of shapes and sizes. The mixes can be swapped between designs too – there's no reason not to replace the ginger spice cake with chocolate cake to make my Winter Wonderland Cake (p.124), for instance, or butter biscuit dough with gingerbread when making squirrel cut-outs.

Some of the edible designs take a little time, but none is difficult to achieve. Don't worry if your first bakes have a few rough edges or imperfections, or if it takes you a few tries to get to grips with a piping bag or a palette knife. This is what hand-made, home-baked cakes are all about. I often actively seek an organic, natural look in my bakes – see my Rustic Showstopper (p.106) or Tree Trunk Cakes (p.120), for instance. I'd much rather be served something that looks hand-made and individual than some super-smooth creation, armoured in flawless (and not very tasty) icing. The more you bake, the more your confidence will grow, feeding both your imagination and your appetite.

INGREDIENTS

Combining ingredients and ideas is what I love most about baking. Using basics such as flour, butter and sugar through to nuts, chocolate and spices, you can conjure up a wonderful variety of creations, with all manner of tastes and textures.

FLOUR

Most of the bakes in this book use standard, white self-raising flour. This flour has raising agents already incorporated, so you don't have to add extra baking powder – one less ingredient to worry about! Plain white flour goes into my brownies (which don't need raising agents as they are intended to have a nicely dense texture). I like Doves Farm flours, though good-quality supermarket own-brands are fine too. Whatever you do, make sure your flour is in date. Out-of-date flour can become stale or even rancid, and the raising agents will lose their efficacy.

SUGAR

The heart and soul of cake and biscuit baking, sugar gives character as well as sweetness. I have stuck to five basic varieties for this book (so as not to overwhelm your kitchen cupboards).

• **Standard white caster sugar** is very fine, blends easily into a cake mixture or dough and has the mildest flavour. It's perfect for classic meringues because it dissolves quickly and keeps them snowy-white. It's also a great base for Flavoured Sugar (see p.283) and for Caramel Sauce (p.284).

• **Golden caster sugar** is slightly coarser and a bit less refined, which means it still contains a little of its natural molasses, giving it a slightly more caramelised flavour and golden colour. Use it for butter biscuits and, in conjunction with golden syrup, for brownies, to ensure a gold-star fudgy finish. In meringues, golden caster sugar will give a subtle but sublime butterscotch tinge and taste.

• **Icing sugar** is ground extremely fine, so it mixes very easily into icings and buttercreams. You can use a golden icing sugar or a pure white one. The golden one will give a light brown colour to the mix. Because it is so fine, icing sugar puffs up easily into clouds (make sure you don't breathe in too much of it!). Covering the bowl with a tea towel when you begin mixing icing sugar into anything will stop this cloud of sugar from escaping. It's always a good idea to sift icing sugar before use to get rid of any little lumps.

• **Muscovado sugars**, light brown and dark brown, are full of natural molasses, which gives them a moist, crumbly texture, a dark colour and an amazing toffee flavour. The dark variety has a particularly rich burnt-sugary taste. Muscovado sugars are ideal for cakes that should be deeply coloured and strong in flavour, such as my coffee and walnut cakes, ginger spice cakes and fruit cakes.

GOLDEN SYRUP

I use this golden gem a great deal in my recipes, not just for its lovely, rich flavour but also for its properties. Golden syrup gives gloss and sweetness to my chocolate ganache, makes caramel sauce smooth (you can stir the caramel as it boils without causing crystallisation) and binds flapjacks and tiffins a treat. I'd never be without some in my cupboard. Syrup in a squeezy bottle is very easy to measure out, but I also like the 454g Lyle's tins because, once empty, they make great baking tins (see p.114), not to mention perfect holders for paintbrushes, pens and spatulas.

HONEY

With its incomparable flavour and moisture-holding qualities, honey is a lovely ingredient. It's slightly tricky to use in cake mixtures because it alters their consistency and you will need to adjust other ingredients accordingly. But I often use honey when I make flapjacks and tiffins, and orange blossom honey greatly enhances the flavour of my Orange Blossom Marzipan (see p.286).

BUTTER

Butter gives a beautiful flavour to cakes, as well as richness. I love the taste of slightly salted butter and use it in most of my bakes. You can, of course, use unsalted butter if you prefer.

MASCARPONE & CREAM CHEESE

Mascarpone is a rich, mild, unsalted cheese made from cream. Its very slight acidity means it tastes a little lighter than pure cream, and it makes a fluffy, snowy topping for cakes that has more body and holds its shape longer than whipped cream.

Plain, full-fat cream cheese is more solid in texture but lower in fat than mascarpone. It has a slightly stronger flavour too and is salted. I add it to buttercream to offset the richness of the butter and the sweetness of the sugar, creating a delectable, cheesecake-like flavour. Combined with white chocolate, it also produces a deliciously tangy 'ganache', which is perfect for my sweet Camembert 'cheese' (see p.240).

EGGS

Medium eggs are used in all the recipes in the book (I prefer free-range or organic). Many people keep their eggs in the fridge, but I don't because very cold eggs can cause a cake mixture to split and curdle. If you do store your eggs in the fridge, take them out in good time before you need them so they can come to room temperature.

Medium eggs range from 53g to 63g. With a 60g egg – my preferred weight – you get 35g white and 15g yolk (with the shell making up the remaining 10g). The variation in egg weight can affect your bakes, leaving mixtures a little too loose or a little too dry – so much so that I weigh my eggs on digital scales and write their weights on the shells. I then try to use the lower-weight eggs in biscuit doughs and the bang-on 60g ones to make up cake mixtures. You can mix your eggs to achieve a similar result: i.e. in a 3-egg cake mix, you could use three 60g eggs, or one 58g plus one 62g plus one 60g. If I only have 'heavy' eggs – i.e. over 60g – I sometimes don't add all the white to the mixture.

CHOCOLATE

One of the most important ingredients in the book! Luckily, good-quality chocolate is very easy to find these days. I like Green & Black's, which comes in a wide range of flavours. The gold foil wrapping on their bars is an added bonus as it's great for decorating bakes.

Whichever shade of chocolate you are using, go for one with a relatively high cocoa solids content – this means you'll get a good, rich chocolate flavour and a better, cleaner texture. With dark chocolate, look for one with 60–72 per cent cocoa solids. You can get higher-cocoa dark chocolate but it can taste quite bitter.

You'll find a lot of other kinds of chocolate used in my bakes because I get inspiration from a very wide range of popular confectionery and classic sweets, from Cadbury chocolate buttons to Rolos, Munchies, Ferrero Rocher and Reese's Mini Peanut Butter Cups.

COCOA POWDER

For the best flavour, I recommend using a high-quality cocoa powder when baking – my favourite is Green & Black's. Unsweetened cocoa powder has a much richer cocoa flavour than drinking chocolate powder, which contains sugar, and its deep brown colour makes it perfect for creating dramatic stencilled designs on your bakes – see my

Coffee Barcode Cake (p.89), for example. For a stylish tonal design you could use a mix of cocoa powders (Cadbury Bournville is lighter than Green & Black's) or contrast with drinking chocolate powder.

NUTS

Nuts of all kinds – from big, chunky brazils to finely ground almonds and hazelnuts – are a much-used ingredient in my kitchen. Pistachios, with their amazing green colour, are especially useful: when ground up, they make perfect 'grass', or can be turned into marzipan and used to create leaves and other greenery.

Buy nuts in the quantities you need, rather than in bulk, and use them quickly because nuts left in the cupboard for long periods can go stale or rancid. Whether used whole, roughly chopped or finely ground, lightly toasting the nuts first – about 5–10 minutes at 180°C/160°c fan/gas 4 – will really help to enhance their flavour.

Ready-ground almonds are easy to find, and ground roasted hazelnuts are available in some supermarkets, healthfood shops and online. But grinding nuts is easy in a small food processor or spice/coffee grinder. Just blitz them to a fine texture, stopping as soon as you get the consistency you want. If you over-process nuts, they can start to release their oils, which will cause them to become greasy and clump together.

BARLEY MALT EXTRACT

I've always had an affection for this ingredient, a by-product of the brewing industry. Its sweetness, its deep, malty 'Horlicks' taste and its dark colour make it useful in many of my recipes, including Malted Milk & Cookies (see p.182) and Bourbon Brick Brownies (p.174).

JAMS & CURDS

If you're not making your own jams and curds for filling cakes (see recipes on pp.272–3), then shop around to find a good-quality brand that you like. Tiptree is a favourite of mine: their preserves are delicious and British-made to boot.

CITRUS FRUIT

If you want to grate the zest from citrus fruit, try to buy unwaxed fruit – oranges and limes can be hard to find but lemons are readily available – or get organic citrus, all of which is unwaxed. If you only have waxed fruit, scrub it in hot, soapy water, rinse well and dry before taking the zest.

FREEZE-DRIED BERRIES

These are relatively new ingredients and I'm a real convert – they're like Nature's hundreds and thousands! The dehydrated fruit retains a concentrated flavour and colour, giving you an intense fruity experience. Freeze-dried berries can be bought whole, as small pieces or as a powder. For most baking purposes, the pieces are most useful as they can be sprinkled on bakes or ground down – it's a good idea to sift out the seeds from powders such as raspberry and strawberry, to ensure your marzipans and meringues are smooth rather than speckled. Larger pieces of freeze-dried fruit make stunning decorations (see my Edible Confetti on p.295). Freeze-dried fruit can be found in some supermarkets and healthfood shops, and there are plenty of online suppliers (see directory, p.307).

VANILLA

This quintessential baking ingredient brings its unique, sweetly pungent, aromatic flavour to so many cakes and biscuits. I love the way its richness enhances simple mixtures and toppings, making them so much more exciting. I always use vanilla extract, rather than anything labelled 'flavouring' or 'essence'. These may contain no real vanilla at all and tend to have a synthetic and very inferior flavour. I also sometimes use vanilla bean paste – a thicker mixture full of real vanilla seeds, which look lovely suspended in a sponge or custard. Finally, a vanilla bean grinder – which you can buy for a few pounds, with the vanilla pods already in it – allows you to grind pure vanilla into a dark powder that makes a perfect sweet seasoning (you can also buy ready-ground vanilla powder). I use it to mimic black pepper to serve alongside my Fish & Chip Cakes (see p.34).

SPICES

Ground mixed spice, ginger and cinnamon find their way into many of my cakes, biscuits and flavoured sugars. Ready-ground spices can lose their flavour and freshness relatively quickly, so buy them in small quantities. Ground spices past their use-by date may be disappointingly bland.

FLOWER-SCENTED WATERS

Rose water and orange blossom water (also called orange flower water) contribute a distinct, perfumed flavour to marzipans, meringues and toppings. Always add them carefully, a little at a time, as different brands can vary quite a lot in their strength. Nielsen Massey flower waters and extracts are my preferred choice.

EQUIPMENT

My kitchen is an extension of my creative space, so the equipment and utensils I use are as much design-related as they are baking. My worktops are full of jars and tins brimming with spoons, spatulas, rulers, paintbrushes, wooden latte stirrers and cocktail sticks. Even the lid of the cocktail stick container is put to good use to cut out gingerbread biscuits. Although I encourage you to use everyday items for creating your bakes, I also recommend that you invest in some essential equipment and tools to make your baking easier and help ensure successful results.

YOUR OVEN

Nobody knows your oven better than you. All ovens differ slightly and the more you bake, the better you will understand your own. An oven thermometer is very useful for gauging exactly what temperature an oven is at (I sometimes take my thermometer with me if I'm baking away from home): the dial is not always completely accurate and the temperature can fluctuate. You may find your oven is a little 'hot', or a little 'cool', or that it tends to brown things very quickly, or the opposite. As you get to know your oven, you'll be able to compensate for its idiosyncrasies by allowing an extra minute here,

or turning down the temperature a few degrees there. Generally, I bake all my cakes in the middle of the oven but you can move them up or down, or turn them around, to speed or slow browning.

DIGITAL SCALES

I couldn't be without this essential bit of kit. Salter is a good brand. Apart from weighing out ingredients very accurately, which is so important when you are baking, digital scales are brilliant for dividing up biscuit doughs and marzipan precisely, and even weighing cake mixtures into tins or muffin cases to ensure even sizing (see p.22 for more information about this). And, because you can weigh everything into one bowl, just 'zero-ing' the scales between ingredients, digital scales can really help save on the washing-up.

CAKE TINS & BAKING TRAYS

Always buy top-quality tins and baking trays: cheap ones are a false economy as they will warp, which can lead to uneven baking and even burning. Solid, non-stick tins and baking trays, such as those made by Master Class and Alan Silverwood (see directory, p.308), are excellent.

If you kit yourself out with the following tins you'll be able to make most of the cakes in the book:
- 10cm, 15cm, 20cm and 23cm round, loose-bottomed tins (7–8cm deep)
- 20cm square loose-bottomed tin (4cm deep)
- 900g (2lb) loaf tin (mine is 21 x 11cm and 7cm deep)
- 20 x 27cm brownie tin (3.5cm deep)
- 12-hole muffin tin (7 x 2.5cm hole)
- 24-hole mini-muffin tin (4 x 2cm hole)

CALCULATOR, RULER, PENS & PAPER

These may not sound like obvious bits of baking equipment but they are 'Quinn-tessential' to me. My bakes start as graphic designs: sketching, measuring and some basic maths are all part of the process of realising them. Arm yourself with these tools and you'll be able to reproduce my designs – and your own – with ease.

MEASURING SPOONS

These are vital to ensure ingredients such as spices and extracts are measured precisely. Inexpensive sets (I'd recommend those made from stainless steel) can be bought at supermarkets as well as baking suppliers. The base of the spoon 'bowl' also makes a handy tool for pressing into biscuit dough to create debossed buttons etc.

BAKING PARCHMENT

Use this non-stick, silicone-coated paper to line all of your tins and trays. Don't confuse it with greaseproof paper, which is not non-stick. When baking biscuits, sheets of parchment can be turned over and re-used – sometimes more than once. The paper is also great for drying out fruit and vegetables to make Edible Confetti (see p.295).

MIXER/HAND WHISK

I am very fond of my free-standing mixer as it allows me to do two jobs at once, and it beats, whisks and whips mixtures very efficiently. But there's nothing in this book that can't be made equally well using a hand-held electric whisk – and, indeed, smaller quantities, such as one-egg cake batches, are easier to beat with a hand-held whisk as they would get a bit 'lost' in a big mixer bowl.

FOOD PROCESSOR/SPICE GRINDER

A food processor will chop nuts fast, although you can of course do this by hand with a sharp knife. For grinding small quantities of nuts, pulverising freeze-dried fruit or blitzing desiccated coconut to make coconut marzipan, I use an electric coffee grinder or a mini electric chopper. You can also use an electric spice grinder, or a small food mill attachment on a processor for these jobs – or even a Nutribullet blender. It's difficult to get a very fine-textured result in a large food processor or by hand.

MICROPLANE FINE GRATER

I find this very fine, sharp grater a whiz for grating citrus zests for marzipans, cakes and curds.

CUTTERS

There's an amazing range of biscuit and pastry cutters available now, from the classic fluted-edged round ones in various sizes, to pretty much any other design you can think of. I generally prefer to use metal cutters, as they produce a sharper outline. That said, I'm a big fan of plastic 'plunger' cutters (see directory, pp.308–9) for small and intricate shapes, such as leaves and snowflakes. These don't just cut the dough, but also indent it with added detail and then allow you to pop out the shape very neatly with the use of a little plunger attached to the cutter.

Aside from these purpose-made tools, my kitchen is full of objects to be used to create shapes, including hexagonal lids from cocktail stick containers, pen lids and bottle caps. I also often use the wide top of piping nozzles as cutters.

PIZZA CUTTER & HERB CUTTER

A pizza cutter is a single, sharp cutting wheel that's incredibly useful when you need to cut straight, even lines, such as for marzipan 'ribbons' or biscuit 'chips' and 'matches'. Herb roller cutters, which have several parallel blades, can also be used to create multiple strips of biscuit dough or marzipan.

PALETTE KNIFE

A flexible palette knife enables you to spread icing smoothly and evenly. I use a small one for covering cupcakes and a larger one for big cakes. A cranked palette knife, where the blade is angled downwards from the handle and then angled flat again, is very useful for smoothing out cake mixtures in the tin and lifting biscuits off trays.

LATTE STIRRERS & COCKTAIL STICKS

You'll find wooden latte stirrer sticks (the kind you get in coffee shops) have a multitude of uses when you're creating edible designs. I use them for sculpting, marking, stencilling and measuring. You can buy them online in large quantities – around 1000 – for just a few pounds, or ask your local barista. Basic wooden cocktail sticks are another invaluable tool.

BRUSHES

I use medium- and fine-tipped paintbrushes to apply melted chocolate, ganache and gold leaf in a controlled manner. The blunt end of a paintbrush can also come in handy for making holes. There's no need to buy expensive brushes, but I would recommend some decent-quality ones from an art supply shop. Larger pastry brushes are brilliant for applying sugar syrups, or for putting edible 'paint' on to my Painter's Palette biscuits (see p.216).

SILICONE SPATULA

This is so useful for stirring and smoothly picking up caramel/sugar from the base and sides of a saucepan and scraping every last bit of mix from a bowl.

DEHYDRATOR

Although not an essential bit of kit, this food-drying machine is something I now wouldn't be without. It allows you to dry fruit and veg (for my Edible Confetti on p.295, for instance) in a precise and controlled way, and I think it preserves the colours of fruit better than oven-drying. A dehydrator will also perfume your house beautifully with fruity fragrance while it works. Dehydrators can be expensive, but if you shop around you can get one online for as little as £20 (see directory, p.309).

BISCUIT MAKER

This may not be a piece of equipment you use often, but it can come in handy. It's like a gun that you 'load' with biscuit dough, then push out the dough through different plates to make a variety of shapes. Unconventionally, I use it to produce long strands of dough for my Sweet Bombay Mix (see p.214). You can buy biscuit makers online (see directory, p.308).

TECHNIQUES

As with anything, the more you bake, the more your confidence and skill in the kitchen will grow. The basic techniques explained here – from lining tins to creating stencils – will give you a good foundation for making all the recipes that follow.

Baking parchment is best for lining tins and baking trays because it really is non-stick and you don't need to brush it with grease or fat. However, I use a little butter (the paper from a pack of butter is very handy for this) or cake-release spray to grease the tin or tray first so that the parchment sticks to it.

To **fully line** a round, square or rectangular tin, simply draw around the base of the tin on the parchment, then cut out the piece from just inside the drawn line to fit neatly on to the base of the tin. Then cut strips, a little wider than the depth of the tin, to line the sides; overlap the strips slightly to make sure all the interior of the tin is covered.

For wetter cake mixtures, you may want to set loose-bottomed tins on a baking tray, or line using what I like to call the **'snip-snip' method**. Cut out two pieces of parchment for the base rather than one, and lay one in place. Cut the strip(s) for the sides 5cm wider than the depth of the tin. Fold in 2.5cm along one long edge of the strip(s), then with scissors snip the fold up to the crease at 1cm intervals. Line the sides of the tin with the strip(s) so that the snipped fold lies flat on the base. Lay the second base piece on top of this 'fringe'.

The lining paper can help you to remove a bake from its tin – particularly useful if your tin isn't loose-bottomed. For square and rectangular tins (including loaf tins), line the base and two sides with one long, continuous piece of parchment that overhangs on either side. I call this a **'seatbelt strap'**. The overhang will act as 'handles' that enable you to lift out the cake once baked. Line the remaining two sides with separate strips of parchment.

I usually line muffin tins with paper or foil cases, but you can sometimes use seatbelt straps. First lightly grease the holes of the muffin tin, then cut a fairly narrow strip of parchment (1–2cm wide, depending on the size of the hole) for each and lay it inside, making sure the ends come up above the rim of the hole on opposite sides.

BEATING BUTTER & SUGAR TOGETHER
This is a crucial first step when making any kind of sponge cake, such as my vanilla, lemon and coffee and walnut cakes, as it incorporates lots of air into the

mixture and makes for a light finish. When you taste a cake, you can tell whether the butter and sugar were beaten properly – if not, the cake has a heavier, coarser feel. Start with really soft butter and use a free-standing mixer or a hand-held electric whisk (you can do it by hand with a wooden spoon but it's very hard work and you'll never achieve quite the same level of fluffiness). Beat the butter and sugar together, starting off at a medium speed and building up to full speed. Stop and scrape down the side of the bowl and the beaters a few times if you need to. Keep beating for at least 5 minutes and up to 10 or until the mixture has grown significantly paler – if you're using caster sugar, the mix should become almost white – and is very light and moussey-looking. I generally use my mixer for this step and leave it running while I complete other tasks, such as lining tins, chopping nuts and weighing out other ingredients.

FOLDING IN

Once you've beaten all that air into the butter/sugar/egg base, it's important not to knock it all out again, so other ingredients such as flour or chopped nuts should be folded in. This means using a light scooping and cutting motion, rather than a stirring action. Take a large metal spoon or a spatula, pass it edgeways on through the middle of the mixture, scoop underneath and fold some of the mixture over on itself. Give the bowl a quarter turn and repeat, until all the ingredients are just combined.

USING SCALES TO DIVIDE MIXTURES

When baking small individual cakes, I like to use digital scales to calculate exactly how much mixture needs to go into each muffin case or other container. I sometimes do this when dividing mixtures between larger tins too. I weigh the empty mixing bowl first, then weigh it again when the mixture is in it. If you deduct the weight of the bowl you are left with the weight of the mixture, which you can then divide by 12 or 24 (or however many cases or tins you want to fill). This will give you the amount of mixture you need to put into each one. After filling one case and having seen how much mixture ½th or ¼th fills, you can continue filling by eye. Or set each muffin case or other container on the scales and fill with the right weight of mixture before placing back into the muffin tin.

MELTING CHOCOLATE

Chocolate will 'split' and turn grainy if it gets too hot (and once that has happened, it can be hard to rectify the situation, although stirring in some milk or syrup can help), so it's important to melt it gently. Begin by chopping the chocolate into small pieces to speed the melting time. You can use a DIY bain-marie: a heatproof bowl set over a pan of just simmering water. Make sure that the base of the bowl doesn't actually touch the water, but is just heated by the steam in the pan. Watch the chocolate carefully, stir gently from time to time and remove from the heat as soon as it is soft and melted. Alternatively, use a microwave, set at a low to medium power, heating the chocolate in short blasts and keeping a close eye on it (especially white chocolate) so that it doesn't burn.

FILLING PIPING BAGS & PIPING

Piping bags are brilliant because they give you so much control – and you don't have to be some kind of sugarcraft genius in order to use one! I'm not much of a one for piping delicate swirls and rosettes, but instead use a piping bag to help fill muffin cases (you can also use a teaspoon, but I think piping is much easier and less fiddly); to apply icings and toppings accurately before spreading them out with a palette knife; and to fill a cake in a neat, even layer. The bags are also great if you want to pipe chocolate: you can melt the chocolate in the bag itself, set in a jug of hot water (a nifty technique first shared with me by my baking friend Jo).

I use disposable plastic piping bags, which you can buy on a roll. They come with their pointed end still sealed – you just snip it off to create the size of aperture you need. For quite accurate piping, you can slot a piping nozzle into the end of the bag.

To fill a piping bag, place it, pointed end down, inside a tall jug or vase – this will support the bag while you spoon your filling into it. As you spoon, shake the bag gently to help move the filling down inside. If air is trapped at the pointed end of the bag, stopping the filling from moving down, snip off the tip of the bag. Be sure not to fill the bag to the very top or you will get into an awful mess when you try to close the end – you can always pipe in two batches if necessary. Twist the open end of the bag to seal it, then twist further to move the filling down to the opening. Do your piping by twisting the top of the bag, and applying pressure from this end, rather than by squeezing the bag in the middle.

ROLLING OUT DOUGHS & MARZIPAN

I like to do my rolling out between sheets of baking parchment, rather than on a flour- or sugar-dusted surface – though you can always add a light dusting of flour if your dough seems very sticky. One great advantage to using parchment is that once you have rolled out the dough and peeled off the top layer of parchment, you can cut out your shapes or biscuits on the base parchment, then

remove the excess dough from around them and lift them, still on the parchment, directly on to a baking tray. This means you don't have to move the shapes, which could distort them. The excess dough you've removed can be squashed together and re-rolled between the removed layer of parchment and a fresh sheet so you can cut more shapes.

CREATING TEMPLATES & STENCILS

Some of my bakes use a template or stencil to add a design or decoration. You can trace my drawings from the book, or photocopy the page, or draw your own decorative shape freehand on a piece of thin card, such as an old cereal box. If you've used tracing paper or made a photocopy, stick it to a piece of card, then cut out the shape with scissors or a scalpel, leaving the outer card in one piece.

Use the cut-out shape as a template – when making biscuits, for example, lay it on the rolled-out dough and cut around it. The rest of the card with the empty shape in the centre can be used as a stencil: lay it on or near a surface, such as the top of a cake, and dust with icing sugar, cocoa or other powder, then lift off the card to reveal the shape on the cake.

CUTTING OUT CORES FROM CUPCAKES

This is a nifty technique that allows you to create cupcakes with delicious, hidden centres of jam, cream or other fillings. A specially designed cupcake corer makes this very easy, but you can just use a small cutter or knife. Take a 3.5cm diameter 'core' from each cupcake, cutting down to a depth of about 2.5cm. Once you have put your filling in the hole and gently pushed the 'core' back in, it will protrude slightly. This doesn't matter if you are going to be covering it with a topping; if you're not, take a slice off the base of the 'core' before you put it back in.

VANILLA CAKE

Light, fluffy and golden, this cake is true to the spirit of a classic Victoria sponge. However, it contains much more vanilla than Victoria is used to, which is why I've re-christened it. The delicacy of the cake and its sweet vanilla flavour make it particularly good paired with fresh fruit and cream – perfect for an old-fashioned high tea.

If you'd like to see those delicious vanilla seeds in the cake crumb, as well as taste them, feel free to use a seed-flecked vanilla bean paste rather than a liquid vanilla extract. But please keep it pure and simple: whatever you do, don't use anything called vanilla 'essence' – it will be synthetic and the flavour will let you down.

BASIC VANILLA CAKE

FOR THE CAKE
50g butter, softened
50g caster sugar
1 egg (at room temperature)
1 tsp vanilla extract
50g self-raising flour
1 tsp warm water

EQUIPMENT
10cm round, deep, loose-
 bottomed tin (pork-pie size),
 greased and fully lined

Preheat the oven to 180°C/160°C fan/gas 4.

Using a hand-held electric whisk (it's tricky to beat this small quantity in a free-standing mixer), beat the butter and sugar together for 5–10 minutes or until very light, pale and creamy.

Break the egg into a mug or jug (this makes it easy and less messy to pour into the mixture). Add the vanilla extract to the egg and beat with a fork. Gradually add the egg to the creamed butter and sugar mixture, beating well after each addition. Should the mixture look like it's curdling, add a spoonful of the flour.

Sift the flour into the cake mixture and fold in until just combined. (If you are making one of the larger quantities – see table opposite – sift and fold in the flour in several batches.)

Gently fold in the warm water, which will loosen the mixture and lighten the finished cake. You will now have a cake mixture with a soft dropping consistency – i.e. if you take a dollop of it on a spoon and turn the spoon on its side, the mixture will drop off of its own accord. Scrape the cake mixture into the prepared tin and spread it out level with a spatula.

Bake for 20–25 minutes or until risen and golden, and a skewer inserted into the centre of the cake comes out clean with no damp cake mixture adhering to it. Leave to cool in the tin for 10 minutes before removing the cake and transferring to a wire rack to cool completely.

TO FINISH

This lovely vanilla sponge is particularly good split into two layers and then sandwiched back together with fresh whipped cream and jam. I also like it topped in Buttercream (see p.276) or Sweetened Mascarpone Cream (p.278) and decorated with fresh fruit and flowers and my Edible Confetti (p.295). You can use the mixture to make mini- and muffin-sized cupcakes too, and decorate them with all sorts of finishes and flavours.

TO MAKE DIFFERENT-SIZED VANILLA CAKES, USE THE TABLE OPPOSITE >>

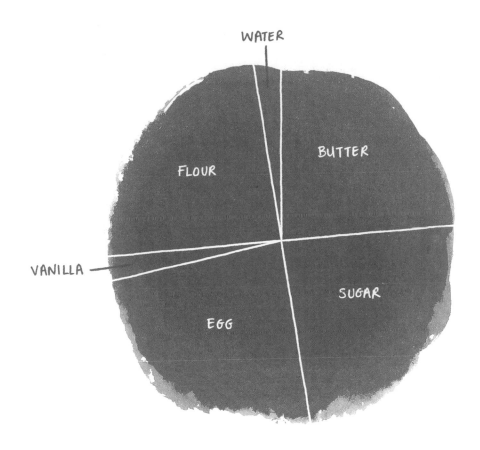

24-HOLE MINI-MUFFIN TIN	12-HOLE MUFFIN TIN	20CM SQUARE TIN	20CM ROUND DEEP TIN	900G (2LB) LOAF TIN	INGREDIENTS
50g	150g	150g	200g	200g	Butter, softened
50g	150g	150g	200g	200g	Caster sugar
1	3	3	4	4	Egg(s)
1 tsp	3 tsp	3 tsp	4 tsp	4 tsp	Vanilla extract
50g	150g	150g	200g	200g	Self-raising flour
1 tsp	3 tsp	3 tsp	4 tsp	4 tsp	Warm water

BAKE IN AN OVEN PREHEATED TO 180°C/160°C FAN/GAS 4					
for 10–12 minutes	for 15–20 minutes	for 25–30 minutes	for 45–50 minutes, or in 2 sandwich tins for 20–25 minutes	for 45–50 minutes	

STRAWBERRY SHORTCAKE

MAKES A 10CM CAKE;
SERVES 2–3

FOR THE CAKE
50g butter, softened
50g caster sugar
1 egg (at room temperature)
1 tsp vanilla extract
50g self-raising flour
1 tsp warm water

TO DECORATE
50g strawberry jam –
    homemade (see p.272)
    or shop-bought
50ml double cream
½ tbsp icing sugar
Few drops of vanilla extract
9 shortcake biscuits
1 medium and 2 small
    strawberries
About 1 tsp freeze-dried
    strawberry pieces

EQUIPMENT
10cm round, deep, loose-
    bottomed tin (pork-pie size),
    greased and fully lined

Here you can have your cake and eat it, together with a biscuit or two! This fusion of vanilla sponge, jam, cream, strawberries and the all-important, buttery shortcake biscuits sums up British summertime at its sweetest. I use the classic, fluted-edged shop-bought shortbread biscuits for this, which measure 6 x 3.5cm. Serve with extra strawberries, if you like.

Preheat the oven to 180°C/160°C fan/gas 4.

Using a hand-held electric whisk (it's tricky to beat this small quantity in a free-standing mixer), beat the butter and sugar together for 5–10 minutes or until very light, pale and creamy. Lightly beat the egg with the vanilla extract. Gradually add the egg to the butter and sugar mixture, beating well after each addition. Sift the flour into the mixture and fold in until just combined, then gently fold in the warm water. Scrape the cake mixture into the prepared tin and spread it out level with a spatula.

Bake for 20–25 minutes or until a skewer inserted into the centre of the cake comes out clean. Leave to cool in the tin for 10 minutes before removing the cake and transferring to a wire rack to cool completely.

Use a long, serrated knife, such as a bread knife, to carefully slice the cake horizontally into two equal layers. If the cake is very domed, you can also level off the top to create a smooth, flat surface for the topping. However, a slightly domed top is fine.

Place the bottom cake layer on your chosen cake board or stand. Spread a few teaspoons of jam over the cut surface – don't be too generous because you don't want the jam to spill out too much. Place the other cake layer on top. Put the cream in a bowl with the icing sugar and vanilla extract, and whip until the cream holds soft to medium peaks. Spoon the cream on top of the cake and smooth it out with a palette knife, creating a slightly textured finish.

Spread some jam over the back of each shortcake biscuit to act as 'glue': spread the jam over three-quarters of the biscuit, leaving the top quarter uncovered. If your jam contains chunks of fruit, avoid them, because any lumps will create an uneven finish.

CONTINUED OVERLEAF >>

STRAWBERRY SHORTCAKE (CONTINUED)

Press the biscuits around the side of the cake, with the un-jammed sections uppermost, to give a clean finish. The nine biscuits won't be wedged tightly up against one another: there should be a few millimetres between them, creating neat spaces for cutting the cake into even slices.

Decorate the top of the cake with the three strawberries, placing the larger one in the centre and the smaller two alongside, slightly off-centre. Scatter the freeze-dried strawberry pieces over the top.

Extra strawberries and freeze-dried strawberry pieces look lovely scattered around the cake, and I like to serve extra whipped cream alongside the cake in a pretty bowl.

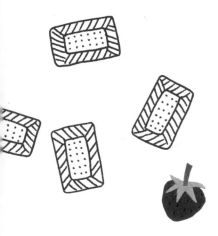

WIMBLEDON CUPCAKES

MAKES 12 CUPCAKES

FOR THE CAKES
150g butter, softened
150g caster sugar
3 eggs (at room temperature)
1 tbsp vanilla extract
150g self-raising flour
1 tbsp warm water

FOR THE BISCUIT RACKETS
220g Basic Butter Biscuits dough
   (⅓ quantity; see p.206)

FOR THE TENNIS BALLS
A little lemon juice or water
12 lemon bonbons
100g icing sugar

TO DECORATE
300g strawberry jam –
   homemade (see p.272) or
   shop-bought
50g ground pistachios, optional
   (see directory, p.307)
12 small strawberries

FOR THE CHANTILLY CREAM
300ml double cream
3 tbsp icing sugar
A few drops of vanilla extract

EQUIPMENT
12-hole muffin tin
12 gold-foil muffin cases
Tennis racket template
   (see overleaf)
Wooden latte stirrer or
   cocktail stick
Small piping bag fitted with
   a fine, round nozzle
3.5cm round biscuit cutter

These fruit-topped cakes celebrate strawberries and Wimbledon: a perfect match. Covered in cream, with the option of ground pistachio 'grass', each cake is served up with a biscuit tennis racket and a lemon bonbon tennis ball. To ensure these cakes score an ace, a drop shot of jam can be found hidden at the centre of each one. Make the biscuit dough ahead of time so it can chill; you can put it in the freezer to speed up the firming time.

Preheat the oven to 180°C/160°C fan/gas 4, and line the muffin tin with the foil muffin cases.

To make the cake mixture, using either a hand-held electric whisk, or in a free-standing mixer, beat the butter and sugar together for 5–10 minutes or until very light, pale and creamy. Lightly beat the eggs with the vanilla extract. Gradually add the eggs to the butter and sugar mixture, beating well after each addition. Sift the flour into the mixture in batches, folding in each batch until just combined, then gently fold in the warm water. Spoon the cake mixture into the muffin cases.

Bake for 15–20 minutes or until the cakes have risen and are lightly golden brown, and a skewer inserted into the centre comes out clean. Set aside for 10 minutes to cool slightly before removing the cupcakes from the tin, still in their foil cases, to a wire rack to finish cooling. Leave the oven on.

While the cupcakes are baking, place the biscuit dough between two sheets of baking parchment and roll out to about 5mm thickness. (I snip off the rounded end of a wooden lollipop stick or coffee stirrer, then mark a 5mm measurement on the stick, to use as a guide when rolling out dough.)

Peel off the top layer of parchment and use the tennis racket template to cut out six biscuits. Pull up the surrounding dough and re-roll it between more parchment paper to cut another six biscuits (remove the surrounding dough). Lift the rackets, on their parchment, on to two baking trays.

Use a latte stirrer or the back of a sharp knife to create indented lines on the handles of the rackets. To create the indented outline within the racket head, cut a 2cm-wide strip of cardboard that is roughly 12cm long – I use a piece cut from a cereal packet or from a baking parchment box – and tape it into an oval-ring shape that will fit within the head of the racket. Press this shape into the dough, going just under halfway through, to create an oval imprint.

CONTINUED OVERLEAF >>

WIMBLEDON CUPCAKES (CONTINUED)

Use the back of the small sharp knife to run diagonal lines across the racket head, keeping within the indented oval. Repeat in the opposite direction to create a criss-cross racket string effect. Transfer the trays of biscuits to the fridge to chill while you make the bonbon tennis balls.

Start by wetting a sheet of kitchen paper or a clean sponge with a little lemon juice or water, then dab the bonbons with it in order to remove some of their powdered sugar coating. This will intensify their yellow colour and make them look more like tennis balls.

For the markings on the bonbon balls, make up some icing by sifting the icing sugar into a bowl and stirring in a little water or lemon juice, a few drops at a time, until you have a smooth, spreadable consistency. Transfer the icing to the piping bag fitted with the fine nozzle. Dab a little blob of icing on each bonbon to hold it in place and put it on a board, then carefully pipe curved tennis ball markings on to the bonbon. Leave the icing to set.

Take the tennis racket biscuits from the fridge and bake (at 180°C/160°C fan/gas 4) for 10–15 minutes or until lightly golden and firm. If you find the racket handles are browning quicker than the heads, you can wrap them carefully in little foil 'gloves', then return the rackets to the oven to finish baking. Leave the biscuits to cool on the baking tray for about 5 minutes before transferring to a wire rack to cool fully.

To assemble your cakes, use the biscuit cutter or a small sharp knife (or the wide end of a sharp metal piping nozzle) to cut out and remove a 'core' from each cupcake. The ideal diameter of the cut piece is 3.5cm and the ideal depth about 2.5cm. (Don't go right through to the base.) Keep these cut-out pieces.

Spoon about 1 tablespoon strawberry jam into the hole in each cupcake. Return the cut-out pieces to the cakes, on top of the jam, and press down like a plug, but not so firmly that the jam spills out over the top. Each cut-out piece will now protrude slightly above the surface of the cake.

To make the Chantilly cream, pour the cream into a bowl. Sift over the icing sugar and add the vanilla extract. With a hand-held electric whisk, whip the cream to soft medium peaks. Dollop a heaped tablespoonful of cream on to the top of each cupcake and use a small palette knife to spread the cream evenly over the cake. If using the ground pistachios, scatter over the cakes to mimic grass. Place a tennis racket biscuit on top of each cupcake, together with a bonbon tennis ball and a small strawberry.

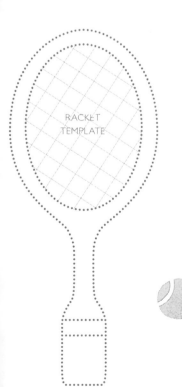

RACKET TEMPLATE

FISH & CHIP CAKES

FOR THE CAKES
50g butter, softened
50g caster sugar
1 egg (at room temperature)
1 tsp vanilla extract
50g self-raising flour
1 tsp warm water

TO DECORATE
220g Basic Butter Biscuits dough
    (⅓ quantity; see p.206)
50g Pistachio Marzipan (p.287)
Pistachio paste (see directory,
    p.307)

FOR THE BUTTERCREAM
50g butter, softened
100g icing sugar, sifted
½ tbsp lemon juice
½ tsp lemon extract or
    the finely grated zest
    of ½ lemon

EQUIPMENT
24-hole mini-muffin tin
24 paper take-away sauce pots
    – 1fl oz (25ml) capacity
    (see directory, p.308)
Fish template (see below) or
    mini fish-shaped cutter
    (see directory, p.308)
Cocktail sticks
2 large piping bags with optional
    1.5cm round nozzle
Wooden latte stirrer

FISH TEMPLATE

These aren't your typical fish cakes: they're mini vanilla cakes decorated with buttery, sweet 'fish' and tiny biscuit 'chips'. They're not baked in typical cake cases either: I've used little paper sauce pots to play on the take-away nature of fish and chips. You can take the chip shop theme even further by making a vanilla syrup (see p.282), topping it up with the lemon juice left over from the lemon buttercream, and displaying it in a retro vinegar bottle to accompany the cakes. You can even add salt and pepper pots filled with vanilla sugar (p.283) and ground vanilla seeds or vanilla powder (see directory, p.307). With a side of pistachio marzipan peas – mushy peas, if you like – and displayed on sheets of newspaper, these cakes are anything but yesterday's news.

Start with the biscuit fish for decoration. You will need 48 biscuits if you want to decorate each cake with two fish. Place half of your biscuit dough between two sheets of baking parchment and roll out to the thickness of a £1 coin. Peel off the top layer of parchment and, using the mini fish cutter or template, cut out your fish shapes. Pull up the surrounding dough and re-roll between fresh parchment to cut more fish. Peel away the excess dough.

Lift the fish, on their parchment, on to a baking tray. Use a cocktail stick to mark their eyes and create smiley mouths (if you want happy fish). Put into the fridge to chill for about 15 minutes.

Next create your biscuit 'chips' using the remaining dough. Again roll out between two sheets of baking parchment to about £1 coin thickness. Peel off the top layer of parchment. Using a ruler and a sharp knife or pizza cutter, cut the dough into 'chips' about 5mm wide (about the width of a wooden latte stirrer) and about 15cm long. It helps to run the knife or pizza cutter through some flour between cuts to prevent the dough from sticking.

Pick the chips up and lay them back down on their parchment so there is a little space between them. You need 10 chips per cake but it's a good idea to make more so you can choose the best. Roll out the dough trimmings and mark out a second batch of chips. You'll probably need two pieces of parchment for all the chips.

Lift the chips, on their parchment, on to two baking trays and chill for about 15 minutes. If you don't have three baking trays (one for the fish biscuits, two for the chips), chill one lot of biscuits at a time and get the next batch into the fridge while the previous batch is baking.

CONTINUED OVERLEAF >>

FISH & CHIP CAKES (CONTINUED)

While the biscuits are chilling, preheat the oven to 180°C/160°C fan/gas 4, and line the muffin tin with the sauce pots.

Next make your cakes. Using a hand-held electric whisk (it's tricky to beat this small quantity in a free-standing mixer), beat the butter and sugar together for 5–10 minutes or until very light, pale and creamy. Break the egg into a mug or jug. Add the vanilla and beat with a fork. Gradually add the egg to the creamed butter and sugar mixture, beating well after each addition. Should the mixture look like it's curdling at any stage, add a spoonful of the flour. Sift the flour into the mixture and fold in until just combined. Gently fold in the warm water to make a cake mixture with a soft dropping consistency.

Transfer the mixture to a piping bag fitted with the 1.5cm nozzle; if you are using a disposable piping bag, you can just snip off a similar-sized opening from the tip. Pipe into the sauce pots. (Alternatively, you can fill the pots using a teaspoon, but the piping bag makes it a lot quicker and less fiddly.) I like to weigh the mixture first and divide by 24 so I know exactly how much to put into each pot (see p.22 for more information), but this isn't essential.

Bake for 10–12 minutes or until the cakes are risen and lightly golden brown and a skewer inserted into the centre comes out clean. Leave to cool in the tin for 5 minutes before removing, still in the sauce pots, and transferring to a wire rack to cool completely. Leave the oven on for the biscuits.

Remove the chilled fish and chip biscuits from the fridge and bake them for 5–10 minutes or until lightly golden. Watch carefully because the biscuits can easily burn as they are so small. Leave to cool on the trays for a few minutes before transferring, on the parchment paper, to a wire rack to cool completely.

While the cakes and biscuits are cooling, make your pistachio peas. For each pea, pull off a tiny bit of the marzipan and, with your fingertips, roll into a mini ball. You'll need five or six peas for each cake so if you want to add peas to all 24 fish and chip cakes, that means about 150 peas in total. I'd recommend offering some cakes without peas – or creating them while you're watching a good film or listening to music. Leave the peas on a plate to firm up. >>

Once the cakes and biscuits have cooled, make the lemon buttercream. Using a hand-held electric whisk, beat the butter in a medium bowl until soft and pale, then sift the icing sugar into the bowl in batches, working in the sugar with a spoon before adding the lemon juice and extract or zest. Beat at full speed until the buttercream is really light and fluffy.

Transfer the buttercream to the second piping bag fitted with the 1.5cm nozzle; if using a disposable piping bag, you can just snip off a similar-sized opening from the tip. Pipe small peaks of buttercream on to the cakes, then smooth over with a small palette knife to cover the surface.

If, like me, you love mushy peas, use some pistachio paste as a 'sauce' to serve your peas in. Dollop a little sauce on to the buttercream with the end of a latte stirrer, then use a cocktail stick to place the pistachio peas in the sauce.

Break your chips down to size: you want at least five 3cm chips and five 2cm chips per cake. Place the fish biscuits and chip biscuits on the cakes.

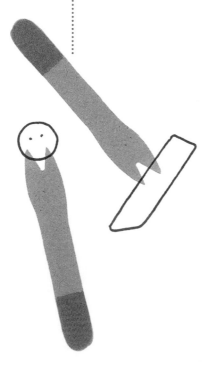

SANDWICH & TOAST CAKES

MAKES I GIANT JAM
SANDWICH CAKE; SERVES 8–10

FOR THE CAKE

200g butter, softened

200g caster sugar

4 eggs (at room temperature)

4 tsp vanilla extract

200g self-raising flour

4 tsp warm water

FOR THE FILLING

100g butter, softened

200g icing sugar, sifted

1 tbsp whole milk

1 tsp vanilla extract

200g strawberry or raspberry
    jam, preferably homemade
    (see p.272)

EQUIPMENT

Sandwich-shaped silicone cake
    mould (see directory, p.308),
    greased and lightly dusted
    with flour

Baked in a slice-of-bread-shaped mould, this cake is filled with buttercream and jam to make it look like a giant jam sandwich. I couldn't resist thinking up some more ambitious fillings and toppings too – see my variations on pp.42–3. If you don't have a sandwich-shaped mould, you can bake your cake in a loaf tin and cut it into slices of 'bread' or 'toast'. Or you can use mini-loaf tins to create sandwiches that would suit the Borrowers.

Preheat the oven to 180°C/160°C fan/gas 4. Place the greased mould on a flat baking tray to make it easy to move the cake in and out of the oven.

Using a hand-held electric whisk, or in a free-standing mixer, beat the butter and sugar together for 5–10 minutes or until very light, pale and creamy. Break the eggs into a mug or jug. Add the vanilla and beat with a fork. Gradually add the egg to the creamed butter and sugar mixture, beating well after each addition. Should the mixture look like it's curdling, add a spoonful of the flour. Sift in the flour and fold in until just combined. Gently fold in the warm water.

Scrape the cake mixture into the prepared mould and level it with a spatula. Bake for 40–45 minutes or until the cake is risen and lightly golden brown and a skewer inserted into the centre comes out clean. Leave to cool slightly on the baking tray before moving the cake, still in the mould, on to a wire rack. Once fully cooled, remove the cake from the mould.

Next, make the buttercream for the filling. If you have a free-standing mixer, put the butter, sugar, milk and vanilla extract into the bowl, cover the bowl with a tea towel to prevent a cloud of sugar from escaping and start beating slowly. Increase the speed and beat the mixture until it is fluffy and almost white, stopping a few times to scrape down the side of the bowl. I beat for up to 10 minutes at full speed to create a really light finish. If using a hand-held electric whisk, beat the butter in a bowl until soft and pale, then sift in the icing sugar in batches, working it into the butter with a spoon before adding the milk and vanilla. Beat at full speed until the buttercream is light and fluffy.

Using a long, serrated knife, carefully slice off the browned top and base of the cake to reveal the golden inside. Then slice the cake horizontally into two equal layers, which will be the two halves of the 'sandwich'. Place the base layer on your cake board or stand and spread over half of the buttercream. Top with the jam. Spread the underside of the second layer with the rest of the buttercream and place on top. Or, divide the jam between the buttercream-topped layers and leave as 'open sandwiches'.

CONTINUED ON P.42 >>

SANDWICH & TOAST CAKES (CONTINUED)

TO MAKE DIFFERENT-SIZED SANDWICH CAKES

- To make one large loaf, bake the mixture in a straight-sided 900g (2lb) loaf tin for 45–50 minutes.
- To make three mini loaves, make the mixture using the basic vanilla cake quantities given in the table on p.27 for 24 mini muffins, but bake in three mini-loaf tins (I use 8 x 4cm disposable cardboard moulds; see directory, p.308). Bake for 15–20 minutes.

Once cooled, cut the loaf cakes into slices about 1cm thick. You will get about 20 slices from the 900g (2lb) loaf and 7–8 slices from each mini loaf.

SANDWICH VARIATIONS

Butter & jam sandwich For a less sweet filling, spread with softened butter rather than using buttercream. Sandwich together or leave open.

Chocolate spread sandwich Cover each layer with chocolate hazelnut spread, or homemade Dark or Milk Chocolate Ganache (see p.279). Scatter a handful of chopped toasted hazelnuts evenly over the chocolate topping. Sandwich together or leave open.

Peanut butter & jam sandwich Spread each layer with peanut butter and cover with raspberry or strawberry jam. Sandwich together or leave open.

Peanut butter & banana sandwich Spread each layer with peanut butter and cover with slices of banana. Sandwich together or leave open.

Cheese & pickle sandwich Spread each layer with brandy butter before covering with mincemeat, to look like pickle. Then coarsely grate natural or golden marzipan over the mincemeat to resemble cheese (it helps to firm up the marzipan in the freezer before grating, ideally overnight, but an hour or two will do). Sandwich together or leave open.

TOASTED CAKES VARIATIONS

To turn your sandwich layers or loaf cake slices into 'toast' (as shown on pp.40–1), place them side by side on a baking tray lined with baking parchment or foil and toast under a moderate grill until golden brown on both sides. Leave to cool before spreading with softened butter and then adding your chosen topping. You can leave the 'open sandwiches' whole or cut them into quarters, squares or triangles. >>

Toast & Marmite Spread each layer or slice with softened butter before marbling with a little black treacle, to look like Marmite.

Toast & marmalade, jam or honey Spread each layer or slice with softened butter, then cover with marmalade, jam or honey, or with peanut butter, chocolate spread (shop-bought or homemade ganache) or lemon curd.

Cheese on toast Spread each layer or slice with softened butter, then cover with a grating of natural or golden marzipan to resemble grated cheese (freezing the marzipan first will make it easier to grate). Grill to melt and lightly brown the marzipan, or use a kitchen blowtorch.

Sweet beans or hoops on toast A dab of orange food colouring, such as Sugarflair tangerine/apricot colour paste (see directory, p.308), added to my basic caramel sauce (see below) gives you a sweet 'tomato' sauce. You can then add peanuts to resemble baked beans, or hoop-shaped cereal for spaghetti hoops. Both look like the real thing, especially when poured on to toasted slices of cake.

To make the caramel sauce, weigh 75g golden syrup into a medium saucepan. Sprinkle 75g caster sugar over the surface of the golden syrup. Set the pan over a medium heat and stir with a wooden spoon or silicone spatula until the sugar has dissolved. Cook, stirring constantly as the caramel bubbles, for 3–4 minutes or until it reaches a rich amber colour.

Remove the pan from the heat and pour in 150ml double cream, stirring as it bubbles up until everything is fully combined. Stir in a pinch of salt if you like (this is not necessary if you are using salted peanuts for the beans on toast). If you find there are bits of sugar that have formed into toffee pieces, set the pan back on the heat and stir to melt these pieces into the sauce. Don't heat it for too long though, or your caramel will thicken too much.

Finally, use the end of a spoon or wooden latte stirrer to add a small amount of food colouring, stirring it through the caramel to create a tomato sauce shade. Once the desired colour has been reached, stir through 200g salted peanuts or 50g hoop-shaped cereal.

Leave the mixture for 5–10 minutes to cool and thicken slightly while you toast and butter your slices, then spoon over the beans/hoops from the pan. If you are creating just one giant slice of 'toast', you can pour half the mixture into a clean 200g bean or spaghetti hoops tin to serve alongside the cake.

BANANA
CAKE

· ·

Although you could bake this in a loaf tin, it definitely isn't
what I'd call a banana bread. Don't get me wrong: I love that big
brother of the banana cake, thickly sliced and spread with butter
– but this is a fluffier and less dense affair, much better suited to
sweet fillings, tempting toppings and nifty decorations. Packed with
pecans, the nuts in this cake add a satisfying crunch, while their
butterscotchy character complements the banana, muscovado and
vanilla flavours in the bake. (If you'd like a less nutty cake, cut the
quantity of pecans in half.) I give the nuts a gentle toasting before
using, which really brings out their buttery taste and adds an extra
dimension to the finished cake. Be sure your bananas are really ripe –
best if blackened, almost weeping their juice – sad, crying bananas
lead to a moist, merry cake.

FOR THE CAKE
50g pecans
50g butter, softened
50g light muscovado sugar
50g very ripe banana flesh
   (from about ½ medium
   banana)
1 egg (at room temperature)
1 tsp vanilla extract
50g self-raising flour

EQUIPMENT
10cm round, deep, loose-
   bottomed tin (pork-pie size),
   greased and fully lined

BASIC BANANA CAKE

Preheat the oven to 180°C/160°C fan/gas 4.

Spread the pecans on a baking tray and toast in the oven for 5–10 minutes or until lightly golden and fragrant. Leave to cool, then chop the nuts with a sharp knife (if chopping a large amount – see table opposite – I'd advise doing this in batches). You can use a food processor, but it's best to process in batches and use the pulse function to avoid your nuts turning to a powder.

Using a hand-held electric whisk (it's tricky to beat this small quantity in a free-standing mixer), beat the butter and sugar together for 5–10 minutes or until the mix is very light and creamy and takes on a pale café-au-lait shade.

Put the banana flesh in a bowl and smush into a purée using a fork or spatula. If you're making one of the larger cakes (see table opposite), you can purée the bananas quickly in the food processor after chopping the nuts.

Break the egg into a mug or jug, add the vanilla and beat with a fork. Gradually add the egg to the creamed butter and sugar mixture, beating well after each addition. Should the mixture look like it's curdling at any point, add a spoonful of the flour.

Sift the flour into the mixture and fold in until just combined. (If you are making one of the larger quantities – see opposite – sift and fold in the flour in several batches.) Finally, stir through the puréed banana and chopped pecans.

Spoon the cake mixture into your prepared tin and bake for 25–30 minutes or until the cake has risen and a skewer pushed into the centre comes out fairly clean. Leave to cool in the tin for about 10 minutes before removing the cake and transferring to a wire rack to cool completely.

TO FINISH
I like this cake slathered with White or Milk Chocolate Ganache (see p.279) with extra chocolate shavings on top. However, you can also use the mix to make cupcakes and top with Cream Cheese Buttercream (p.277) plus Banana Buttons (p.293) or shop-bought banana chips. Then again, for a real banoffee treat, cover the cake(s) with Mascarpone Caramel Cream (p.278) and scatter toffee, banana or chocolate chips over the top – or all three together!

TO MAKE DIFFERENT-SIZED BANANA CAKES, USE THE TABLE OPPOSITE >>

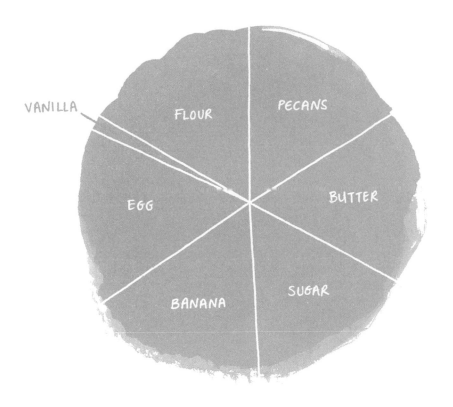

24-HOLE MINI-MUFFIN TIN	12-HOLE MUFFIN TIN	20CM SQUARE TIN	20CM ROUND DEEP TIN	900G (2LB) LOAF TIN	INGREDIENTS
50g	150g	150g	200g	150g	Pecans
50g	150g	150g	200g	150g	Butter, softened
50g	150g	150g	200g	150g	Light muscovado sugar
50g	150g	150g	200g	150g	Very ripe banana flesh
1	3	3	4	3	Egg(s)
1 tsp	3 tsp	3 tsp	4 tsp	3 tsp	Vanilla extract
50g	150g	150g	200g	150g	Self-raising flour
BAKE IN AN OVEN PREHEATED TO 180°C/160°C FAN/GAS 4					
for 10–12 minutes	for 15–20 minutes	for 30–35 minutes	for 50–60 minutes, or in 2 sandwich tins for 25–30 minutes	for 50–60 minutes	

BANOFFEE BUTTERFLY PRETZEL CAKES

MAKES 24 MINI CAKES

FOR THE CARAMEL TOPPING
25g golden syrup
25g caster sugar
25ml double cream
Pinch of salt, optional
100g mascarpone

FOR THE CAKES
50g pecans, toasted (see p.46)
50g butter, softened
50g light muscovado sugar
50g very ripe banana flesh
    (from about ½ medium
    banana)
1 egg (at room temperature)
1 tsp vanilla extract
50g self-raising flour

FOR THE PRETZEL WINGS
65g hard toffees, such as
    Werther's Originals
48 small pretzels (about 65g)

EQUIPMENT
24-hole mini-muffin tin
24 paper mini-muffin cases
Large disposable piping bag,
    optional
Small piping bag with optional
    1.5cm round nozzle

These cakes are bound to take off. I love pretzels just as they are, but add toffee to them and they become sweet as well as salty, and twice as moreish. Here they make toffee wings for my banoffee butterflies. The cake topping combines mascarpone with a simple homemade caramel (although, as a short-cut, you can whip up a quick caramel mascarpone by beating together 100g mascarpone with 50g light muscovado sugar). Halved pecans act as the butterflies' bodies.

If you are making your caramel from scratch, do this first as it will need time to cool. Weigh the golden syrup into a small saucepan. Sprinkle the caster sugar over the surface of the golden syrup. Set on a medium heat and cook, stirring occasionally with a silicone spatula or a wooden spoon, until the sugar has dissolved. Continue to cook the syrup for about 2 minutes or until it turns a rich amber colour. Remove the pan from the heat and add the double cream, stirring as it bubbles up to fully combine everything. Add the salt if you are creating a salted caramel. Transfer to a medium bowl to cool.

Next make your cakes. Preheat the oven to 180°C/160°C fan/gas 4. Line the mini-muffin tin with the muffin cases. Reserve 12 of the toasted pecans for decoration and chop the rest (see p.46).

Using a hand-held electric whisk (it's tricky to beat this small quantity in a free-standing mixer), beat the butter and sugar together for 5–10 minutes or until the mixture is very light and creamy and takes on a pale café-au-lait shade. Put the banana flesh in a bowl and smush it into a purée using a fork or spatula. Break the egg into a mug, add the vanilla and beat together with a fork. Gradually add the egg to the creamed butter and sugar mixture, beating well after each addition and scraping down the side of the bowl as you go. Should the mixture look like it's curdling, add a spoonful of the flour. Sift the flour into the mixture and fold it in until just combined. Finally, stir through the mashed banana and chopped pecans.

Spoon the cake mixture into your cases, dividing it equally. Alternatively, pipe it in (I find this quicker and neater): use a large, disposable piping bag and snip off a 2cm opening from the tip. Bake for 10–12 minutes or until the cakes have risen and a skewer pushed into the centre comes out clean. Cool slightly in the tin for about 5 minutes, then transfer (still in the paper cases) to a wire rack to cool completely. Leave the oven on for the pretzel butterfly wings.

CONTINUED OVERLEAF >>

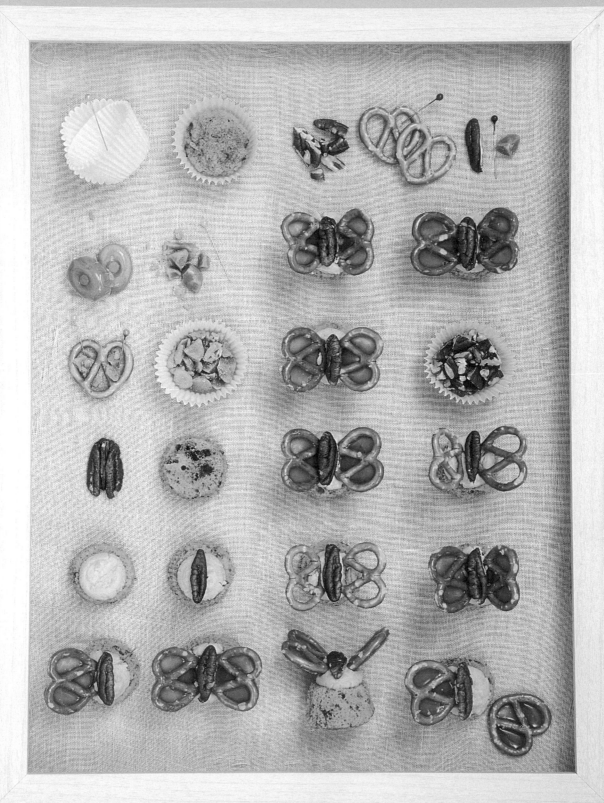

BANOFFEE BUTTERFLY
PRETZEL CAKES (CONTINUED)

Put the toffees, still in their wrappers, in a sandwich bag
wrapped in a tea towel (to prevent the sweets flying loose).
Crush them with a rolling pin. Remove the wrappers from
the bag and transfer the crushed sweets to a bowl.

Line a large baking tray with baking parchment and place your pretzels on it.
Make sure you lay them on the tray salt-studded side up, as this helps them lie
flat and makes it less likely the molten toffee will leak out. Carefully place the
crushed toffee into the gaps within the pretzels – I find it best to do this using
a ¼ teaspoon measure. The crushed toffee should be roughly level with the
top of the pretzels. Bake for 2–5 minutes or until the sweets have melted
inside the pretzels. Leave to cool completely on the tray. If you
are not using them straight away, store the pretzel wings
in an airtight container between layers of baking
parchment. They'll keep for a few days. >>

To finish the caramel cream topping, beat the mascarpone into the cooled caramel until smooth and creamy. Transfer the mixture to the small piping bag fitted with the 1.5cm nozzle; if you are using a disposable piping bag, you can just snip off a similar-sized opening from the tip. Remove the cakes from their cases (like butterflies emerging from their chrysalises) and turn them over. Pipe the topping on to the centre of each cake, creating a gently domed shape.

Cut the reserved whole pecans in half vertically, to make 24 pieces. Press a pecan piece, cut side down, into the topping on each cake. Position a toffee pretzel on either side of each pecan and press gently into the cream to create the impression of the butterfly's wings.

BANOFFEE
TUMBLER TRIFLES

MAKES 4 TRIFLES

FOR THE CUSTARD
200ml double cream
2 egg yolks (at room
    temperature)
20g caster sugar
½ tsp vanilla extract

FOR THE CAKES
50g butter, softened
50g light muscovado sugar
50g very ripe banana flesh
    (from about ½ medium
    banana)
1 egg (at room temperature)
1 tsp vanilla extract
50g self-raising flour
50g pecans, toasted and
    chopped (see p.46)

FOR THE CARAMEL
50g golden syrup
50g caster sugar
100ml double cream
Pinch of salt, optional

TO DECORATE
50g hard banana chips (see
    directory, p.307)
50ml dark rum
300ml double cream
4 small, medium-ripe bananas
50g butterscotch chips
Cocoa powder, to dust

EQUIPMENT
6- or 12-hole muffin tin
4 paper muffin cases
4 x 35ml glass 'barrel' tumblers

Banoffee pie and trifle are two classic, crowd-pleasing English creations, and these little puds raise a glass to both of them – quite literally. Presented in tumblers, you can see all the layers, from the banana cake through to the caramel. To give the dish an extra banana kick, add a blitzed-up banana to the caramel after stirring in the cream. If you want to see little black specks of vanilla seed in your homemade custard, use vanilla bean paste instead of extract. When you're short of time, you can use 175g shop-bought dulce de leche and 200ml ready-made custard to layer your trifles.

If you're making your own custard, pour the cream into a medium saucepan and set over a gentle heat. Bring to just below simmering. Meanwhile, whisk together the egg yolks, sugar and vanilla in a medium heatproof bowl. Add the hot cream to the bowl, whisking all the time to combine the ingredients. Immediately pour the mixture back into the pan, using a heatproof plastic or silicone spatula to get it all out of the bowl. With the spatula, or a wooden spoon, stir over a gentle heat until the custard thickens enough to coat the back of the spatula/spoon. Pour the custard back into the bowl and cover the surface directly with clingfilm to stop a skin from forming. Leave to cool.

Next make the cakes. Preheat the oven to 180°C/160°C fan/gas 4. Put the four muffin cases into the muffin tin.

Using a hand-held electric whisk (it's tricky to beat this small quantity in a free-standing mixer), beat the butter and sugar together for 5–10 minutes or until the mix is very light and creamy and takes on a pale café-au-lait shade. Put the banana flesh in a bowl and smush it into a purée using a fork or spatula. Break the egg into a mug or jug, add the vanilla and beat together with a fork. Gradually add the egg to the creamed butter and sugar mixture, beating well after each addition and scraping down the side of the bowl as you go. Should the mixture look like it's starting to curdle, add a spoonful of the flour. Sift the flour into the mixture and fold it in until just combined. Finally, stir through the puréed banana and chopped pecans.

Spoon the cake mixture into your four cases, dividing it equally, and bake for 15–20 minutes or until the cakes have risen and a skewer pushed into the centre comes out clean. Leave to cool in the tin for about 5 minutes, then transfer, still in the paper cases, to a wire rack to cool completely.

CONTINUED OVERLEAF >>

BANOFFEE TUMBLER TRIFLES (CONTINUED)

Meanwhile, make the caramel sauce. Weigh the golden syrup into a small saucepan. Sprinkle the caster sugar over the surface of the golden syrup. Cook over a medium heat, stirring occasionally with a silicone spatula or wooden spoon, until the sugar has dissolved. Continue to cook gently for about 3 minutes or until the syrup has turned a rich amber colour. Remove the pan from the heat and pour in the double cream, stirring as it bubbles up to thoroughly combine everything. Add the salt if you are creating a salted caramel. Transfer to a medium bowl to cool.

Once the cakes and caramel have cooled, you can assemble your trifles. Set aside four of the best-looking banana chips and break the remainder into small pieces – do this with a sharp knife or your fingers.

Remove the banana cakes from their paper cases and cut or crumble them into bite-sized pieces. You will use one cake per tumbler: put the cake pieces in the base of the tumbler and sprinkle with 1 tablespoon rum. Press the cake down with a spoon and set aside to soak.

Meanwhile, use a hand-held electric whisk to whip the double cream to soft-to-medium peaks; set aside. Cover the cake in the tumblers with the caramel, dividing it evenly. Scatter the broken banana chips over the caramel.

Cut the fresh bananas into 5mm slices – you will be using one banana per trifle so you might find it easier to work on one trifle at a time. Arrange some of the banana slices around the inside of each tumbler, pressing the slices up against the side so the whole of the slice is visible. Put the remaining slices within this ring of upright banana.

Next cover the bananas with the custard, dividing it equally among the four tumblers. Use a spoon or small palette knife to smooth the surface of the custard. Keep back a few butterscotch chips to decorate the trifles; scatter the remainder over the custard. Top with the softly whipped cream, using a palette knife to smooth it out a bit but still keeping a slightly rustic finish. Sift a little cocoa powder over the centre of each cream-topped trifle and decorate with a dried banana chip and the reserved butterscotch pieces.

BANANA BUTTON BITES

FOR THE CAKE
150g butter, softened
150g light muscovado sugar
150g very ripe banana flesh
    (from about 1½ medium
    bananas)
3 eggs (at room temperature)
1 tbsp vanilla extract
150g self-raising flour
150g pecans, toasted and
    chopped (see p.46)

TO DECORATE
1–1½ medium-ripe medium-
    sized bananas (or 25 shop-
    bought chewy, dried banana
    slices; see directory, p.307)
30 giant chocolate buttons

FOR THE BUTTERCREAM
50g butter, softened
100g icing sugar, sifted
½ tbsp whole milk
½ tsp vanilla extract
75g full-fat cream cheese

EQUIPMENT
20cm square, loose-bottomed
    tin, greased and lined with
    seatbelt straps (see p.21)
2.5cm plain, round cutter,
    optional
Medium paintbrush

My banana buttons – oven-dried banana slices – are very simple to make and have an irresistible chewy texture and caramel flavour. They're delicious eaten on their own, but when stuck on top of a giant milk chocolate button, they're even better. (You can, if you're in a hurry, use shop-bought chewy, dried banana slices.) These double buttons sit very well on a layer of cream cheese buttercream, making this a bake I come back to time and again. I sometimes like to serve the finished cakes with a few more giant chocolate buttons, made to look like real buttons by pressing holes through them with a heated metal skewer.

Preheat the oven to 180°C/160°C fan/gas 4.

Using a hand-held electric whisk, or in a free-standing mixer, beat the butter and sugar together for 5–10 minutes or until the mixture is very light and creamy and takes on a pale café-au-lait shade. Put the banana flesh in a bowl and smush it into a purée using a fork or spatula. Break the eggs into a mug or jug, add the vanilla and beat together with a fork. Gradually add the egg to the creamed butter and sugar mixture, beating well after each addition and scraping down the side of the bowl as you go. Should the mixture look like it's curdling at any stage, add a spoonful of the flour. Sift the flour into the mixture and fold it in until just combined. Finally, stir through the puréed banana and chopped pecans.

Spoon the cake mixture into your prepared tin and level it out. Bake for 30–35 minutes or until the cake has risen and a skewer pushed into the centre comes out clean. Leave to cool in the tin for about 15 minutes before removing the cake and transferring to a wire rack to cool completely. Turn the oven down to 120°C/100°C fan/gas ½ for drying the banana buttons – opening the oven door a little will speed the cooling.

Peel the bananas for decorating and cut them into slices about the thickness of a £1 coin. In order to fit on to the chocolate buttons, the slices should be about 2.5cm in diameter – if yours are larger than this, cut them down to size with the 2.5cm cutter or the wide end of a metal piping nozzle. Lay the slices on a large baking tray lined with baking parchment. Once the oven has reached the right temperature, bake the banana buttons for 1¼–1½ hours or until dried out and chewy – they'll be slightly reduced in size.

CONTINUED OVERLEAF >>

Leave the banana buttons to cool – ideally in the switched-off oven with the door ajar – this will enhance their toffee colour and thoroughly dry them out. (You could also use a dehydrator for the whole banana-drying process if you have one; see directory, p.309.) If you are not using them straight away, store the banana buttons in an airtight container such as a clean jam jar. They can be kept for up to a week.

Once the banana buttons have cooled, lay out 25 of the giant chocolate buttons on a tray. Melt the five remaining chocolate buttons in a microwave, or in a heatproof bowl set over a pan of simmering water (bain-marie). Allow the chocolate to cool slightly before dabbing a little on to each chocolate button with the paintbrush. Stick a banana button on top and leave to set.

Next make the cream cheese buttercream. Using a hand-held electric whisk, beat the butter in a medium bowl until soft and pale. Sift the icing sugar into the bowl in batches, working in the sugar with a spoon before adding the milk and vanilla. Beat at full speed until the buttercream is really light and fluffy. Finally, beat in the cream cheese for about 1 minute (not much more – if you overbeat at this stage the cream cheese can 'split' and loosen the buttercream; if this does happen, place it in the fridge to firm up slightly).

Use a palette knife to spread the cream cheese buttercream over the cake. Chill it for 30 minutes to firm up the buttercream slightly, which will make it easier to cut squares neatly.

Place the banana buttons on top of the cake in five rows of five, evenly spaced apart. Cut the cake into equal, bite-sized pieces using a sharp knife. For really precise bites, you can trim off the sides of the cake before cutting into squares.

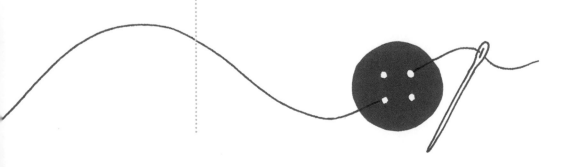

BANANA-LLAMA

FOR THE CAKE
50g butter, softened
50g light muscovado sugar
50g very ripe banana flesh
(from about ½ medium
banana)
1 egg (at room temperature)
1 tsp vanilla extract
50g self-raising flour
50g pecans, toasted and
chopped (see p.46)

FOR THE GANACHE
25g dark chocolate
25ml double cream

TO DECORATE
1½ tbsp icing sugar
125ml double cream
½ tsp cocoa powder
1 hard, dried banana chip (see
directory, p.307)
2 butterscotch pieces
1 cream-filled chocolate biscuit,
such as an Oreo (you will
only need a tiny bit)
1 bourbon biscuit (you will
only need a tiny bit)
A little melted dark chocolate

EQUIPMENT
10cm round, deep, loose-
bottomed tin (pork-pie size),
greased and fully lined
Large disposable piping bag
fitted with a 1.5cm wide
6-point star nozzle
Llama template (see overleaf)
Fine paintbrush

If you're a fan of bananas and have an affection for llamas – and who doesn't? – this is the cake for you. There's no drama to this llama – it's very simple to make. The only tricky bit is piping the creamy creature itself, and that simply requires a relatively steady hand. Give the finished bake to your best llama-loving friend to ensure good karma.

Preheat the oven to 180°C/160°C fan/gas 4.

Using a hand-held electric whisk (it's tricky to beat this small quantity in a free-standing mixer), beat the butter and sugar together for 5–10 minutes or until the mixture is very light and creamy and takes on a pale café-au-lait shade. Put the banana flesh in a bowl and smush it into a purée using a fork or spatula. Break the egg into a mug or jug, add the vanilla and beat together with a fork. Gradually add the egg to the creamed butter and sugar mixture, beating well after each addition and scraping down the side of the bowl as you go. Should the mixture look like it's curdling, add a spoonful of the flour. Sift the flour into the mixture and fold it in until just combined. Finally, stir through the mashed banana and chopped pecans.

Spoon the cake mixture into your prepared tin and level it out. Bake for 25–30 minutes or until the cake has risen and a skewer pushed into the centre comes out clean. Leave to cool in the tin for about 10 minutes before removing the cake and transferring to a wire rack to cool completely.

While the cake is baking and cooling, make the ganache for the filling. As you are using a very small quantity of both cream and chocolate, I advise warming them together in a heatproof bowl set over a pan of simmering water (bain-marie), or heating them in short blasts in the microwave, to melt the chocolate. Stir together until smooth, then leave the ganache to cool until it has reached a soft, spreadable consistency. (Alternatively, you could use 50g leftover ganache from another recipe, or the same quantity of chocolate spread.)

If the cake has domed on top, trim off the domed centre (not the whole top surface of the cake) using a long serrated knife such as a bread knife, then cut the cake horizontally into two equal layers.

Set the bottom cake layer on your chosen plate or stand. Spread the ganache smoothly over the cut surface of this cake layer using a palette knife, ensuring you spread the ganache right out to the edge.

CONTINUED OVERLEAF >>

LLAMA
TEMPLATE

BANANA-LLAMA (CONTINUED)

For the decoration, sift the icing sugar into a bowl and pour in the double cream. Using a hand-held electric whisk or a hand whisk, whip the cream until it forms soft-to-medium peaks. With a palette knife, spread 2–3 tablespoons of the cream over the top cake layer, making sure it looks neat around the edges. If the cream thickens up a lot as you work, making it difficult to spread, dip the palette knife in some unwhipped cream or milk to help smooth things along. Transfer the rest of the cream to the piping bag fitted with the star nozzle.

Take a piece of thin cardboard and, using the loose base of the cake tin as a guide, draw a circle on the card. Place the llama template within this and draw the outline of the llama's head. Cut out the llama shape and place it on the cream-covered cake surface.

Sift the cocoa powder over the cake, then carefully remove the card template, revealing the silhouette of the llama's head. (It's difficult to pipe cream directly on to cocoa powder, so apart from acting as a guideline, the template keeps the silhouette area clear of cocoa.)

Pipe the cream into the llama shape in blobs, holding the bag directly vertical over the cake, and pulling the bag up as you pipe each blob to create a tuft-like appearance. The star nozzle will help you produce a textured, fluffy finish. Aim to make the cream shape about 2cm high. Then pipe a second layer of cream within the llama's face area so it forms a peak at the nose 3–4cm high.

Cut the tip off the piping bag and remove the nozzle, then pipe the remainder of the cream over the ganache-covered surface of the bottom cake layer. Smooth with a palette knife (it's easier to get a smooth cream filling without the star nozzle). Gently set the decorated top layer in place. >>

Break the banana chip into llama ear-shaped pieces and stick into the top of the llama's head. Place the butterscotch pieces on the banana chips to look like the inside of the ears. Break up the chocolate biscuit and use some of the pieces to create the llama's eyes and nose. Break up the bourbon biscuit and choose a roundish piece to be the llama's muzzle – you can cut it down to size with a sharp knife. Paint a smile on this piece using the paintbrush and some melted dark chocolate – or use a black edible ink pen if you're feeling less dextrous. Position this under the biscuit nose.

CARROT CAKE

· ·

Carrots just happen to be my favourite vegetable, which is perhaps why I'm such a fan of this cake. Granted, it contains as much sugar and butter as it does carrot but, when I'm making it, I tend to snack on lots of raw carrot too, so I tell myself it's a pretty healthy option. I like to grate my carrots finely for this cake: the thin shreds make it easier to cut or carve into when baked. Many carrot cake recipes use oil as an ingredient. I prefer butter for the incomparable flavour and slightly more crumbly, friable texture it provides. With orange zest, aromatic cinnamon and toasted pistachios all in the mix too, this bake elevates a humble vegetable into a rooty-tooting terrific treat. If you're not a great fan of nuts, just halve the quantity of pistachios.

BASIC CARROT CAKE

50g pistachios
50g butter, softened
50g light muscovado sugar
1 egg (at room temperature)
50g self-raising flour
1 tsp ground cinnamon
Finely grated zest of ½ orange
50g finely grated carrot (about
    ½ medium carrot)

EQUIPMENT
10cm round, deep, loose-
    bottomed tin (pork-pie size),
    greased and fully lined

Preheat the oven to 180°C/160°C fan/gas 4.

Spread the pistachios on a baking tray and toast in the oven for 5–10 minutes or until lightly browned and fragrant. Leave to cool, then chop the nuts with a sharp knife (if chopping a large amount – see table opposite – I'd advise doing this in batches). You can use a food processor, but it's best to process in batches and use the pulse function to avoid your nuts turning to a powder.

Using a hand-held electric whisk (it's tricky to beat this small a quantity in a free-standing mixer), beat the butter and sugar together for 5–10 minutes or until the mixture is very light and creamy and a pale café-au-lait shade.

Break the egg into a mug and beat with a fork. Gradually add the egg to the butter and sugar mixture, beating well after each addition.

Sift the flour and cinnamon into the mixture and fold in (if you're baking one of the larger quantities – see opposite – do this in several batches). Finally, stir through the orange zest, carrot and chopped pistachios.

Spoon the cake mixture into your prepared tin. Bake for 25–30 minutes or until the cake has risen and a skewer pushed into the centre comes out fairly clean. Leave to cool in the tin for about 15 minutes before removing the cake and transferring to a wire rack to cool completely.

TO FINISH

Good old Cream Cheese Buttercream (see p.277) is always a winner with carrot cake – particularly when it's finished off with a scattering of coarsely chopped pistachios and a dusting of cinnamon. Chocolate Orange Ganache (p.279) is another irresistible topping and enhances the flavour of orange in the cake.

TO MAKE DIFFERENT-SIZED CARROT CAKES, USE THE TABLE OPPOSITE >>

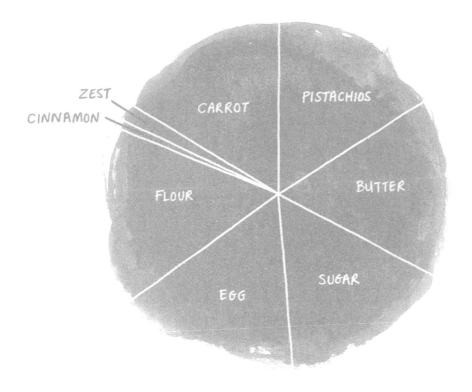

ZEST

CINNAMON

CARROT

PISTACHIOS

FLOUR

BUTTER

EGG

SUGAR

24-HOLE MINI-MUFFIN TIN	12-HOLE MUFFIN TIN	20CM SQUARE TIN	20CM ROUND DEEP TIN	900G (2LB) LOAF TIN	INGREDIENTS
50g	150g	150g	200g	150g	Pistachios
50g	150g	150g	200g	150g	Butter, softened
50g	150g	150g	200g	150g	Light muscovado sugar
1	3	3	4	3	Egg(s)
50g	150g	150g	200g	150g	Self-raising flour
1 tsp	3 tsp	3 tsp	4 tsp	3 tsp	Ground cinnamon
½ orange	1½ oranges	1½ oranges	2 oranges	1½ oranges	Zest of orange
50g	150g	150g	200g	150g	Finely grated carrot

BAKE IN AN OVEN PREHEATED TO 180°C/160°C FAN/GAS 4					
for 10–12 minutes	for 15–20 minutes	for 30–35 minutes	for 50–60 minutes, or in 2 sandwich tins for 25–30 minutes	for 50–60 minutes	

WHITE RABBIT CAKES

50g pistachios, toasted
(see p.64)
50g butter, softened
50g light muscovado sugar
1 egg (at room temperature)
50g self-raising flour
1 tsp ground cinnamon
Finely grated zest of ½ orange
50g finely grated carrot (about
½ medium carrot)
12 pitted soft-dried dates
(50–100g)

FOR THE MARZIPAN
100g desiccated coconut
½ egg white (15–17g; reserve
the rest of the white for
decoration) (at room
temperature)
2 tsp lemon juice
100g icing sugar
½ tsp freeze-dried strawberry
powder

EQUIPMENT
24-hole mini-muffin tin
24 gold-foil mini-muffin cases
Curved-edge modelling tool
(see directory, p.308) or
wooden latte stirrer
Medium paintbrush
Large piping bag with optional
1.5cm round nozzle

INGREDIENTS CONTINUED
OVERLEAF >>

These Lewis Carroll-inspired white rabbits are ideal for any tea party – not just Alice's. The cakes are baked in gold foil cases, which makes them look extra special, and is a reference to the gold watch the white rabbit carries. Half the cakes have coconut marzipan ears, while the others sport bunny tails. In both cases, desiccated coconut makes the perfect rabbit fur. I've even hidden a very important 'date' in the centre of each mini cake. Don't worry: no one will be late when these are on the table.

Preheat the oven to 180°C/160°C fan/gas 4. Line the mini-muffin tin with the foil cases. After toasting the pistachios, set aside 24 whole nuts and chop the rest (see p.64).

Using a hand-held electric whisk (it's tricky to beat this small a quantity in a free-standing mixer), beat the butter and sugar together for 5–10 minutes or until the mixture is very light and creamy and a pale café-au-lait shade. Break the egg into a mug or jug and beat with a fork. Gradually add the egg to the butter and sugar mixture, beating well after each addition. Sift the flour and cinnamon into the mixture and fold in. Finally, stir through the orange zest, carrot and chopped pistachios.

Spoon the mixture into your cases, dividing it equally. Cut the dates in half lengthways and stuff each half with one of the reserved whole pistachios. Press a stuffed date, cut side up, into the centre of the mixture in each case (if some or all of your dates are very long, you might need to cut them down to fit into the cakes). Use a teaspoon to cover the dates with cake mix.

Bake for 10–12 minutes or until the cakes have risen and a skewer pushed in (around the dates) comes out fairly clean. Leave to cool in the tin for 10 minutes before transferring the cakes, still in their foil cases, to a wire rack to cool completely.

While the cakes are baking and cooling, make your coconut marzipan. Put the desiccated coconut in a food processor, or coffee or spice grinder, and grind to a really fine powder (in batches, if necessary). Put the egg white into a medium bowl with the lemon juice and mix together. Sift in the icing sugar, then add the ground coconut and stir to bring together into a ball, using a spatula to pick up all the mixture from around the side of the bowl.

CONTINUED OVERLEAF >>

WHITE RABBIT CAKES (CONTINUED)

TO DECORATE
50g desiccated coconut

FOR THE BUTTERCREAM
50g butter, softened
100g icing sugar, sifted
½ tbsp lemon juice
½ tsp lemon extract
75g full-fat cream cheese

Remove a quarter of this coconut marzipan and place in a separate bowl. Sift in the freeze-dried strawberry powder through a fine sieve (to remove any seeds). Knead into the marzipan to tint it a pale pink. Add an extra drop of lemon juice or egg white to moisten, if necessary. Keep the pink marzipan wrapped in clingfilm until needed.

To create the rabbit ears, pull 24 pieces from the remaining white coconut marzipan, each weighing about 4g. Roll each piece into a sausage shape 4cm long and narrower at one end than the other. Flatten each shape slightly with your fingertips and mould into a rabbit ear. Lay the ears on a sheet of baking parchment or foil and, with the curved-edge modelling tool or latte stirrer, create a lengthways indent within each rabbit ear.

Pull off 24 little pieces from the pink marzipan – about 2g each. Roll each piece between your thumb and forefinger until it is 3cm long, then press into the indent in a rabbit ear with your modelling tool or stirrer. You can use a little lemon juice or egg white, applied with the paintbrush, to help the marzipan stick, if necessary. Leave to set while you create your rabbits' tails.

Pull off 12 pieces, about 4g each, from the remaining white coconut marzipan and roll each into a hazelnut-sized ball. Place on a plate and, holding each ball at the sides, press down slightly to create a flat base. Lightly paint these rabbit tails with egg white and sprinkle over some of the 50g desiccated coconut to cover. Leave to set. >>

Next make the lemon cream cheese buttercream. Using a hand-held electric whisk, beat the butter in a medium bowl until soft and pale. Sift the icing sugar into the bowl in batches, working in the sugar with a spoon before adding the lemon juice and extract. Beat at full speed until the buttercream is really light and fluffy. Finally, beat in the cream cheese for about 1 minute (not much more – if you overbeat at this stage the cream cheese could 'split' and loosen the buttercream; if this does happen, place it in the fridge to firm up slightly).

Transfer the buttercream to the piping bag fitted with the 1.5cm nozzle; if you are using a disposable piping bag, you can just snip off a similar-sized opening from the tip. Pipe the buttercream on to your cakes in a domed shape, covering the cake's surface to ensure a fully 'white' rabbit. Sprinkle with the rest of the desiccated coconut for decoration, then chill for 15 minutes to firm up the buttercream slightly. Place two coconut marzipan ears in the buttercream on 12 of the cakes, and a tail on each of the others.

FOR THE CAKE

200g butter, softened

200g light muscovado sugar

4 eggs (at room temperature)

200g self-raising flour

4 tsp ground cinnamon

Finely grated zest of 2 oranges

200g finely grated carrots
(about 2 medium carrots)

200g pistachios, toasted and
chopped (see p.64)

FOR THE BUTTERCREAM

50g butter, softened

100g icing sugar, sifted

½ tbsp whole milk

½ tsp vanilla extract

75g full-fat cream cheese

FOR THE GANACHE

100g dark chocolate, chopped
into small pieces

1 tbsp orange blossom honey
or golden syrup

1 tsp vanilla extract

150ml double cream

TO DECORATE

Icing sugar, to create the moon

Edible silver glitter, to dust

A selection of white chocolate
stars; white shimmer
pearls; mini white shimmer
pearls; mini silver stars (see
directory, p.307)

EQUIPMENT

20cm round, deep, loose-
bottomed tin (or 2 x 20cm
round, loose-bottomed
sandwich tins), greased and
fully lined

SEE-IN-THE-DARK CAKE

Carrots, as we know, are good for your eyes – and what better excuse could there be to eat cake? Maybe at a midnight feast... Dark chocolate ganache is an amazingly good partner to carrot cake, and forms a velvety backdrop to the crescent moon and shining stars. If you're a fan of chocolate and orange, use an orange-flavoured dark chocolate or orange extract in place of the vanilla. The cream cheese filling not only plays on the idea that the moon is made of cheese but, when the cake is cut, its white mass creates a dramatic contrast to the dark chocolate ganache and night sky.

Preheat the oven to 180°C/160°C fan/gas 4.

Using a hand-held electric whisk, or in a free-standing mixer, beat the butter and sugar together for 5–10 minutes or until the mixture is very light and creamy and a pale café-au-lait shade. Break the eggs into a jug and beat with a fork. Gradually add the egg to the butter and sugar mixture, beating well after each addition. Should the mixture look like it's curdling, add a spoonful of the flour. Sift the flour and cinnamon into the mixture in two or three batches, folding in each batch gently. Finally, stir through the orange zest, carrots and pistachios. Spoon the mixture into your prepared tin(s).

Bake the larger cake for 50–60 minutes, the two sandwich cakes for 25–30 minutes, or until risen and a skewer pushed into the centre comes out fairly clean. Leave to cool in the tin(s) for about 10 minutes before removing the cake(s) and transferring to a wire rack to cool completely.

Meanwhile, make the cream cheese buttercream. If you have a free-standing mixer, put the butter, sugar, milk and vanilla extract into the bowl, cover the bowl with a tea towel to prevent a cloud of sugar from escaping and start beating slowly. Increase the speed and beat until the mixture is fluffy, creamy and almost white, stopping a few times to scrape down the side of the bowl. I beat for up to 10 minutes at full speed to create a really light finish. If you are using a hand-held electric whisk, beat the butter in a medium bowl until soft and pale, then sift the icing sugar into the bowl in batches, working in the sugar with a spoon before adding the milk and vanilla. Beat at full speed until the buttercream is really light and fluffy. Finally, beat in the cream cheese for about 1 minute (not much more – if you overbeat at this stage the cream cheese can 'split' and loosen the buttercream; if this does happen, place it in the fridge to firm up slightly).

CONTINUED OVERLEAF >>

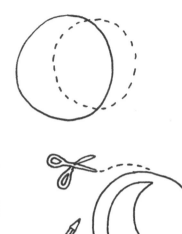

SEE-IN-THE-DARK CAKE (CONTINUED)

Trim the top of the cake(s) if domed. If you have used one deep tin, slice the cooled cake horizontally into two equal layers. Set the top layer (or one of the two smaller cakes) on some foil. Use a palette knife to spread the cream cheese buttercream over the surface. Turn the other cake layer (or second cake) upside down and set it in place on the buttercream – this will give you a flat, smooth surface on top to decorate. Chill the cake for about 15 minutes to firm up the buttercream.

Meanwhile, make the ganache. Put the chocolate in a medium-sized heatproof bowl with the honey or syrup and vanilla. Gently heat the cream in a medium saucepan over a medium heat. When it's just coming to the boil, pour it over the chocolate and leave to sit for a few minutes before stirring gently until the mixture is smooth and shiny.

Remove the cake from the fridge and place it on a wire rack set on a baking tray or on a sheet of foil or baking parchment (to collect any ganache that overflows). Pour the ganache over the cake, encouraging it to flow all over the top and down the side by carefully moving the rack from side to side. You might need to smooth the ganache on the side with a palette knife to ensure all the cake is covered.

Leave the ganache to set slightly before transferring the cake, with the help of a cake lifter or fish slices, to your chosen cake board or plate. If you leave doing this until the ganache has completely set, you risk the ganache cracking.

To make your moon stencil, use the base of the cake tin as a guide and cut out a circle of card. Draw a crescent moon shape on the circle, then cut it out and discard. Hold the stencil over the cake, a few millimetres above the ganache to prevent the stencil from sticking to the surface, and dust with icing sugar and a sprinkling of edible glitter. Remove the stencil to leave a pale, sparkling moon on the cake surface. Position your sparkling stars and shimmering pearl planets on the cake in a cluster.

VARIATION
You can also create an Orange Syrup (see p.282) with the juice after zesting your oranges for the cake. Apply this to the surface of the cake layers before adding the buttercream and ganache. Or, more simply, prick the surface with a cocktail stick, squeeze some juice over the layers and allow to soak in.

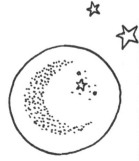

CARROT CANDLE CAKES

MAKES 12 CUPCAKES

FOR THE CANDLES

50g white chocolate (without vanilla seeds), chopped into small pieces
About 1 tsp desiccated coconut
Edible gold glitter

FOR THE CAKE

150g butter, softened
150g light muscovado sugar
3 eggs (at room temperature)
150g self-raising flour
1 tbsp ground cinnamon
Finely grated zest of 1½ oranges
150g finely grated carrots (about 1½ medium carrots)
150g pistachios, toasted and chopped (see p.64)

FOR THE BUTTERCREAM

100g butter, softened
200g icing sugar, sifted
1 tbsp whole milk
1 tsp vanilla extract
150g full-fat cream cheese

EQUIPMENT

12-hole muffin tin
12 gold-foil muffin cases
2 piping bags (1 small disposable and 1 large) plus optional wide star nozzle or 1.5cm round nozzle
5 drinking straws, 21cm long and ideally 7.5mm diameter, each cut into 3 equal pieces
Fine paintbrush or wooden latte stirrer

These white chocolate candle-topped carrot cakes are great to serve up at a birthday party and make the perfect edible present if given away individually – especially if accompanied by a box of extra candles and Biscuit Matches (see p.208) to really set the gift alight! To make your cakes extra special, you can sprinkle on some edible gold glitter and apply extra melted white chocolate down the sides of the candles to look like melted wax.

Start with the candles. Boil the kettle; while waiting, put the white chocolate pieces into a small disposable piping bag and twist the end closed. Once the water has boiled, pour it into a jug and put the piping bag into it. Leave the chocolate to melt inside the bag, then remove the bag from the jug and wipe dry with a tea towel. Wait for the chocolate to firm up a little: you don't want to pipe it into the straws while it's still really runny or it will flood out again.

Meanwhile, line your cut-down straws with baking parchment – this will ensure that the chocolate candles can be pushed out of the straws without getting stuck. To line the straws, cut strips of parchment 10 x 7.5cm, then cut these down into 7.5 x 2.5cm strips. Wrap each strip around the end of a slim-handled paintbrush (or a drinking straw smaller in diameter than the ones you are using to create your candles) and slide inside a piece of straw. Gently pull out the paintbrush or smaller straw.

Once the chocolate has reached a paste-like consistency, snip the very tip off the piping bag so it will fit snugly inside your the straws. Pipe the chocolate into each piece of straw, filling it almost fully. Lay the straws flat to firm up.

Meanwhile, toast the desiccated coconut lightly in a frying pan (this makes the shreds look like wicks that have been alight). You can leave some of the coconut untoasted to create a mixture of candles. Before the chocolate has fully set in the straws, carefully insert a coconut shred into the tip of each 'candle'. Leave the candles to set completely in the fridge. Once hard, remove them from the straws by pushing them out with the end of the paintbrush.

When you're ready to bake, preheat the oven to 180°C/160°C fan/gas 4. Line the muffin tin with the foil cases.

Using a hand-held electric whisk, or in a free-standing mixer, beat the butter and sugar together for 5–10 minutes or until the mixture is very light and creamy and a pale café-au-lait shade.

CONTINUED OVERLEAF >>

CARROT CANDLE CAKES (CONTINUED)

Break the eggs into a mug or jug and beat with a fork. Gradually add the eggs to the butter and sugar mixture, beating well after each addition. Should the mixture look like it's curdling, add a spoonful of the flour. Sift the flour and cinnamon into the mixture in two or three batches, folding in each batch gently. Finally, stir through the orange zest, carrots and pistachios. Spoon the mixture into the muffin cases, dividing it evenly.

Bake for 15–20 minutes or until the cakes have risen and a skewer pushed into the centre comes out fairly clean. Leave to cool in the tin for about 10 minutes, then transfer, in the foil cases, to a wire rack to cool completely.

While the cakes are cooling, make the cream cheese buttercream. If you have a free-standing mixer, put the butter, sugar, milk and vanilla into the bowl, cover the bowl with a tea towel to prevent a cloud of sugar from escaping and start beating slowly. Increase the speed and beat until the mixture is fluffy, creamy and almost white, stopping a few times to scrape down the side of the bowl. I beat for up to 10 minutes at full speed to create a really light finish. If you are using a hand-held electric whisk, beat the butter in a medium bowl until soft and pale, then sift the icing sugar into the bowl in batches, working in the sugar with a spoon before adding the milk and vanilla. Beat at full speed until the buttercream is really light and fluffy. Finally, beat in the cream cheese for about 1 minute (not much more – if you overbeat at this stage the cream cheese can 'split' and loosen the buttercream; if this does happen, place it in the fridge to firm up slightly).

Put the buttercream into a large piping bag fitted with the star or round nozzle, depending on the finish you want; if you are using a disposable piping bag, you can just snip off a 1.5–2cm opening from the tip. Pipe the buttercream over the cakes. If using the plain nozzle, smooth over the buttercream, without flattening its height, using a small palette knife. You could also just cover the cakes with buttercream using a teaspoon.

Allow the buttercream to firm up slightly before sticking a white chocolate candle into the top of each cake (for an extra special cake, add lots of candles like the one photographed). Sprinkle lightly with some edible gold glitter. To add drips of 'melted wax', melt a little extra white chocolate and apply to the sides of the candles with the fine paintbrush or latte stirrer.

HIDDEN CARROT CAKE

150g butter, roughly chopped

150g light muscovado sugar

150g golden syrup

150g dark chocolate, chopped
into small pieces

150ml whole milk

3 eggs (at room temperature)

I tbsp vanilla extract

3 tbsp cocoa powder

150g self-raising flour

100g butter, softened

100g light muscovado sugar

2 eggs (at room temperature)

100g self-raising flour

2 tsp vanilla extract

Finely grated zest of I orange

100g finely grated carrot (about
I medium carrot)

Orange food colouring, such as
Sugarflair tangerine/apricot
colour paste (see directory,
p.308)

900g (2lb) loaf tin (21 x 11cm)
greased and lined with
seatbelt straps (see p.21)

4 disposable mini-loaf cases,
8 x 4cm (see directory,
p.308)

3.5cm round biscuit cutter

Fine paintbrush

Cocktail stick

INGREDIENTS CONTINUED
OVERLEAF >>

Designed on the same lines as my Hidden Bulb Cakes (see p.138), this loaf-shaped bake conceals sweet, marzipan-topped carrot-cake carrots within a chocolate veg patch. With a scattering of dark chocolate 'topsoil', it makes a beautiful bake for the gardener in your life – or you could serve it up for tea outside on a summer's day. It's best to make both the chocolate and carrot cakes the day before assembling: the mini loaves need to be frozen and the chocolate cake needs time to firm up.

Preheat the oven to 180°C/160°C fan/gas 4.

Start with the chocolate cake. Put the butter, sugar and golden syrup in a saucepan set over a medium heat. Stir occasionally until the sugar has fully dissolved. Remove from the heat, add the chocolate and stir until melted and smooth. Transfer to a large bowl and leave for 5 minutes to cool slightly.

Meanwhile, measure the milk in a jug and beat in the eggs and vanilla. Pour the milk and egg mixture into the warm syrup mixture and beat to combine. Sift the cocoa and flour into the mixture in two batches, mixing to make a very wet batter. Pour into the prepared loaf tin. Bake for 50–60 minutes, covering with foil if the top of the cake seems to be browning too fast, until a skewer pushed into the centre of the cake comes out fairly clean.

Remove from the oven (leave the oven on) and cool in the tin for 30 minutes before removing the cake and transferring to a wire rack. When the cake is cold, store it in an airtight container overnight to firm up a little.

Next make the mini carrot cake loaves. Using a hand-held electric whisk, or in a free-standing mixer, beat the butter and sugar together for 5–10 minutes or until the mixture is very light and creamy and a pale café-au-lait shade. Break the eggs into a mug or jug and beat with a fork. Gradually add the eggs to the butter and sugar mixture, beating well after each addition. Should the mixture look like it's curdling, add a spoonful of the flour. Sift the flour into the mix and fold in gently, then stir through the vanilla, orange zest, carrot and enough food colouring to tint the mixture a deep carrot-orange shade.

Place the mini-loaf cases on a baking tray. Spoon the carrot mixture into them, dividing it evenly (the mixture will make four loaves and you will only use three of them, but it's a good idea to have an extra one to play with). Bake for 20–25 minutes or until the cakes have risen and a skewer pushed into the centre comes out fairly clean.

CONTINUED OVERLEAF >>

FOR THE MARZIPAN

1 egg (at room temperature)
1 tbsp orange blossom water
1 tbsp orange blossom honey
Finely grated zest of 3 oranges
⅓ tsp orange food colouring, such as Sugarflair tangerine/apricot colour paste (see directory, p.308)
300g ground almonds
300g icing sugar, sifted
1 tbsp ground cinnamon

FOR THE GANACHE

150g dark chocolate
1½ tbsp golden syrup
1½ tsp vanilla extract
150ml double cream

TO FINISH THE CARROTS

3 pistachios
A few sprigs of curly leaf parsley

Leave to cool on the tray for about 10 minutes, then transfer the loaves, still in their cases, to a wire rack to cool completely. Once cooled, put the mini loaves, in their cases, in a freezer bag and freeze them – this will make it easier to carve them into carrot shapes later.

To make the marzipan, put the egg in a medium bowl and add the orange blossom water, honey, orange zest and food colouring. Mix together well to make a paste. Add the ground almonds and icing sugar and start mixing them in with a spoon, then bring the mixture together into a ball with your hands. (I wear disposable silicone gloves when doing this to prevent my hands from turning orange.) At the beginning, it may seem that the mixture is too dry, but keep going and the marzipan will come together like pastry.

Break off a 75g chunk of the orange marzipan and set it aside. Knead the cinnamon into the remaining marzipan to give it a terracotta colour. Add a splash of orange juice or water if the mixture seems too dry. Keep both pieces of marzipan wrapped in clingfilm to prevent them from drying out.

Once your chocolate cake has firmed up overnight and the mini carrot loaves have been frozen, you can make the ganache. Chop the chocolate into small pieces or blitz it in a food processor to create a topsoil-like texture. Remove a quarter of the chocolate to use later as 'topsoil' and set aside. Put the remaining chopped chocolate into a medium-sized heatproof bowl with the syrup and vanilla. Gently heat the cream in a small saucepan over a medium heat. When it's just coming to the boil, pour it over the chocolate and stir gently until smooth and shiny. Keep a spoonful of the ganache aside at room temperature – you want to keep this runny so you can use it to assemble the hidden carrots. The rest of the ganache needs to have a soft, spreading consistency, so, once cooled, you may want to put it in the fridge to firm up.

Use the biscuit cutter to mark out three evenly spaced holes on the top of the chocolate loaf cake. Use a spoon and sharp knife to carve out a carrot-shaped hole inside each circle, which will be filled with the cake carrots. Put the chocolate sponge carvings into a bowl and break into crumbs to use later.

Remove your frozen mini loaves from the freezer. Using a small knife, trim the short ends of each loaf to create two flat surfaces. Stand the loaf up on end. Place the biscuit cutter on top of your now vertical loaf and use it as a guide for the top of the carrot. Carve down into the loaf to create a carrot shape. >>

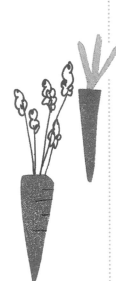

Insert the 'carrots' into the carrot-shaped holes in the chocolate cake to help you get the shape and size of the holes right. Then take them out again. Using the paintbrush, paint some of the still-liquid chocolate ganache inside the carved-out holes. Return the carrot-shaped carrot cakes to the holes and fill in any gaps with some of the reserved chocolate cake crumbs.

Next create the marzipan carrot tops. Take three pieces of the orange marzipan, each weighing about 25g, and form each into a carrot-top shape. Using the biscuit cutter as a guide, ensure that the base of each carrot top is the same diameter as the carrot cakes stuck inside the chocolate cake. With a sharp knife, mark horizontal lines around the carrot tops to make them look realistically lumpy and bumpy. Press a pistachio into the centre of each carrot top. Chill in the fridge while you make your terracotta pot.

Spread a thin layer of the thickened chocolate ganache around the sides of the chocolate loaf cake using a palette knife; set aside while you roll out the terracotta-coloured marzipan to make the 'pot' for the cake to sit in. First roll the marzipan into a sausage shape about 65cm long and set it on an equally long strip of baking parchment. Roll out the marzipan until it is about 1cm thick and roughly 7.5cm wide (or the right dimensions to go all the way round the sides of your loaf cake to cover them – measure this using a piece of string). Trim the edges to neaten (this is easiest with a pizza cutter and ruler), then wrap the marzipan around the cake. Seal the ends together and smooth with your thumb and fingers. Using a ruler or knife, score a line around the 'pot', 2cm from the top, for definition.

Remove your carrot tops from the fridge and position them over the carrot cake pieces in the cake, using some honey to secure them, if necessary. Spread the rest of the ganache around the marzipan carrot tops and over the top of the loaf. Scatter the reserved chopped chocolate and crumbled chocolate cake over the top to look like topsoil.

When ready to serve, carefully remove the pistachio from each carrot top and insert a tiny sprig of parsley with the help of the cocktail stick, then press the pistachio back in place (the parsley will wilt if you do this too far ahead of time). If you like, write 'Carrot Cake' on a seed label with the date or any other text you wish, or use an edible biscuit plant label (see Seedlings, p.184), and insert into the cake.

CARROT CAKE

COFFEE &
WALNUT CAKE

· ·

Coffee, cake and crunch. This classic combination is pretty irresistible and one I've brought to life in various new guises for you to have your very own 'shot' at. The best way to flavour a coffee cake is a matter of debate among baking aficionados. Espresso? Coffee extract? I find that instant coffee creates the right depth of flavour and gives an appealing café-au-lait shade to the cake. To match up against the sizeable amount of walnuts (which you can halve if you want a less nutty cake), I use a dark roast coffee, but you can use a medium roast if you prefer a milder coffee hit. Try to toast the walnuts, as this adds a wonderful flavour to the bake.

BASIC COFFEE & WALNUT CAKE

MAKES A 10CM CAKE;
SERVES 2–3

FOR THE CAKE

50g walnuts
1 tbsp instant coffee
1 tbsp freshly boiled hot water
1 tbsp whole milk
50g butter, softened
50g light muscovado sugar
1 egg (at room temperature)
50g self-raising flour

EQUIPMENT

10cm round, deep, loose-
   bottomed tin (pork-pie size),
   greased and fully lined

Preheat the oven to 180°C/160°C fan/gas 4.

Spread the walnuts on a baking tray and toast in the oven for 5–10 minutes or until lightly golden and fragrant. If you're short on time, you can use the nuts as they are, but toasting them really brings out their flavour. Leave to cool, then chop the nuts with a sharp knife (if chopping a large amount – see table opposite – I'd advise doing this in batches). You can use a food processor, but it's best to process in batches and use the pulse function to avoid your nuts turning to a powder.

Mix the coffee with the hot water, then stir in the milk. Set aside to cool. Using a hand-held electric whisk (it's tricky to beat this small quantity in a free-standing mixer), beat the butter and sugar together for 5–10 minutes or until very light and creamy. Use a spatula to scrape the mixture down from the side of the bowl and off the beater every now and again. The mixture will turn from a rich toffee brown to a pale café-au-lait shade. Break the egg into a mug or jug and beat with a fork. Gradually add the egg to the creamed butter and sugar mixture, beating well after each addition and scraping down the side of the bowl as you beat. Should the mixture look like it's curdling at any point, add a spoonful of the flour.

Sift the flour into the mixture and fold in until just combined. Finally, stir through the coffee and chopped walnuts. (If you are making one of the larger quantities – see opposite – sift and fold in the flour, and stir through the coffee and walnuts, in several batches.)

Spoon the mixture into the prepared tin and bake for 25–30 minutes or until the cake has risen and a skewer pushed into the centre comes out clean. Leave to cool in the tin for about 15 minutes before removing the cake and transferring to a wire rack to cool completely.

TO FINISH

The classic coffee and walnut cake is filled and smothered with Coffee Buttercream (see p.276) and topped with a generous scattering of fat walnuts, either halves or chopped. Or, for a moreish mocha hit, try topping this cake with a Semi-sweet Milk Chocolate Ganache (p.279) and decorating it with chocolate-covered coffee beans. For a tiramisu-style twist, drizzle a boozy Coffee Syrup (p.282) over the cake and coat it in a cloud of Sweetened Mascarpone Cream (p.278).

TO MAKE DIFFERENT-SIZED COFFEE CAKES, USE THE TABLE OPPOSITE >>

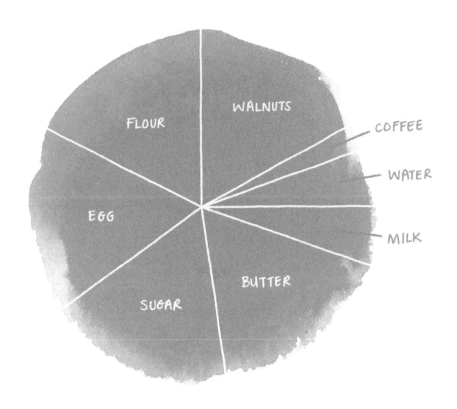

24-HOLE MINI-MUFFIN TIN	12-HOLE MUFFIN TIN	20CM SQUARE TIN	20CM ROUND DEEP TIN	900G (2LB) LOAF TIN	INGREDIENTS
50g	150g	150g	200g	150g	Walnuts
1 tbsp	3 tbsp	3 tbsp	4 tbsp	3 tbsp	Instant coffee
1 tbsp	3 tbsp	3 tbsp	4 tbsp	3 tbsp	Hot water
1 tbsp	3 tbsp	3 tbsp	4 tbsp	3 tbsp	Whole milk
50g	150g	150g	200g	150g	Butter, softened
50g	150g	150g	200g	150g	Light muscovado sugar
1	3	3	4	3	Egg(s)
50g	150g	150g	200g	150g	Self-raising flour

BAKE IN AN OVEN PREHEATED TO 180°C/160°C FAN/GAS 4					
for 10–12 minutes	for 15–20 minutes	for 30–35 minutes	for 50–60 minutes, or in 2 sandwich tins for 20–25 minutes	for 50–60 minutes	

COFFEE SHOT 'CUP' CAKES

MAKES 12 SMALL CAKES

FOR THE CAKES
3 tbsp instant coffee
3 tbsp freshly boiled hot water
3 tbsp whole milk
150g butter, softened
150g light muscovado sugar
3 eggs (at room temperature)
150g self-raising flour
150g walnuts, toasted and
    chopped (see p.82)

FOR THE COFFEE SYRUP
½ tbsp instant coffee
50ml boiling water
50g caster sugar
½ tbsp coffee liqueur, such as
    Tia Maria, optional

FOR THE TOPPING
250g mascarpone
Few drops of vanilla extract
50g icing sugar
Dash of milk or cream, if needed

TO DECORATE
Cocoa powder

EQUIPMENT
12-hole muffin tin
12 espresso-sized (115ml/4oz)
    paper cups – ideally kraft
    ripple (see directory, p.308)
Cocktail stick
Medium paintbrush
Coffee-bean stencil (see below)
    or other stencil, optional

COFFEE-BEAN
STENCIL

Baked and served in take-away coffee cups, these cakes will bring out your inner barista. They are soaked in a coffee syrup with, if you like, a shot of coffee liqueur, before being topped with sweetened mascarpone cream (or use whipped cream if you prefer). You can find paper espresso cups online or, even better, make friends with your local coffee shop and buy the cups from them. I would definitely advise using the brown kraft ripple cups, as the outer rippled layer will conceal any butteriness that can soak through from the cake through the inner cardboard.

Preheat the oven to 180°C/160°C fan/gas 4. Line the muffin tin with the cups.

Mix the coffee with the hot water, then stir in the milk. Set aside to cool. Using a hand-held electric whisk, or in a free-standing mixer, beat the butter and sugar together for 5–10 minutes or until very light and creamy. The mixture will turn from a rich toffee brown to a pale café-au-lait shade. Break the eggs into a mug or jug and beat with a fork. Gradually add the eggs to the creamed butter and sugar mixture, beating well after each addition. Should the mixture look like it's curdling, add a spoonful of the flour. Sift in the flour and fold in until just combined. Finally, stir through the coffee and chopped walnuts.

Spoon the mixture into the paper cups and bake for 15–20 minutes or until the cakes have risen and a skewer pushed into the centre comes out clean.

While the cakes are baking, make the syrup. Put the coffee in a small pan, add the boiling water and stir to dissolve the granules. Stir in the sugar. Set the pan over a medium heat and bring to the boil. Reduce the heat and simmer gently for a few minutes or until the sugar is completely dissolved and you are left with a runny syrup. Remove from the heat and stir in the liqueur, if using.

Once the cakes are baked, remove from the oven and leave to cool in the tin for about 5 minutes. During this time, prick them all over with a cocktail stick and brush over the coffee syrup using a paintbrush or pastry brush, allowing the syrup to soak into the sponge. Use about ½ tablespoon syrup per cup. Remove the cakes from the tin, still in their cups, and leave to cool completely on a wire rack.

Put the mascarpone and vanilla in a bowl and sift in the icing sugar. Beat together until creamy and well combined, adding a dash of milk or cream to slacken the mix slightly, if necessary. Spoon some on to each cake and spread level with a palette knife. Sift the cocoa on top, either all over or through a coffee-bean stencil to create some barista art.

WALNUT WHIPPIES

MAKES 24 WHIPPIES

Inspired by walnut whips and ice-cream van treats, my mini walnut whippies are baked inside their very own bespoke waffle cones. Each with a mini flake, they're great to hand around at parties. To make these '99s' 100 per cent impressive, I like to coat the top of some of the cones in dark chocolate (a coffee-flavoured one if possible) and chopped walnuts. As well as being baked in paper espresso cups, which support the cones in the oven, these mini treats can be displayed in them too, emphasising the coffee theme.

FOR THE CAKES
1 tbsp instant coffee
1 tbsp freshly boiled hot water
1 tbsp whole milk
24 waffle ice-cream cones (plus a few spares)
50g butter, softened
50g light muscovado sugar
1 egg (at room temperature)
50g self-raising flour
50g walnuts, toasted and chopped (see p.82)

TO DECORATE
2 chocolate flake bars (about 32g each), such as Cadbury
50g dark chocolate, coffee-flavoured if possible, chopped into small pieces

FOR THE TOPPING
250g mascarpone
½ tsp vanilla extract
50g icing sugar
Dash of milk or cream, if needed

EQUIPMENT
12-hole muffin tin
8 espresso-sized (115ml/4oz) paper cups (see directory, p.308)
2 large disposable piping bags plus a large star nozzle

Preheat the oven to 180°C/160°C fan/gas 4. Mix the coffee with the hot water, then stir in the milk. Set aside to cool.

To prepare your mini waffle cones, place a folded tea towel on your work surface and lay a waffle cone on it (the towel will cushion the cone as you cut it down to size). With a serrated knife, gently score a line all around the cone 8cm up from the tip. Very carefully cut through the scored line, trying not to break the cone. Repeat this process to create 24 mini cones. You won't need the top sections, so you can break them up and use them in Tiffin (see p.180), or grind them into a powder to look like sand and display with your cones, as shown in the photograph.

Place the eight disposable coffee cups in the muffin tin and put three mini waffle cones inside each cup so that they support each other. Set aside.

Using a hand-held electric whisk (it's tricky to beat this small quantity in a free-standing mixer), beat the butter and sugar together for 5–10 minutes or until very light and creamy. The mixture will turn from a rich toffee brown to a pale café-au-lait shade. Break the egg into a mug or jug and beat with a fork. Gradually add the egg to the creamed butter and sugar mixture, beating well after each addition. Should the mixture look like it's curdling, add a spoonful of the flour. Sift in the flour and fold in until just combined. Finally, stir through the coffee and half of the chopped walnuts.

Transfer the mixture to a piping bag and snip off a 2cm opening from the tip. Pipe the mixture into the mini cones, filling them just over three-quarters full. Bake for 10–12 minutes or until the cake filling is lightly golden and a skewer inserted into the centre comes out clean. Leave the cake-filled cones in the coffee cups, in the tin, to cool completely.

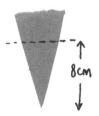

8cm

CONTINUED OVERLEAF >>

WALNUT WHIPPIES (CONTINUED)

Meanwhile, use a small, sharp knife to cut each chocolate flake bar across into four 3cm lengths, then cut each length vertically into four mini-flakes. Don't worry if some of them crumble – you have a few extra to play with. Cutting the flake on a few sheets of kitchen paper will help to cushion it.

If you want to coat the rims of the waffle cones with chocolate and nuts, melt the chocolate in a microwave or a heatproof bowl set over a pan of simmering water (bain-marie). Paint some chocolate on to the tops of the cones, then sprinkle on the chopped walnuts. Leave to set on a sheet of baking parchment or a silicone mat.

Put the mascarpone and vanilla extract in a bowl and sift over the icing sugar. Beat until creamy and well combined, adding a dash of milk or cream to slacken the mix slightly, if necessary. Transfer the mixture to a piping bag fitted with the star nozzle. Carefully pipe the sweetened mascarpone on to each mini cone in a high peak – like ice cream. If you haven't put the chopped walnuts around the rim of the cones, scatter them over the mascarpone. Top each cone with a mini flake.

COFFEE BARCODE CAKE

3 tbsp instant coffee
3 tbsp freshly boiled hot water
3 tbsp whole milk
150g butter, softened
150g light muscovado sugar
3 eggs (at room temperature)
150g self-raising flour
150g walnuts, toasted and
    chopped (see p.82)

FOR THE SYRUP
½ tbsp instant coffee
50ml freshly boiled hot water
50g caster sugar
½ tbsp coffee liqueur, such
    as Tia Maria

FOR THE TOPPING
250g mascarpone
½ tsp vanilla extract
50g icing sugar
Dash of milk or cream,
    if needed

TO DECORATE
Cocoa powder
About 100g chocolate
    cappuccino flutes, such
    as Elizabeth Shaw's

EQUIPMENT
20 x 27cm brownie tin, greased
    and lined with seatbelt
    straps (see p.21)
Cocktail stick
Stencil with numbers 2cm
    in height
Mini sieve

The ingredients in this cake – sweetened mascarpone cream, coffee liqueur syrup, chocolate and cocoa – combine to give a flavour reminiscent of tiramisu. I use coffee-chocolate 'flutes' to create a barcode pattern on the cake, and make the numbers at the base with the aid of a classic stencil. You can create a special, personalised barcode (perhaps someone's date of birth) or keep it as simple as 1,2,3. The one photographed here is actually the barcode on the back of this book!

Preheat the oven to 180°C/160°C fan/gas 4. Mix the coffee with the hot water, then stir in the milk. Set aside to cool.

Using a hand-held electric whisk, or in a free-standing mixer, beat the butter and sugar together for 5–10 minutes or until very light and creamy. The mixture will turn from a rich toffee brown to a pale café-au-lait shade. Break the eggs into a mug or jug and beat with a fork. Gradually add the egg to the creamed butter and sugar mixture, beating well after each addition. Should the mixture look like it's curdling, add a spoonful of the flour. Sift in the flour, then fold in until just combined. Finally, stir through the coffee and chopped walnuts.

Spoon the mixture into your tin and level the surface with a cranked palette knife. Bake for 25–30 minutes or until the cake has risen and a skewer pushed into the centre comes out clean.

While the cake is baking, make the syrup. Put the coffee in a small pan, add the hot water and stir to dissolve the granules (to save boiling the kettle twice, you can do this when you create your coffee paste for the cake). Stir in the sugar. Set the pan over a medium heat and bring to the boil. Reduce the heat and simmer gently for a few minutes or until the sugar has completely dissolved and you are left with a runny syrup. Remove from the heat and stir in the coffee liqueur. Keep warm.

Once the cake is baked, remove it from the oven. Prick the surface all over with a cocktail stick or fork and brush with the syrup. Leave it to soak in, then give the cake a second brushing of syrup. Once the cake has cooled in the tin for about 15 minutes, remove it and transfer to a wire rack to cool completely.

CONTINUED OVERLEAF >>

COFFEE BARCODE CAKE (CONTINUED)

To make the sweetened mascarpone topping, put the mascarpone and vanilla extract in a bowl and sift in the icing sugar. Beat together until creamy and well combined, adding a dash of milk or cream to slacken the mixture slightly, if necessary. Spoon dollops of the mascarpone cream over the cake and spread with a palette knife to create a smooth, level surface.

Position the numerical stencil along one long edge of the cake (this will be the base of the barcode pattern), leaving a 1cm gap between the edge of the cake and the bottom of the numbers. Place a strip of thin card or paper lightly over this 1cm border below the stencil and another strip above the numbers – this will prevent any cocoa powder from going on to the cake where you don't want it. Using a small sieve (or a tea strainer), carefully sift cocoa powder over the stencil. Remove the protective strips and the stencil to reveal the row of numbers. If you want to create a bespoke barcode, you'll need to cover up the unwanted numbers in the stencil and dust in stages.

Now create your barcode lines with the chocolate flutes. Starting 2cm in from a short side of the cake and 1 cm from the top, arrange the flutes and slightly press them into the topping – follow the arrangement seen in the photograph opposite. You should have a few flutes left over: cut one of them into 2cm pieces and place pieces at the end of the two outermost flutes and one at the end of the middle flute to re-create the authentic barcode pattern.

The cocoa powder numbers will get darker, and tie in better with the chocolate flutes, if the cake is left in the fridge for an hour or so. But bring it back to room temperature before serving.

COFFEE & WALNUT WALL

MAKES A 20CM SQUARE CAKE;
SERVES 12

FOR THE CAKE
3 tbsp instant coffee
3 tbsp freshly boiled hot water
3 tbsp whole milk
150g butter, softened
150g light muscovado sugar
3 eggs (at room temperature)
150g self-raising flour
150g walnuts, toasted and
   chopped (see p.82)

FOR THE TOPPING
250g mascarpone
½ tsp vanilla extract
50g icing sugar
Dash of milk or cream,
   if needed

TO DECORATE
1 tbsp cocoa powder
1 tbsp cinnamon sugar –
   homemade (see p.283)
   or shop-bought
1 tsp ground cinnamon

EQUIPMENT
20cm square, loose-bottomed
   tin, greased and lined with
   seatbelt straps (see p.21)
8 wooden latte stirrers,
   19cm long

Building a cake has never been more fun. This coffee cake is plastered in sweetened mascarpone cream, which becomes 'mortar' when covered with a stencilled pattern of delicious brickwork. Both chocolate and cinnamon are put to good use here to produce differing colours and textures of brick.

Preheat the oven to 180°C/160°C fan/gas 4. Mix the instant coffee with the hot water, then stir in the milk. Set aside to cool.

Using a hand-held electric whisk, or in a free-standing mixer, beat the butter and sugar together for 5–10 minutes or until the mixture is very light and creamy and has taken on a pale café-au-lait shade. Break the eggs into a mug or jug and beat with a fork. Gradually add the egg to the creamed butter and sugar mixture, beating well after each addition. Should the mixture look like it's curdling at any point, add a spoonful of the flour. Sift in the flour and fold it in until just combined. Finally, stir through the coffee and chopped walnuts.

Spoon the mixture into your tin and smooth the surface with a cranked palette knife. Bake for 30–35 minutes or until the cake has risen and a skewer pushed into the centre comes out clean. Leave to cool in the tin for 15 minutes before removing the cake and transferring to a wire rack to cool completely.

Once the cake has cooled, make the sweetened mascarpone topping. Put the mascarpone and vanilla extract in a bowl and sift in the icing sugar. Beat together until creamy and well combined, adding a dash of milk or cream to slacken the mix slightly, if necessary. Spoon on to the cake in dollops and spread over with a palette knife to create a smooth, level surface.

To create your brickwork pattern, lay four of the wooden latte stirrers on the cake, flat side down, to form four horizontal parallel lines with a 3.5cm gap between each stick. Cut the remaining sticks into 4cm pieces – you will need 15 pieces in total. Lay these pieces vertically between the horizontal sticks to create a varying brickwork pattern. Your smallest brick should be no less than 3cm wide and your biggest no more than 5.5cm.

Sift cocoa powder into some of the brick shapes and cinnamon sugar into the others, creating two different shades of brickwork. Finish with a light dusting of cinnamon to create depth and shadow. Carefully remove the latte stirrers to reveal your brick wall. If you leave the cake in the fridge for an hour, the moisture from the topping will darken and enhance the colours of the bricks. Bring the cake back to room temperature before serving.

LEMON
CAKE

With or without a final zingy drizzle, this lemon cake is packed full of zesty flavour: your tastebuds will go 'ping!' along with the kitchen timer once it's baked. I use ground almonds to give the crumb a lovely moistness and to complement the lemon flavour. But if you don't like almonds, or can't eat nuts, you can leave them out (if you do this, reduce the tablespoon of lemon juice to a teaspoon). I always use unwaxed lemons for this cake so I know that all I'm grating into the mixture is delicious, unadulterated zest.

BASIC LEMON CAKE

MAKES A 10CM CAKE;
SERVES 2–3

FOR THE CAKE

50g butter, softened
50g caster sugar
Finely grated zest of 1 lemon
1 egg (at room temperature)
50g self-raising flour
1 tbsp ground almonds
1 tbsp lemon juice

EQUIPMENT

10cm round, deep, loose-
bottomed tin (pork-pie size),
greased and fully lined

Preheat the oven to 180°C/160°C fan/gas 4.

Using a hand-held electric whisk (it's tricky to beat this small quantity in a free-standing mixer), beat the butter and sugar together for 5–10 minutes or until very light, pale and creamy.

Add the lemon zest and beat it in. Break the egg into a mug or jug (which makes it easy and less messy to pour into the mixture) and beat with a fork. Gradually add the egg to the creamed butter and sugar mixture, beating well after each addition. If the mixture looks like it's curdling, beat in a spoonful of the flour.

Sift the flour and ground almonds into the mixture and fold them in until just combined. (If you are making one of the larger quantities – see opposite – sift and fold in the flour with the almonds in several batches.)

Gently fold in the lemon juice, which will loosen the mixture and lighten the finished cake. You will now have a cake mixture with a soft dropping consistency – i.e. if you take a dollop of it on a spoon and turn the spoon on its side, the mixture will drop off of its own accord. Scrape the mixture into the prepared tin and level it out with a spatula.

Bake for 20–25 minutes or until risen and golden, and a skewer inserted into the centre of the cake comes out clean. Leave to cool in the tin for 15 minutes before removing the cake and transferring to a wire rack to cool completely.

TO FINISH

To give your cake a classic lemon drizzle, prick it all over with a cocktail stick while still warm, then trickle some Lemon Syrup (see p.282) over it and leave to soak in. Alternatively, for a sharper, super-quick lemon downpour, squeeze fresh lemon juice directly over the cake and sprinkle with sugar. This cake is also delicious sandwiched or topped with Chantilly Cream (p.277) or Sweetened Mascarpone Cream (p.278) plus Lemon Curd (p.273) and fresh raspberries, with a sprig of mint for a final flourish and striking hit of colour.

TO MAKE DIFFERENT-SIZED LEMON CAKES, USE THE TABLE OPPOSITE >>

ALMONDS

BUTTER

FLOUR

EGG

SUGAR

LEMON

24-HOLE MINI-MUFFIN TIN	12-HOLE MUFFIN TIN	20CM SQUARE TIN	20CM ROUND DEEP TIN	900G (2LB) LOAF TIN	INGREDIENTS
50g	150g	150g	200g	200g	Butter, softened
50g	150g	150g	200g	200g	Caster sugar
Zest of 1 lemon, 1 tbsp juice	Zest of 3 lemons, 3 tbsp juice	Zest of 3 lemons, 3 tbsp juice	Zest of 4 lemons, 4 tbsp juice	Zest of 4 lemons, 4 tbsp juice	Zest and juice of lemon
1	3	3	4	4	Egg(s)
50g	150g	150g	200g	200g	Self-raising flour
1 tbsp	3 tbsp	3 tbsp	4 tbsp	4 tbsp	Ground almonds

BAKE IN AN OVEN PREHEATED TO 180°C/160°C FAN/GAS 4					
for 10–12 minutes	for 15–20 minutes	for 25–30 minutes	for 45–50 minutes, or in 2 sandwich tins for 20–25 minutes	for 45–50 minutes	

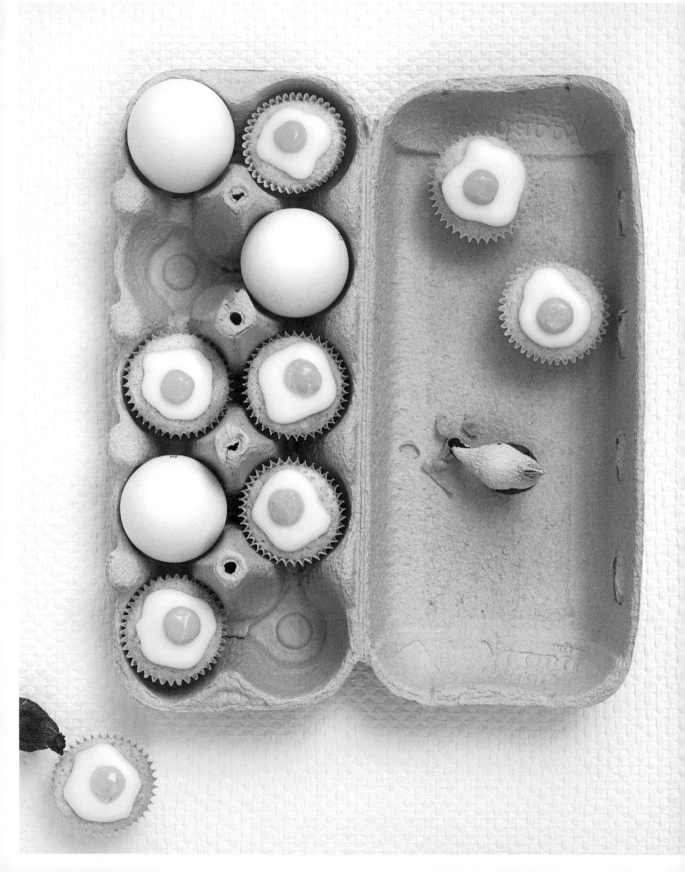

FRIED EGG CAKES

These egg-cellent bite-sized treats are made with my essential lemon cake mix. To make them extra citrussy, the bright yolk at the centre of each egg is formed with a blob of delicious orange curd. Serve up the cakes in real egg cartons for a great gift. To make them even sweeter, include a side of my butter biscuit chips too (see p.35).

FOR THE CAKES

50g butter, softened
50g caster sugar
Finely grated zest of 1 lemon
1 egg (at room temperature)
50g self-raising flour
1 tbsp ground almonds
1 tbsp lemon juice

FOR THE FRIED EGGS

50g icing sugar
About ½ tbsp lemon juice
25g Orange Curd (see p.273)

EQUIPMENT

24-hole mini-muffin tin
24 white or yellow paper
    mini-muffin cases
Wooden latte stirrer
Egg boxes, to serve, optional

Preheat the oven to 180°C/160°C fan/gas 4. Line the mini-muffin tin with the muffin cases.

Using a hand-held electric whisk (it's tricky to beat this small quantity in a free-standing mixer), beat the butter and sugar together for 5–10 minutes or until very light, pale and creamy. Add the lemon zest and beat it in.

Break the egg into a mug or jug and beat with a fork. Gradually add the egg to the creamed butter and sugar mixture, beating well after each addition. If the mixture looks like it's curdling, beat in a spoonful of the flour. Sift the flour and almonds into the bowl and fold them in until just combined. Gently stir in the lemon juice. Spoon the mixture into the muffin cases, dividing it equally.

Bake for 10–12 minutes or until the cakes are risen and lightly golden brown, and a skewer inserted into the centre comes out clean. Leave the cakes to cool in the tin for 5 minutes before transferring them, still in their paper cases, to a wire rack to cool completely.

To make a lemon water icing for the fried eggs, sift the icing sugar into a bowl and stir in a little lemon juice, a few drops at a time, until you have a smooth, thick paste. Carefully spoon a little of the icing on to the top of each cake, creating an uneven shape that suggests the white of a fried egg. Use the latte stirrer to help you spread the icing into the right shape. Then, with the stirrer, apply a blob of orange curd to the centre of each egg. Leave to set.

Before serving, carefully place your cakes inside egg boxes, if using.

VARIATION

Instead of the icing and curd eggs, you can use fried egg sweets, securing one to the top of each cake with a little honey, some water icing or curd.

RAINBOW CAKE

FOR THE CAKE

Cake-release spray for the tin
100g butter, softened
100g caster sugar
2 lemons
2 eggs (at room temperature)
100g self-raising flour
2 tbsp ground almonds

FOR THE LEMON SYRUP

100g caster sugar

TO DECORATE

300ml double cream
1 kiwi fruit
1 mango
150g strawberries
50g blueberries

EQUIPMENT

23cm round, deep, loose-
    bottomed tin, greased
    and fully lined
Empty golden syrup tin
    (454g size)
Cocktail stick
Medium paintbrush

This colourful cake looks spectacular but is very simple to make. You can use a ring-shaped savarin tin to bake the cake, but I quite like the DIY approach of putting an empty golden syrup tin inside a round cake tin – a pot of gold in more ways than one. Either way, with its clouds of cream and rows of glistening, lemon-glazed fruit, this bake will 'rain' supreme!

Preheat the oven to 180°C/160°C fan/gas 4. Lightly grease the outside of the syrup tin with cake-release spray, then wrap it in baking parchment. Place it in the centre of the lined round tin.

Using a hand-held electric whisk, or in a free-standing mixer, beat the butter and sugar together for 5–10 minutes or until very light, pale and creamy. Grate the zest from the lemons into the mix and beat it in.

Lightly beat the eggs in a mug or jug. Gradually add the egg to the butter and sugar mixture, beating well after each addition. If the mixture looks like it's curdling, add a spoonful of the flour. Sift the flour and almonds into the mixture, in batches, folding in each batch until just combined.

Squeeze all the juice from the lemons. Gently stir 2 tablespoons of the juice into the cake mixture. Set the rest of the juice aside.

Spoon the cake mixture into your tin, taking care to keep the syrup tin central as you spread the mixture around it. Bake for 20–25 minutes or until the cake is risen and lightly golden brown, and a skewer inserted into it comes out clean.

While the cake is baking, make the lemon syrup. Measure the reserved lemon juice and add water, if necessary, to make it up to 100ml. Pour into a saucepan. Add the caster sugar and set the saucepan over a medium-high heat. Warm for several minutes, stirring occasionally, until the sugar has dissolved, then remove from the heat and allow to cool.

Once the cake is baked, and while it is still warm, prick the surface all over with the cocktail stick. Brush over some of the lemon syrup using the paintbrush or a pastry brush, allowing the syrup to soak into the sponge. Set aside the remaining syrup to glaze the fruit later.

CONTINUED OVERLEAF >>

RAINBOW CAKE (CONTINUED)

Leave the cake to cool slightly before carefully lifting out the syrup tin. Set the cake, still in its round tin, on a wire rack to cool completely.

Remove the cooled cake from the tin. Using a ruler as a guide, cut the cake across in half to make two rainbow shapes.

Whip the cream with a hand-held electric whisk until it forms soft-to-medium peaks. Using a small palette knife, spread half the cream over each rainbow-shaped cake, creating a slightly textured finish. Place one cream-covered rainbow cake on top of the other.

Cut the top and bottom off the kiwi fruit, then slice the skin away in strips. Use a small, sharp knife to peel the mango, then slice the flesh off the central stone in large pieces; you'll only need about half of this, depending on the mango's size. Cut the kiwi, mango and strawberries into neat 1–2cm pieces. >>

Arrange all the pieces of fruit on top of the cake in neat rows, to create the appearance of a rainbow. Brush the remaining lemon syrup over the fruit as a glaze. (Any leftover syrup can be kept in the fridge for up to a week and used to flavour other cakes.)

VARIATION

I also like to present the finished cake on a slate board that is dusted with icing sugar clouds, made by sifting icing sugar over a cloud stencil (use the cloud template shape on p.213 to cut a stencil from a sheet of card). To add to the display, fill a golden syrup tin with lemon drops and gold chocolate coins and put it at the end of the rainbow cake to represent the pot of gold.

CONFETTI CUPCAKES

Cupcakes needn't be all about sugary frostings and sprinkles. For me, they should be delicious cakes in their own right topped off with a combination of ingredients that offers varying textures and colours. Decorated with fruit and flowers, these cupcakes have the added bonus of a hidden lemon curd and raspberry centre, plus edible confetti that makes them a feast for your tastebuds as well as your eyes. Adorn the cakes with marzipan bees and pineapple flowers too, if you choose.

FOR THE CAKES
150g butter, softened
150g caster sugar
Finely grated zest of 3 lemons
3 eggs (at room temperature)
150g self-raising flour
3 tbsp ground almonds
3 tbsp lemon juice

FOR THE FILLING
250g Lemon Curd (see p.273)
12 raspberries, plus extra to
  decorate the cakes

FOR THE TOPPING
500g mascarpone
100g icing sugar

TO DECORATE
Edible Confetti: Summer
  (see p.295)
Blueberries
Small strawberries
Cherries
Flowers (unsprayed)
Fresh mint
Marzipan bees (see Honey Bee
  Bites, p.194), optional
Pineapple Flowers (p.290),
  optional

EQUIPMENT
12-hole muffin tin
12 paper muffin cases
3.5cm round biscuit cutter

Preheat the oven to 180°C/160°C fan/gas 4. Line the muffin tin with the cases.

Using a hand-held electric whisk, or in a free-standing mixer, beat the butter and sugar together for 5–10 minutes or until very light, pale and creamy. Add the lemon zest and beat it in. Lightly beat the eggs in a mug or jug. Gradually add the egg to the butter and sugar mixture, beating well after each addition. Sift the flour and almonds into the mixture, in batches, folding in each batch until just combined. Gently stir in the lemon juice.

Spoon the mixture into the cases. Bake for 15–20 minutes or until the cakes have risen and are lightly golden brown, and a skewer inserted into the centre comes out clean. Leave to cool in the tin for 10 minutes before transferring the cupcakes, still in their paper cases, to a wire rack to cool completely.

To assemble your cakes, use the biscuit cutter or sharp wide end of a piping nozzle (or a small sharp knife) to cut out a 3.5cm diameter 'core' from each cupcake – cut down to a depth of about 2.5cm and don't go through to the base. Keep these cut-out pieces. Spoon about 1 tablespoon of lemon curd into the hole in each cupcake and put a fresh raspberry into each one. Return the cut-out pieces to the cakes and press down like a plug, but not so firmly that the curd spills out. Each piece will protrude slightly above the surface of its cake, but the topping will disguise this.

To make the mascarpone cream topping, put the mascarpone in a bowl and sift over the icing sugar. With a hand-held electric whisk, whip until creamy. If too stiff, add a little lemon juice. Spoon about 2 tablespoons of the mascarpone cream on to the top of each cupcake and spread with a small palette knife to create a slightly textured finish. Scatter on the confetti and add fresh fruit, flowers and herbs, plus marzipan bees and pineapple flowers, if using.

For serving you can leave the cupcakes in their cases or unwrap them for a more natural look. Remember to remove any non-edible flowers before eating.

RUSTIC SHOWSTOPPER

A total of:

950g butter, softened

950g caster sugar

Finely grated zest and juice of
19 lemons

19 eggs (at room temperature)

950g self-raising flour

About 150g ground almonds

All the extra lemon juice from
the lemons (you can freeze
this if making the sponge
layers in advance)

The same weight in caster sugar

2 x 10cm round, loose-
bottomed sandwich tins,
greased and fully lined

3 x 15cm round, loose-
bottomed sandwich tins,
greased and fully lined

3 x 20cm round, loose-
bottomed sandwich tins,
greased and fully lined

3 x 25cm round, loose-
bottomed sandwich tins,
greased and fully lined

Medium paintbrush

Cake paddle

15 plastic straws

Long length of 5mm round
dowelling

Cocktail sticks

INGREDIENTS CONTINUED
OVERLEAF >>

This spectacular cake can be adapted to suit any season or celebration. It makes the perfect centrepiece at a wedding – you can adorn it with shortbread hearts, which can also be used as wedding favours. The fruit, flowers and foliage are entirely up to you. Keep your flowers and fruit to different shades of one colour or mix them up for a natural effect. I like a variety of different sizes, shapes and textures, and to present this beautifully rustic creation on a tree-trunk cake stand (see directory, p.309).

2 X 10CM ROUND TINS	3 X 15CM ROUND TINS	3 X 20CM ROUND TINS	3 X 25CM ROUND TINS	INGREDIENTS
50g	150g	300g	450g	Butter, softened
50g	150g	300g	450g	Caster sugar
Zest of 1 lemon, 1 tbsp juice	Zest of 3 lemons, 3 tbsp juice	Zest of 6 lemons, 6 tbsp juice	Zest of 9 lemons, 9 tbsp juice	Zest and juice of lemon
1	3	6	9	Egg(s)
50g	150g	300g	450g	Self-raising flour
1 tbsp	3 tbsp	6 tbsp	9 tbsp	Ground almonds

BAKE IN AN OVEN PREHEATED TO 180°C/160°C FAN/GAS 4			
for 12–15 minutes	for 15–20 minutes	for 20–25 minutes	for 25–30 minutes

TOPPING AND FILLING			
About 100g maschilly and 1 tbsp (about 25g) lemon curd	About 300g maschilly and about 100g lemon curd	About 500g maschilly and about 150g lemon curd	About 700g maschilly and about 200g lemon curd

Preheat the oven to 180°C/160°C fan/gas 4. The table above gives the ingredient quantities to make the the different-sized cakes.

I usually make the larger cakes first. However, if you don't have more than one tin in each size, bake the cakes in batches. For example, bake one 25cm cake and one 20cm cake, repeating three times. You can bake the two smaller cakes while the larger ones are cooling, and you're washing up and re-lining the tins.

CONTINUED OVERLEAF >>

FOR THE MASCHILLY CREAM

FOR THE MASCHILLY CREAM
300g icing sugar
750g mascarpone
750ml double cream
1 tbsp vanilla extract

TO DECORATE
450g Lemon Curd (see p.273),
  or about 1½ jars
  shop-bought curd
About 450g raspberries
Icing sugar, to dust
Assortment of flowers and
  foliage (unsprayed)
450g mixed strawberries and
  redcurrants
Shortbread hearts (see
  Strawberry Hearts, p.224),
  optional

To make each batch of mixture (see the table on p.106), use a hand-held electric whisk, or a free-standing mixer, to beat the butter and sugar together for 5–10 minutes or until very light, pale and creamy. Add the lemon zest and beat it in. Lightly beat the egg(s) with a fork. Gradually add the egg to the butter and sugar mixture, beating well after each addition. Sift the flour and almonds into the mixture in batches, folding in each batch until just combined. Gently stir in the lemon juice – keep the rest of the juice from the lemon(s) to make the lemon syrup.

Spoon the mixture into the tins, dividing it equally, and bake for the required time (see the table on p.106) until the cakes have risen and are lightly golden brown, and a skewer inserted into the centre comes out clean. Cool in the tins for 15 minutes, then remove the cakes and transfer to wire racks to cool completely. Wrap in clingfilm, or layer up interleaved with baking parchment, and store in tins or plastic boxes, or freeze, until ready to assemble.

After all the cakes have been made, measure the amount of lemon juice you have left from making all the batches of mixture – you want to have about 400ml. Pour the juice into a large pan placed on digital scales. Add the same weight of caster sugar to the pan. Warm over a medium-high heat for several minutes, stirring, until the sugar has dissolved, then remove this lemon syrup from the heat and allow to cool. Pour into clean jars or bottles for storage.

When you're ready to assemble the cake (do this on the morning you are going to serve it), prick the surface of each cake all over with a cocktail stick, going about 3cm deep. Brush over some of the lemony syrup with a paintbrush or pastry brush, allowing it to soak into the sponge.

While the syrup is soaking in, make the maschilly cream. It's a large quantity, so I suggest you do this in two batches. Sift half the icing sugar into a bowl. Measure out half the mascarpone and half the cream and add them both to the bowl with half the vanilla. Whip together with a hand-held electric whisk until the mix holds soft peaks. Repeat with the rest of the maschilly ingredients.

Now you can start stacking the cake layers on your chosen surface. If using a tree-trunk stand, put a 25cm cake board on it first. Sit the base cake layer (one of the 25cm cakes) on the board. Spoon half the quantity of maschilly cream (see the table on p.106) in blobs on to the cake and spread out with a palette knife. Drizzle about half the lemon curd over the cream. Scatter a few of the less perfect raspberries on the curd to add a fruity pop. >>

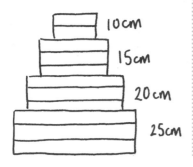

10cm
15cm
20cm
25cm

Using a cake paddle, carefully put the next 25cm cake layer in place on top of the first and repeat the filling stage. Top with the remaining 25cm cake layer, but flip it over first so its base becomes the top, providing a flatter surface to decorate. Push six of the straws vertically into the layered cake to form a ring no larger than the 20cm cake you will be placing on top (the straws will help support the structure). Using scissors, snip off the ends of the straws where they protrude from the cake so they are flush with the top and not visible.

Repeat this assembly with the 20cm and 15cm cake layers, using five straws in the layered 20cm cake and four in the layered 15cm cake. Assemble the top two-layered 10cm cake, using the same method but spreading the second half of the maschilly cream (without curd and berries) on the top layer. Take your piece of dowelling and measure it against the height of the entire cake before cutting it to size. Carefully push the dowelling down from the top of the cake through the centre of all the cake layers.

Decorate the cake as close to serving time as possible. First dust the tops of the tiers lightly with icing sugar, then add flowers and foliage – from the garden and/or florist – as well as berries (halved cocktail sticks will help fix any unbalanced strawberries), arranging them all naturally – this is meant to be a 'rustic' celebration cake after all. Depending on the occasion, put some shortbread hearts on the tiers too. Remember to remove any non-edible flowers before eating.

VARIATION

If you don't have two 10cm sandwich tins, you can bake one cake in a 10cm round, deep tin (see the Basic Lemon Cake on p.96). Once cold, carefully slice the cake horizontally into two equal layers using a long, serrated knife, such as a bread knife.

GINGER SPICE CAKE

My ginger cake is so simple to make – like my chocolate cake, it uses the 'melting' method, which is very easy and quick. It's one of the most moist and moreish bakes I know, with the black treacle giving it a lovely richness and depth, and has the added bonus of arguably tasting even better a few days after baking – if it survives that long!

To give your cake an extra kick of ginger plus little gems of satisfying chew, fold through some chopped candied ginger once your mixture is made. You can also decorate your finished cake with candied ginger. Or, to add an oriental dimension to the cake, substitute five spice for the mixed spice.

BASIC GINGER SPICE CAKE

MAKES A 10CM CAKE;
SERVES 2–3

FOR THE CAKE
50g butter, roughly chopped
50g dark muscovado sugar
50g golden syrup
50g black treacle
50ml whole milk
1 egg (at room temperature)
1 tsp ground ginger
1 tsp ground mixed spice
50g self-raising flour

EQUIPMENT
10cm round, deep, loose-
    bottomed tin (pork-pie
    size), greased and fully lined
    or lined using the snip-snip
    method (see p.21)

Preheat the oven to 170°C/150°C fan/gas 3.

Put the butter, sugar, golden syrup and treacle into a saucepan. Set over a medium heat and warm, stirring occasionally, until the butter has melted and the sugar has dissolved. Remove the pan from the heat. Pour the mixture into a large bowl and leave to cool slightly for 5–10 minutes.

Meanwhile, place the lined tin on a baking tray (this will make it easier to transport in and out of the oven). Measure the milk in a jug, add the egg and beat together with a fork.

Pour the milk and egg mixture into the warm syrup mixture and beat to combine – ideally with a hand-held electric whisk. Finally, sift the spices and flour into the mixture and beat until everything is combined and you have a very wet, smooth batter with no visible lumps of flour. Carefully pour the mixture into the prepared tin.

Bake for 35–40 minutes or until a skewer pushed into the centre of the cake comes out clean. Leave to cool in the tin for 15 minutes before removing the cake and transferring to a wire rack to cool completely.

TO FINISH
A good, moist ginger cake can be enjoyed just as it comes. However, I also love this slathered with Sweetened Mascarpone Cream (see p.278) or Cream Cheese Buttercream (p.277) and sprinkled with chopped, toasted nuts – roasted salted nuts being my favourite – to make a mini ginger nut cake.

TO MAKE DIFFERENT-SIZED GINGER SPICE CAKES, USE THE TABLE OPPOSITE >>

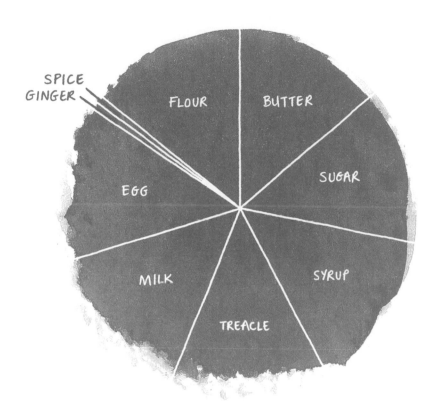

24-HOLE MINI-MUFFIN TIN	12-HOLE MUFFIN TIN	20CM SQUARE TIN	20CM ROUND DEEP TIN	900G (2LB) LOAF TIN	INGREDIENTS
50g	150g	150g	200g	150g	Butter, roughly chopped
50g	150g	150g	200g	150g	Dark muscovado sugar
50g	150g	150g	200g	150g	Golden syrup
50g	150g	150g	200g	150g	Black treacle
50ml	150ml	150ml	200ml	150ml	Whole milk
1	3	3	4	3	Egg(s)
1 tsp	3 tsp	3 tsp	4 tsp	3 tsp	Ground ginger
1 tsp	3 tsp	3 tsp	4 tsp	3 tsp	Ground mixed spice
50g	150g	150g	200g	150g	Self-raising flour

BAKE IN AN OVEN PREHEATED TO 170°C/150°C FAN/GAS 3

24-HOLE MINI-MUFFIN TIN	12-HOLE MUFFIN TIN	20CM SQUARE TIN	20CM ROUND DEEP TIN	900G (2LB) LOAF TIN	
for 12–15 minutes	for 20–25 minutes	for 35–40 minutes	for 55–65 minutes, or in 2 sandwich tins for 30–35 minutes	for 55–60 minutes	

CAKE TINS

FOR THE CAKE

100g butter, roughly chopped

100g dark muscovado sugar

100g golden syrup

100g black treacle

Melted butter or cake-release
spray for the tins

100ml whole milk

2 eggs (at room temperature)

2 tsp ground ginger

2 tsp ground mixed spice

100g self-raising flour

EQUIPMENT

3 Lyle's golden syrup/black
treacle tins (454g), empty
and cleaned

Medium paintbrush

I have always had a strong affection for Lyle's golden syrup and treacle tins. Their iconic designs make them desirable receptacles for everything from paintbrushes to tea. And you can bake cake in them too! As well as being perfect presents, these tins full of cake make great portable feasts or packed lunch treats – you just dip into them with a spoon, as if you were scooping out some treacle, sharing a tin between two if you're feeling generous. My two-egg chocolate cake mix (see the table on p.135) can also be tin-baked. If you don't have Lyle's tins to hand, empty pineapple tins are good alternatives.

Preheat the oven to 170°C/150°C fan/gas 3.

Put the butter, sugar, golden syrup and treacle into a saucepan. Set over a medium heat and warm, stirring occasionally, until the butter has melted and the sugar has dissolved. Transfer the mixture to a large bowl and leave to cool slightly for 5–10 minutes. Meanwhile, grease your tins with butter or cake-release spray. I find a silicone pastry brush the most efficient tool for thoroughly coating the inner surface of each tin.

Measure the milk in a jug, add the eggs and beat together. Pour the milk and egg mixture into the warm syrup mixture and beat to combine – ideally with a hand-held electric whisk. Finally, sift the spices and flour into the mixture and beat until everything is combined and you have a very wet, smooth batter with no visible lumps of flour.

To fill your tins accurately, which will ensure even baking, place them one at a time on digital scales and spoon in the mixture following the guideline weights given at the end of the recipe – i.e. 225g mixture for a 454g tin. The tins will be about two-thirds full. Place the filled tins on a baking tray to make it easier to transport them in and out of the oven.

Bake for 25–30 minutes or until a skewer pushed into the centre of the cake comes out fairly clean. The cakes will rise above the rim of the tins, but they will then sink back slightly during cooling. Transfer the tins to a wire rack and leave to cool completely.

You can enjoy the cakes just as they are, tucking into them with a spoon, but they are delicious topped with a scoop of ice cream. Or, after you've taken a few spoonfuls of cake, try pouring in a little, or a lot of, cream or custard.

CONTINUED OVERLEAF >>

CAKE TINS (CONTINUED)

Alternatively, you could create a syrup or treacle effect. To do this, cut off the domed top of each cake and pour on some ganache, made with golden syrup to add gloss and sweetness – a dark chocolate ganache looks like treacle, so is ideal for a treacle tin cake! A combination of 25g dark chocolate, 25ml double cream and 1 tablespoon golden syrup will make enough to top the three tins – see p.279 for my ganache method. You could also use sieved or shredless marmalade, gently heated to loosen it, as a glaze for a cake baked in a golden syrup tin.

If you leave the cakes plain and stick a couple of indoor sparklers into each, they make great bonfire night treats.

GUIDELINE TIN WEIGHTS

This recipe makes approximately 700g of cake mixture. The following guideline weights will help in filling your chosen tins. You can bake just one or two tin cakes and use the remaining mix for cupcakes – bake these according to the timings in the table on p.113.

454g golden syrup/black treacle tin = 225g mixture; bake for 25–30 minutes
227g pineapple tin = 150g mixture; bake for 20–25 minutes
200–220g baked beans/hoops tin = 125g mixture; bake 15–20 minutes

BONFIRE CUPCAKES

MAKES 12 CUPCAKES

FOR THE CAKES
150g butter, roughly chopped
150g dark muscovado sugar
150g golden syrup
150g black treacle
150ml whole milk
3 eggs (at room temperature)
3 tsp ground ginger
3 tsp ground mixed spice
150g self raising flour

FOR THE GANACHE
150g dark chocolate, chopped
    into small pieces
1½ tbsp golden syrup
½ tbsp vanilla extract
150ml double cream

FOR THE CARAMEL FLAMES
50g golden syrup
50g caster sugar
Edible gold glitter, optional

FOR THE BONFIRE
12 white marshmallows
75g chocolate-covered biscuit
    sticks, such as Mikado
130g chocolate orange sticks,
    such as Matchmakers
50g pretzel sticks

EQUIPMENT
12-hole muffin tin
12 brown paper muffin cases
    (or a mix of brown and
    gold-foil cases)

My ginger cake is not dissimilar to parkin, the lovely, dark, spicy gingerbread that is traditionally eaten on Guy Fawkes' night. Inspired by that association, I've come up with these firecrackers. A whole, ganache-covered marshmallow sits on top of each cake – a reference to toasting marshmallows around a fire – while the sugar flames add a toffee flavour and striking finish.

Preheat the oven to 170°C/150°C fan/gas 3.

Put the butter, sugar, golden syrup and treacle into a saucepan. Set over a medium heat and warm, stirring occasionally, until the butter has melted and the sugar has dissolved. Transfer the mixture to a large bowl and leave to cool slightly for 5–10 minutes.

Meanwhile, line the muffin tin with the muffin cases. Measure the milk in a jug, add the eggs and beat together. Pour the milk and egg mixture into the warm syrup mixture and beat to combine – ideally with a hand-held electric whisk. Finally, sift the spices and flour into the mixture, beating until combined and you have a very wet, smooth batter with no visible lumps of flour.

Carefully pour the mixture into the cases. I like to weigh the mixture first on digital scales (deducting the weight of the bowl), then divide by 12 so I know exactly how much to put into each muffin case (see p.22 for more information) – but this isn't essential.

Bake for 20–25 minutes or until the cakes have risen and a skewer pushed into the centre comes out fairly clean. Leave the cakes to cool in the tin for about 5 minutes, then transfer, in the cases, to a wire rack to cool completely.

Meanwhile, to make the ganache, put the chocolate into a medium-sized heatproof bowl with the golden syrup and vanilla. Gently heat the cream in a small saucepan over a medium heat. When the cream is just coming to the boil, pour it over the chocolate and stir gently until melted, smooth and shiny. Leave to cool. You want the ganache to have a soft spreading consistency, so once cooled you may want to put it in the fridge to firm up a little.

To create the caramel flames, first place two sheets of foil or baking parchment on a flat surface. Make sure you press the foil or parchment down flat to prevent it from lifting up when you come to apply the caramel. A light slick of oil can help to secure it.

CONTINUED OVERLEAF >>

BONFIRE CUPCAKES (CONTINUED)

Put the golden syrup in a pan and heat gently until the syrup has liquefied and coats the base of the pan. Sprinkle the caster sugar over the surface. Cook over a medium heat for 3–4 minutes, stirring occasionally with a wooden spoon, until the sugar has dissolved and the caramel has reached an amber colour (the joy of using golden syrup as well as sugar is that you can stir a caramel happily without fear of crystallisation, thus reducing the chance of the sugar burning).

With a wooden spoon, use about half the caramel to make splodges, dabs and strokes on the foil or parchment to represent flames. Make them 5–7cm in height and about 2cm wide, aiming to give them flame-like, tapered tips. Return the pan to the heat for 1–2 minutes to colour the caramel a bit more. Once it's a deeper amber shade, repeat the spooning and splodging step. You need 36 flames in total – but use all the caramel you have so you can choose the best. Once all the caramel has been used, and before it has fully set, you can sprinkle a very small amount of edible glitter over the tops of the flames, if you wish. Leave the flames to cool and set on the foil or parchment.

Use three-quarters of the ganache to cover the cakes, spreading it on with a palette knife. Press a marshmallow, wide base down, into the ganache on top of each cake. I sometimes toast the base of the marshmallows over a gas flame or candle first, to enhance the bonfire theme and give a caramelised sugar taste and smell. If you do this, make sure you allow the marshmallows to cool slightly before pressing them on to the ganache-covered cakes. When your marshmallows are stuck in place, cover them with the remaining ganache to create chocolate-covered marshmallow molehills. The ganache will act as a 'glue' for all the edible sticks.

Break the chocolate-covered biscuit sticks, chocolate sticks and pretzel sticks into pieces, some longer than others. Press them into the ganache-topped cakes to create the effect of a bonfire. Leave a slight gap at the top of the bonfire to insert the caramel flames. Try to vary the direction and height of the sticks to create a realistic bonfire appearance. Finally, insert two or three caramel flames into each bonfire. Use the sticks to keep the flames in place.

The glowing effect of the gold-dusted caramel flames is accentuated if you serve the cakes cleverly lit with a lamp or candles.

TREE TRUNK CAKES

MAKES 12 SMALL CAKES

FOR THE CAKES

12 chocolate-hazelnut balls, ideally Ferrero Rocher
150g butter, roughly chopped
150g dark muscovado sugar
150g golden syrup
150g black treacle
150ml whole milk
3 eggs (at room temperature)
1 tbsp ground ginger
1 tbsp ground mixed spice
150g self-raising flour

TO DECORATE

250–300g Basic Gingerbread dough (about ½ quantity; see p.238)
6 brazil nuts
15g white chocolate
15g ground toasted hazelnuts
Cocoa powder, to dust
Handful of whole, skin-on hazelnuts
Edible Confetti: Walk in the Woods (p.295), optional

EQUIPMENT

12-hole muffin tin
12 paper tulip muffin cases
Squirrel cutter, 9 x 7cm (see directory, p.308)
Leaf plunger cutter, about 2.5cm long (see directory, p.308)
Wooden latte stirrers
Cocktail stick
Fine paintbrush

INGREDIENTS CONTINUED OVERLEAF >>

A gingerbread squirrel takes centre stage on these mini tree trunks, while layers of ganache and hazelnut buttercream form the trees' textured bark. I recommend baking the cakes and making the biscuit dough up to a day in advance. This allows the cakes time to firm up and enhances their flavour, and makes the biscuit dough easier to handle. Ground toasted hazelnuts are available in some supermarkets, or you can create your own by grinding pre-toasted chopped or whole hazelnuts.

Preheat the oven to 170°C/150°C fan/gas 3. Place the wrapped chocolates in the freezer to firm up.

Put the butter, sugar, golden syrup and treacle into a saucepan. Set over a medium heat and warm, stirring occasionally, until the butter has melted and the sugar has dissolved. Transfer the mixture to a large bowl and leave to cool slightly for 5–10 minutes. Meanwhile, line the muffin tin with your tulip cases.

Measure the milk in a jug, add the eggs and beat in. Pour the milk and egg mixture into the warm syrup mixture and beat to combine – ideally with a hand-held electric whisk. Finally, sift the spices and flour into the mixture and beat until combined and you have a very wet, smooth batter with no visible lumps of flour.

Unwrap the frozen chocolates and put one into each paper case. Carefully pour the cake mixture into the cases – a soup ladle or measuring cup makes this easier. Press the chocolate down into the mixture if necessary, so it isn't bobbing on the surface.

Bake for 20–25 minutes or until the cakes have risen and a skewer pushed in (not into the hidden chocolate) comes out fairly clean. Leave to cool in the tin for about 5 minutes before transferring, in the cases, to a wire rack to cool completely. Leave the oven on to bake the biscuits.

To make the biscuits, roll out the gingerbread dough between two sheets of baking parchment to the thickness of a £1 coin. Peel off the top layer of parchment and cut out as many gingerbread squirrels as you can. Pull up the trimmings, re-roll them between fresh parchment and cut out more squirrels until you have 12 in total. Lift the squirrels, on the parchment paper, on to two baking trays and refrigerate for 15 minutes.

CONTINUED OVERLEAF >>

TREE TRUNK CAKES (CONTINUED)

FOR THE GANACHE
150g dark chocolate, chopped
   into small pieces
1½ tbsp golden syrup
½ tbsp vanilla extract
150ml double cream

FOR THE BUTTERCREAM
50g butter, softened
100g icing sugar, sifted
½ tbsp whole milk
½ tsp vanilla extract
1 tbsp ground toasted hazelnuts

To create your gingerbread acorns, remove a 30g chunk from the remaining gingerbread dough and divide into six 5g balls. Roll each into a rounded-end cylinder, 3cm long and 1.5cm thick. Place these on one of the trays of squirrel biscuits and leave to chill.

Roll out the rest of the gingerbread dough between sheets of parchment to the thickness of a 50-pence piece. Peel off the top layer and cut out 12 small gingerbread leaves. Peel away the surrounding dough and re-roll to cut out more leaves. Chill the leaves, on their parchment, on a baking tray in the fridge. If you don't have lots of baking trays, re-use one of those the squirrels and acorns are on, once baked.

Remove your trays of squirrels and acorns from the fridge. Use the end of a latte stirrer or a small sharp knife to create a fur pattern on the squirrels' tails, pressing the tip into the dough at random angles. Use a cocktail stick to create the squirrels' eyes, then press the stick at an angle into the squirrels' faces to create smiling mouths. Bake the squirrels and acorns for 8–12 minutes or until deep golden. Leave the squirrels to cool on their trays for a few minutes before transferring, on the parchment, to a wire rack to cool completely. While still warm, cut the gingerbread cylinders in half across their middles to form two acorn caps. Leave to cool with the squirrels.

Transfer the gingerbread leaves, on their parchment, to a baking tray and bake for 5–7 minutes or until golden brown around the edges. Leave to firm up a bit on the tray before lifting on to a wire rack.

While the cakes and biscuits are baking and cooling, make the ganache. Put the chocolate into a medium-sized heatproof bowl with the golden syrup and vanilla. Gently heat the cream in a small saucepan over a medium heat. When the cream is just coming to the boil, pour it over the chocolate. Leave to sit for a few minutes so that the heat from the cream melts the chocolate, then stir gently until smooth and shiny.

Cut the brazil nuts in half across the middle – these will form the acorns themselves. You want the nut pieces to be roughly the same length, or a little bit longer, than the gingerbread acorn caps. You also want the cut surface of each brazil nut half to be as flat as possible, to make it easy to join to the gingerbread cap. If your brazil nuts still have a lot of dark skin on them, scrape some of it off with a small sharp knife. >>

Use the paintbrush to apply a little still runny ganache to the cut surface of each gingerbread acorn cap – you don't want to cover the whole surface, you just need a dab. Press a brazil nut half on to the chocolate to form an acorn. Leave to set. Leave the rest of the ganache to cool and firm up slightly while you make the hazelnut buttercream. Using a hand-held electric whisk, beat the butter in a medium bowl until soft and pale. Sift the icing sugar into the bowl in batches, working in the sugar with a spoon before adding the milk and vanilla. Beat at full speed until the buttercream is really light and fluffy. Finally, mix in the ground toasted hazelnuts.

Remove the cakes from their tulip cases. If the tops are very domed, trim them a little to flatten, being careful not to trim off any of the concealed chocolate. Turn the cakes upside down so their broader tops become the base of the tree trunks. Use a palette knife to spread the hazelnut buttercream over the top and about a third of the way down the side of each cake. Spread the ganache all around the side of each cake using a round-ended table knife or small palette knife. Mix and merge the buttercream and ganache over the tree trunk tops to create a marbled brown-and-cream shade. Leave to set slightly while you decorate your squirrel biscuits.

Melt the white chocolate in a microwave or heatproof bowl set over a pan of simmering water (bain-marie), then use the paintbrush to paint the chocolate on to the chests of the biscuit squirrels. Sprinkle a fine dusting of ground hazelnuts over the chocolate. Leave to set.

Now return to the cakes: with a fork and the tip of a sharp knife or cocktail stick, work into the chocolate ganache to create the striated effect of bark. Use a cocktail stick to create the appearance of tree rings on the buttercream tops. Dust over some ground hazelnuts and cocoa powder to add a textured finish. Decorate each cake with a biscuit squirrel, a biscuit leaf, a gingerbread acorn and a whole hazelnut. Add some edible confetti, if using. I often serve the cakes on a tree-trunk cake board (see directory, p.309).

VARIATION

I like to bake these cakes in 'tulip' muffin cases as the larger size gives more space for the squirreled-away chocolate. However, you can use standard muffin cases and omit the hidden chocolates.

WINTER WONDERLAND CAKE

MAKES 1 CAKE;
SERVES 8–12

TO DECORATE

Icing sugar, to dust
100g white fondant icing or
    Coconut Marzipan
    (see p.287)
20 small edible silver balls
100g desiccated coconut
4 clear mints, such as Fox's
    Glacier Mints (about 20g)
10 mint imperial sweets
    (about 20g)
5 white-covered milk chocolate
    balls, such as Cadbury
    Snowbites (about 20g)
Edible silver glitter, to dust

FOR THE CAKE

Melted butter or cake-release
    spray, for the tin
200g butter, roughly chopped
200g dark muscovado sugar
200g golden syrup
200g black treacle
200ml whole milk
4 eggs (at room temperature)
4 tsp ground ginger
4 tsp ground mixed spice
200g self-raising flour

EQUIPMENT

Holiday tree bundt tin (see
    directory, p.309)
Snowflake plunger cutters
    in different sizes (see
    directory, p.309)
Mini polar bear cutter, optional
Cocktail stick

Here's a wonderful alternative to a traditional Christmas cake. Surrounded by coconut snow, snowflakes, mint snowballs, mint ice shards and even polar bears, it makes a magical centrepiece for the festive season. The shaped 'holiday tree' cake tin that it's baked in is an investment (it will cost in the region of £35) but I promise you'll be using it year after year – and you can use it to make mini tree cakes too (see variation on p.126–7). Even without the decorations and sparkle, a cake baked in this form is a showstopper all by itself. My basic chocolate cake mix works well in it too (use the quantities in the table on p.113 for a 4-egg cake baked in a 20cm round deep tin). It's a good idea to make the fondant or marzipan snowflakes and snowballs the day before to give them time to harden.

On a surface lightly dusted with icing sugar, or on a sheet of baking parchment, roll out the fondant icing or coconut marzipan to the thickness of a £1 coin. Using snowflake plunger cutters of various sizes, stamp out one large snowflake, eight medium and eleven small. Lay these on a tray lined with baking parchment. Carefully press a silver ball into the centre of each snowflake. If you have a mini-polar-bear cutter, cut out three mini polar bears. With the end of a cocktail stick, mark an eye on each one.

Break the remainder of the fondant/marzipan into little pieces and roll into 'snowballs', making them smaller than the mint imperial and chocolate sweets. Ideally, leave the snowflakes, polar bears and snowballs to harden overnight.

Preheat the oven to 170°C/150°C fan/gas 3. Grease the cake tin liberally with melted butter or cake-release spray, making sure that every nook and cranny is well coated (a silicone pastry brush makes this easy).

To make the cake mixture, put the butter, sugar, golden syrup and treacle into a saucepan. Set over a medium heat and warm, stirring occasionally, until the butter has melted and the sugar has dissolved. Transfer the mixture to a large bowl and leave to cool slightly for 5–10 minutes.

Meanwhile, measure the milk in a jug, add the eggs and beat in. Pour the milk and egg mixture into the warm syrup mixture and beat to combine – ideally with a hand-held electric whisk. Finally, sift the spices and flour into the mixture and beat until everything is combined and you have a very wet, smooth batter with no visible lumps of flour.

CONTINUED OVERLEAF >>

WINTER WONDERLAND CAKE (CONTINUED)

Carefully pour the mixture into your prepared tin. Bake for 35–40 minutes or until a skewer pushed in near the centre of the cake comes out fairly clean. Leave to cool completely in the tin.

Turn the cake out of the tin on to a plate, cake stand, board or white tile. Fill the hollow of the cake with desiccated coconut and scatter the remainder around the sides. Dust the cake with icing sugar.

To create the ice shards, place the clear mint sweets, still in their wrappers, in a plastic bag. Encase it in a tea towel, to prevent the sweets from flying loose, and hit them with a rolling pin to break into pieces. Remove the wrappers.

Decorate the cake with the snowflakes, snowballs, polar bears (if using), clear mint shards and remaining sweets. You can simply lay them against the cake – they should adhere to its slightly sticky surface – or, if necessary, use a dab of golden syrup to help fix them. Finally, lightly dust the whole thing with silver glitter. To make the cake even more magical, you can stick mini indoor sparklers into the tips of the 'trees'.

I like to serve vanilla or coconut ice cream, or just plain whipped cream, alongside this cake. If you're not a fan of desiccated coconut, you can fill and surround the cake with whipped, sweetened double cream instead. Crumbled-up meringue also makes a great alternative to coconut snow and, if used together with cream, will result in an Arctic Eton mess.

VARIATION

Sugar & Spice Snow Globes Make up the ginger spice cake mix using the one-egg quantity (see the table on p.113). Grease the holiday tree cake tin, then place it on digital scales. Pour 15g of the mixture into each tree shape to create mini trees; or use 25g to create slightly larger trees. I like to make a mix of the two sizes. You'll have some of the mixture left over, which you could use for one of my Cake Tins (see p.114). Bake for about 10 minutes. Leave to cool, then carefully remove the trees from the tin with the help of a small sharp knife or cocktail stick. >>

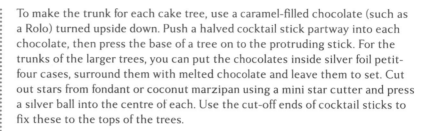

To make the trunk for each cake tree, use a caramel-filled chocolate (such as a Rolo) turned upside down. Push a halved cocktail stick partway into each chocolate, then press the base of a tree on to the protruding stick. For the trunks of the larger trees, you can put the chocolates inside silver foil petit-four cases, surround them with melted chocolate and leave them to set. Cut out stars from fondant or coconut marzipan using a mini star cutter and press a silver ball into the centre of each. Use the cut-off ends of cocktail sticks to fix these to the tops of the trees.

You can also stick a few silver balls on the trees to look like baubles – use some melted chocolate as glue if the stickiness of the ginger cake doesn't hold them in place. Dust the trees with sifted icing sugar and edible silver glitter.

Put each mini cake on the upturned lid of a clean jar. Surround with desiccated coconut, snowflakes, snowballs and clear mint 'ice shards', as for the larger cake. Place the glass jar over the tree to create the snow globe. These look magical on their own, or displayed alongside the Winter Wonderland Cake.

CHOCOLATE CAKE

• •

This is rich, dense and indulgent, a real chocoholic's treat. It's made using the melting method, which means it's particularly easy – no creaming butter with sugar to worry about. I use both melted chocolate and cocoa powder for a really intense flavour. For the best results, choose a dark chocolate with at least 60–70 per cent cocoa solids – not much more than this or the whole thing will be too devilishly dark! As with my brownies (see p.166), you can use a flavoured chocolate such as mint or orange, or add a flavouring extract, to create chocolate cakes with subtly different characters.

BASIC CHOCOLATE CAKE

FOR THE CAKE

50g butter, roughly chopped

50g light muscovado sugar

50g golden syrup

50g dark chocolate, chopped
    into small pieces

50ml whole milk

1 egg (at room temperature)

1 tsp vanilla extract

1 tbsp cocoa powder

50g self-raising flour

EQUIPMENT

10cm round, deep, loose-
    bottomed tin (pork-pie
    size), greased and fully lined
    or lined using the snip-snip
    method (see p.21)

Preheat the oven to 170°C/150°C fan/gas 3.

Put the butter, sugar and golden syrup into a saucepan. Set over a medium heat and warm, stirring occasionally, until the butter has melted and the sugar has dissolved.

Remove the pan from the heat, add the chopped chocolate and stir until melted and smooth. Transfer the mixture to a large bowl and leave to cool for 5–10 minutes – I often place the bowl outside on a cold surface to cool quickly.

Measure the milk in a jug, add the egg and vanilla extract, and beat in with a fork. Pour the milk and egg mixture into the warm syrup mixture and beat to combine – ideally with a hand-held electric whisk. Finally, sift the cocoa powder and flour into the mixture, beating until everything is well combined and no flour is visible in the very wet, smooth batter.

Set your lined tin on a baking tray to make it easier to transport in and out of the oven, then carefully pour the mixture into the tin. Bake for 35–40 minutes or until a skewer pushed into the centre of the cake comes out clean. Leave to cool in the tin for 15 minutes before removing the cake and transferring to a wire rack to cool completely.

TO FINISH

This lovely, tender chocolate cake is incredibly versatile. You can serve it up with crushed raspberries and generous spoonfuls of cream for pudding, or slather it with Caramel Sauce (see p.284) and add a scoop of ice cream. For more of a teatime treat, cut the cake horizontally into two or three layers, then sandwich and top with whipped cream or a ganache (pp.277–9). Add a textural dimension by topping with chopped nuts, chocolate bars and biscuits.

TO MAKE DIFFERENT-SIZED CHOCOLATE CAKES, USE THE TABLE OPPOSITE >>

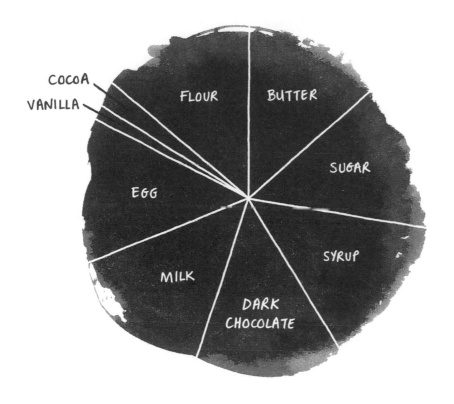

COCOA
VANILLA
FLOUR
BUTTER
SUGAR
EGG
SYRUP
MILK
DARK CHOCOLATE

24-HOLE MINI-MUFFIN TIN	12-HOLE MUFFIN TIN	20CM SQUARE TIN	20CM ROUND DEEP TIN	900G (2LB) LOAF TIN	INGREDIENTS
50g	150g	150g	200g	150g	Butter, roughly chopped
50g	150g	150g	200g	150g	Light muscovado sugar
50g	150g	150g	200g	150g	Golden syrup
50g	150g	150g	200g	150g	Dark chocolate, chopped into small pieces
50ml	150ml	150ml	200ml	150ml	Whole milk
1	3	3	4	3	Egg(s)
1 tsp	3 tsp	3 tsp	4 tsp	3 tsp	Vanilla extract
1 tbsp	3 tbsp	3 tbsp	4 tbsp	3 tbsp	Cocoa powder
50g	150g	150g	200g	150g	Self-raising flour
BAKE IN AN OVEN PREHEATED TO 170°C/150°C FAN/GAS 3					
for 12–15 minutes	for 20–25 minutes	for 35–40 minutes	for 55–65 minutes, or in 2 sandwich tins for 30–35 minutes	for 55–60 minutes	

CRUNCHIE CAKE

FOR THE CAKE

50g butter, roughly chopped

50g light muscovado sugar

50g golden syrup

50g dark chocolate, chopped
into small pieces

50ml whole milk

1 egg (at room temperature)

1 tsp vanilla extract

1 tbsp cocoa powder

50g self-raising flour

FOR THE GANACHE

50g dark chocolate, chopped
into small pieces

½ tbsp golden syrup

½ tsp vanilla extract

100ml double cream

TO DECORATE

1 honeycomb chocolate bar
(about 50g), such as a
Crunchie, or homemade
Honeycomb (see p.285)

EQUIPMENT

10cm round, deep, loose-
bottomed tin (pork-pie
size), greased and fully lined
or lined using the snip-snip
method (see p.21)

This cake will deliver that Friday feeling every day of the week. Its compact size makes it the perfect individual celebration cake – much more impressive than a cupcake and yet small enough to warrant the receiver sharing it with no one! If you do feel like scaling it up, that's easily done (see the table on p.131), and you can try topping it with other chocolate bars too.

Preheat the oven to 170°C/150°C fan/gas 3.

Put the butter, sugar and golden syrup into a saucepan. Set over a medium heat and warm, stirring occasionally, until the butter has melted and the sugar has dissolved. Remove the pan from the heat, add the chopped chocolate and stir until melted and smooth. Transfer the mixture to a large bowl and leave to cool for about 5 minutes.

Measure the milk in a jug, add the egg and vanilla extract, and beat in with a fork. Pour the milk and egg mixture into the warm syrup mixture and beat to combine – ideally with a hand-held electric whisk. Finally, sift the cocoa powder and flour into the mixture, beating until everything is well combined and no flour is visible in the very wet, smooth batter.

Set your prepared tin on a baking tray, then carefully pour the mixture into the tin. Bake for 35–40 minutes or until a skewer pushed into the centre of the cake comes out fairly clean. Leave to cool in the tin for 15 minutes before removing the cake and transferring to a wire rack to cool completely.

While the cake is baking and cooling, make the ganache. Put the chocolate into a medium-sized heatproof bowl with the golden syrup and vanilla extract. Gently heat the cream in a small saucepan over a medium heat. When it's just coming to the boil, pour it over the chocolate and stir gently until smooth and shiny. Alternatively, because this is a very small quantity of ganache, you can put all the ingredients in a heatproof bowl set over a pan of simmering water (bain-marie) and melt together. Leave to cool. You want the ganache to have a soft spreading consistency when you come to use it, so, once cooled, you may want to put it in the fridge to firm up a little.

When the cake has cooled and the ganache reached a spreadable consistency, chop your honeycomb into random-sized pieces.

CONTINUED OVERLEAF >>

CRUNCHIE CAKE (CONTINUED)

Using a long, serrated knife, such as a bread knife, carefully cut the cake horizontally into three equal layers. Place the base layer on a plate, cake board or stand. Use a small palette knife to spread a third of the ganache over the surface of this layer before adding the middle cake layer. Spread another third of the ganache over this. Spread the remainder of the ganache over the surface of the third layer, then set it carefully in place on top of the cake.

Sprinkle the smaller, crumb-like pieces of honeycomb over the ganache on top, then place some of the medium-sized pieces and the largest chunks in the centre of the top, pressing them in lightly. Finish by pressing the remaining small/medium pieces of honeycomb into the ganache between the layers on the side of the cake.

If you're making this cake in advance, don't add the honeycomb decoration until just before serving because the honeycomb will start to dissolve once it comes into contact with the ganache.

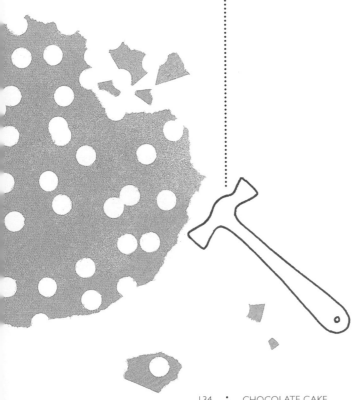

CHOCOLATE FOREST CAKE

MAKES A 15CM CAKE;
SERVES 5–6

FOR THE CAKE
100g butter, roughly chopped
100g light muscovado sugar
100g golden syrup
100g dark chocolate, chopped
  into small pieces
100ml whole milk
2 eggs (at room temperature)
2 tsp vanilla extract
2 tbsp cocoa powder
100g self-raising flour

FOR THE GANACHE
100g dark chocolate, chopped
  into small pieces
1 tbsp golden syrup
1 tsp vanilla extract
150ml double cream

FOR THE FILLING
150ml double cream

FOR THE PINE CONE
Cocoa powder, to dust your
  hands, optional
1 chocolate-covered biscuit
  stick, such as a Mikado
25g toasted flaked almonds

EQUIPMENT
15cm round, deep, loose-
  bottomed tin (pork-pie
  size), greased and fully lined
  or lined using the snip-snip
  method (see p.21)

INGREDIENTS CONTINUED
OVERLEAF >>

Forget the Black Forest – rich, chocolatey-brown is where it's at, and there's not a cherry in sight here. With its abundant, woodland-themed decorations, this bake has a wonderfully organic and generous feel. You could go further and create a whole thicket of forest cakes in different sizes, including some mini-muffin-sized ones (see the table on p.131), and cover them in drifts of sweet pine cones, leaves, acorns and twigs. I can't think of anything better as a birthday cake for someone who loves the wild woods...

Preheat the oven to 170°C/150°C fan/gas 3.

Put the butter, sugar and golden syrup into a saucepan. Set over a medium heat and warm, stirring occasionally, until the butter has melted and the sugar has dissolved. Remove the pan from the heat, add the chopped chocolate and stir until melted and smooth. Transfer the mixture to a large bowl and leave to cool for about 5 minutes.

Measure the milk in a jug, add the eggs and vanilla extract, and beat in with a fork. Pour the milk and egg mixture into the warm syrup mixture and beat to combine – ideally with a hand-held electric whisk. Finally, sift the cocoa powder and flour into the mixture, beating until everything is well combined and no flour is visible in the very wet, smooth batter.

Set your lined tin on a baking tray, then carefully pour the mixture into the tin. Bake for about 50 minutes or until a skewer pushed into the centre of the cake comes out fairly clean. Leave to cool in the tin for 15 minutes before removing the cake and transferring to a wire rack to cool completely.

While the cake is baking and cooling, make the ganache. Put the chocolate into a medium-sized heatproof bowl with the golden syrup and vanilla extract. Gently heat the cream in a small saucepan over a medium heat. When it's just coming to the boil, pour it over the chocolate and stir gently until smooth and shiny. Leave to cool, then put the ganache in the fridge to firm up slightly.

When the ganache has reached a soft spreading consistency, transfer 25g of it (1–2 tablespoons) to a small bowl; you will use this to create your chocolate pine cone. Return this small portion to the fridge to firm up further.

CONTINUED OVERLEAF >>

CHOCOLATE FOREST CAKE (CONTINUED)

TO DECORATE

Some or all of the following:
Biscuit Leaves (see p.300)
I Marzipan Tealight (p.298)
Gingerbread Acorns (p.300)
I pretzel stick
I chocolate-covered biscuit
    stick, such as a Mikado
I chocolate stick, such as a
    Matchmaker
An assortment of nuts, such
    as hazelnuts, walnuts and
    pecans, whole and chopped
I tbsp Edible Confetti: Walk
    in the Woods (p.295)

Using a long, serrated knife, such as a bread knife, carefully cut the cake horizontally into two equal layers. Set the base layer on a plate, cake board or stand (I like to use a tree-trunk cake stand; see directory, p.309).

Whip the cream to fill the cake until medium peaks form. Use a small palette knife to spread the whipped cream over the surface of the bottom cake layer, then place the second layer on top. If necessary, chill the cake to help firm up the cream filling – this will make it easier to cover the cake with ganache.

With a palette knife, spread the ganache all over the side and top of the cake.

To create your pine cone, take the small portion of chilled ganache and mould it with your hands (dusted with cocoa powder, if necessary) into a rough cone shape, about 5cm long and 2cm in diameter at the widest end. Break off about a third of the chocolate-covered biscuit stick and reserve for decorating the cake (as a twig). Carefully push the other longer piece of the stick, broken end down, into the centre top of the chocolate cone. The broken end of the stick will protrude out of the base of the cone. Insert this end into the ganache-covered cake at about 11 o'clock, a few centimetres in from the edge. Beginning at the base of the cone, stick in flaked almonds (using only those that are unbroken) to look like the scales of a pine cone. You can use the remaining almond pieces in the edible foliage.

Surround the pine cone with the rest of your chosen decorations. It looks best if you cover only about half of the cake surface, just scattering some edible confetti over the remainder.

HIDDEN BULB CAKES

MAKES 12 SMALL CAKES

FOR THE CUPCAKES
150g butter, roughly chopped
150g light muscovado sugar
150g golden syrup
150g dark chocolate, chopped
　　into small pieces
150ml whole milk
3 eggs (at room temperature)
1 tbsp vanilla extract
3 tbsp cocoa powder
150g self-raising flour

FOR THE GANACHE
150g dark chocolate, chopped
　　into small pieces
1½ tbsp golden syrup
½ tbsp vanilla extract
150ml double cream

FOR THE BULBS
250g natural marzipan
150g filo pastry – about
　　6 sheets
50g butter, melted
1 tsp cocoa powder

EQUIPMENT
12-hole muffin tin
12 paper tulip muffin cases
24 paper mini-muffin cases
12-hole (or 24-hole) mini-
　　muffin tin
3.5cm round biscuit cutter
Fine paintbrush
Cocktail stick

INGREDIENTS CONTINUED
OVERLEAF >>

These cakes feature marzipan-filled 'bulbs' snuggled in chocolate ganache surrounded by cake crumb 'topsoil'. Slice the cakes in two to reveal an almond cupcake centre with a whole sweet almond at its core. These are ideal as a gift for the green-fingered, and also make a memorable bake for Mother's Day or a sweet springtime alternative to more traditional Easter cakes. I use tulip muffin cases because regular cases would make ridges on the baked sponges, which then would look less like plants.

Preheat the oven to 170°C/150°C fan/gas 3. Line the muffin tin with the tulip paper cases.

Start with the chocolate cupcakes. Put the butter, sugar and golden syrup into a saucepan. Set over a medium heat and warm, stirring occasionally, until the butter has melted and the sugar has dissolved. Remove from the heat. Add the chopped chocolate and stir until melted and smooth. Transfer the mixture to a large bowl and leave to cool for about 5 minutes.

Measure the milk in a jug, add the eggs and vanilla extract, and beat in with a fork. Pour the milk and egg mixture into the warm syrup mixture and beat to combine – ideally with a hand-held electric whisk. Finally, sift the cocoa powder and flour into the mixture, beating until everything is well combined and no flour is visible in the very wet, smooth batter.

Carefully pour the mixture into your tulip cases, dividing it equally. Bake for 20–25 minutes or until the cakes have risen and a skewer inserted into the centre comes out fairly clean. Leave to cool in the tin for 5 minutes before transferring, still in the tulip cases, to a wire rack to cool completely. Leave the oven on for the mini cupcakes.

While the chocolate cupcakes are baking, make the ganache. Put the chocolate into a medium-sized heatproof bowl with the golden syrup and vanilla extract. Gently heat the cream in a small saucepan over a medium heat. When it's just coming to the boil, pour it over the chocolate and stir gently until smooth and shiny. Set aside a little of the ganache for assembling the cakes. You want the remaining ganache to reach a soft spreading consistency, so, once cooled, you may want to put it in the fridge to firm up a little.

Put 12 of the mini-muffin cases into the mini-muffin tin (if using a 24-hole mini-muffin tin, line just half of the holes).

CONTINUED OVERLEAF >>

HIDDEN BULB CAKES (CONTINUED)

FOR THE MINI CUPCAKES
50g butter, softened
50g golden caster sugar
1 egg (at room temperature)
1 tsp almond extract
1 tsp warm water
1 tbsp ground almonds
50g self-raising flour
12 whole, skin-on almonds

FOR THE BULB SHOOTS
100g pistachios
½ egg white (at room temperature)
Finely grated zest of 1 lime
1 tsp lime juice
1 tsp honey
100g icing sugar, sifted

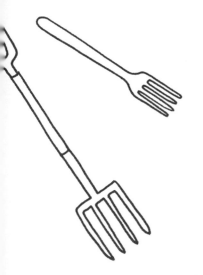

To make the filo bulbs, break the natural marzipan into 12 pieces, each about 20g in weight, and roll into balls. Place these in a plastic tub and put it in the freezer – freezing the marzipan will help to prevent it from leaking out of the filo during baking.

Meanwhile, make the mini almond cupcakes. Place all the ingredients, except the whole almonds, in a bowl and beat together with a hand-held electric whisk for about a minute or until creamed and combined.

Spoon the almond cupcake mixture into the mini-muffin cases, dividing it equally. Bake for 10–12 minutes or until the cakes are risen and a skewer inserted into the centre comes out clean. Leave to cool in the tin for a few minutes before transferring, in the cases, to a wire rack to cool completely. The mini-muffin tin needs to cool too, ready to use for the filo bulbs – I sometimes put the tin outside on a cold surface to speed the cooling. Leave the oven on.

Now return to the filo bulbs. Remove your frozen marzipan balls from the freezer. Unfold the filo but keep it covered with a damp cloth so it doesn't dry out. Take one sheet and brush both sides with melted butter, then cut it into four strips, each about 7cm wide – a pizza cutter can come in handy here. Don't worry if the strips aren't perfect, as this will just add to the organic look of the bulb. Wrap two strips of filo around each marzipan ball, making sure you encase the ball completely in pastry, particularly on what will be the base, to prevent leakage during baking. Pinch and scrunch the filo around the ball roughly as you go, then unfold and curl back some of the layers of pastry to look like the top of a bulb. Repeat with all the filo and marzipan balls.

Place the remaining 12 mini-muffin cases in the mini-muffin tin and put the filo bulbs in them. Bake the filo bulbs for 12–15 minutes or until the filo has turned crisp and golden. Leave to cool in the tin. While still slightly warm, carefully cut off 2cm from the base of each bulb so it sits steady – you will be left with a 5cm tall bulb.

While the bulbs are baking, make your marzipan for the shoots. Grind the pistachios finely in a food processor or, in batches, in a coffee or spice grinder. Put the egg white in a medium bowl and add the lime zest and juice and honey. Mix into a paste. Add the pistachios and icing sugar. Start mixing with a spoon, then bring the mix together into a ball with your hands. You'll need about a quarter of the marzipan for this recipe. The rest can be wrapped in clingfilm and kept in the fridge for up to a week – use it to make peas (see p.34). >>

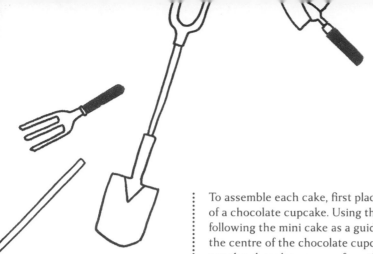

To assemble each cake, first place a mini almond cupcake, upside down, on top of a chocolate cupcake. Using the biscuit cutter or a small sharp knife, and following the mini cake as a guide, cut out an appropriately sized hole from the centre of the chocolate cupcake that the mini cupcake will fit into. Carve out the chocolate sponge from the hole using a teaspoon, put it into a bowl and break into crumbs. This will be the 'topsoil'. Set it aside.

Using the paintbrush, brush some of the reserved ganache inside the carved-out hole in each chocolate cupcake – if necessary, melt the ganache slightly to make it easier to spread. Remove each mini cupcake from its paper case and put into the hole in the chocolate cupcakes, top side down. Carve off any 'muffin top' surround with a knife, if necessary, to fit.

Make an incision in the top of the mini cupcake with the end of a sharp knife and insert a whole almond, pointed end up, pushing it down into the middle of the cake so it is no longer visible.

Place a marzipan filo bulb on top of each cake, using a little ganache to secure it in place. Peel back the paper tulip cases but leave the cakes sitting on them to catch any fallen chocolate 'topsoil'. Spread the rest of the ganache over the top of the cakes around the bulbs. Scatter over some of the reserved chocolate cake crumbs to look like topsoil.

To make each marzipan bulb shoot, take a small piece of pistachio marzipan (about 3g) and roll it into a short sausage, then twist one end to a point. Repeat this to form 12 shoots. Carefully insert a green shoot into the top of each filo bulb, using the end of the paintbrush or a cocktail stick to help.

Use the marzipan trimmings to create mini bulb shoots to sit in and around the central bulb. Insert these into the ganache 'earth' with the aid of a cocktail stick incision. Lightly dust the bulb tops and cakes with cocoa powder to enhance the appearance of the 'topsoil'. Finally, remove the tulip cases completely. Any leftover chocolate crumbs can be scattered around the cakes to provide a realistic earthy finish.

HEART BEET CAKE

FOR THE CAKE AND HEARTS

300g vacuum-packed, plain
    cooked beetroot (without
    vinegar or other flavourings)
150g butter, roughly chopped
150g light muscovado sugar
150g golden syrup
150g dark chocolate, chopped
    into small pieces
150ml whole milk
3 eggs (at room temperature)
1 tbsp vanilla extract
3 tbsp cocoa powder
150g self-raising flour
Icing sugar, to dust, optional

FOR THE TOPPING

250g mascarpone
50g icing sugar
½ tsp rose water

EQUIPMENT

20cm heart-shaped tin,
    preferably loose-bottomed,
    (see directory, p.308),
    greased and fully lined
4cm heart cutter (see
    directory, p.308)

Adding a little puréed beetroot to my basic chocolate cake mixture makes the crumb extra moist and also produces a very subtle red hue – a natural version of the traditional red velvet cake. The dried beetroot hearts used to decorate the cake highlight this unexpected ingredient. They also look rather like dried rose petals – and there's a dash of rose water in the sweetened mascarpone topping too – making this an ideal Valentine's or even wedding cake. Heart-shaped tins are quite easy to come by nowadays. However, if you don't have one, you can create a heart cake by baking your mix in a round or square tin and then cutting out a heart shape using a homemade template.

Preheat the oven to 170°C/150°C fan/gas 3.

Begin by preparing your beetroot hearts. Place some double layers of kitchen paper on your work surface to soak up the moisture from the beetroot. Trim off the top and bottom of the beetroots to create flat ends (reserve the trimmings). Next cut each beetroot horizontally into two or three thick slices, depending on their size. Use your mini heart cutter to stamp out a heart shape from each beetroot slice. Use the cutter to take more pieces from the offcuts of beetroot – they won't be whole hearts, but halves and smaller pieces. These 'broken' hearts will add to the authenticity of the rose petal effect.

Use a sharp knife or a mandoline to very thinly slice the hearts and broken hearts. Lay all the slices on the sheets of kitchen paper. Place more kitchen paper on top and press down gently to blot any excess beetroot juice. Leave to one side.

Weigh out 150g of the remaining beetroot trimmings and offcuts. Put this in a mini food processor and blitz to a purée, adding a splash of water if needed.

To make the cake, put the butter, sugar and golden syrup into a saucepan. Set over a medium heat and warm, stirring occasionally, until the butter has melted and the sugar has dissolved. Remove from the heat, add the chocolate and stir until melted and smooth. Transfer to a large bowl and cool for 5–10 minutes.

Meanwhile, measure the milk in a jug, add the eggs and vanilla, and beat in with a fork. Pour the milk and egg mixture into the warm syrup mixture and beat to combine – preferably with a hand-held electric whisk. Mix in the puréed beetroot. Sift the cocoa powder and flour into the mixture in two batches, mixing until well combined into a very wet, smooth batter.

CONTINUED OVERLEAF >>

HEART BEET CAKE (CONTINUED)

Set your prepared tin on a baking tray. Pour the mixture into the tin and bake for about 50 minutes or until a skewer pushed into the centre of the cake comes out fairly clean. Leave to cool in the tin for 15 minutes before removing the cake and transferring to a wire rack to cool completely. Turn the oven down to 120°C/fan 100°C/gas ½ – opening the oven door and leaving it ajar will speed the cooling-down time.

If you want to create even sweeter-tasting beetroot hearts, lightly dust the beetroot slices with sifted icing sugar while they are still on the kitchen paper. Carefully transfer the beetroot hearts on to two baking trays lined with baking parchment, arranging the hearts in one layer. (I like to use white parchment as the stain left by the beetroot hearts creates a lovely pattern, and you can use the parchment as wrapping paper.) Once the oven has cooled to temperature, use the trays to help you slide the sheets of parchment directly on to the oven shelf. Dry out the beetroot for 1–1¼ hours or until crisp and slightly reduced in size. (You can also dry the beetroot in a dehydrator; see directory, p.309.) Carefully peel the hearts from the parchment, then lay them back on the paper and leave to cool. If you're not using the hearts straight away, store them in a moisture-free container. I find a clean jam jar works well. >>

To make the topping, put the mascarpone into a bowl and sift over the icing sugar. Beat together until smooth and creamy, then add rose water to taste. Spread the sweetened mascarpone over the cake using a palette knife. Scatter most of the dried beetroot hearts on top of the cake and a few more around its base – do this just before you're about to serve, otherwise the beetroot hearts will slowly start to soften and turn the mascarpone topping pink.

VARIATION

To create bite-sized heart beet cakes, scale down the mixture by two-thirds, using the one-egg mix (see the table on p.131) to bake 24 mini cupcakes. Top each with a blob of sweetened mascarpone (make up half the topping quantity listed here) and a single beetroot heart, cut with a 2.5cm mini cutter.

FRUIT CAKE

• •

I'm not content with conventional currants and sultanas alone:
this cake is crammed with a whole fanfare of dried fruits. Dates add
a sticky-toffee-pudding dimension that complements and cuts
through the tang of the cranberries. Golden-brown figs give a festive,
figgy pudding feel, and their seeds pop and crunch nicely in contrast
with velvety, dark prunes. If you don't fancy any of the fruits I've
used, feel free to substitute. I like to start soaking the fruit in the
brandy well ahead of time – up to two days – to make it lusciously
plump and boozy. And I'm a great believer in 'feeding' the finished
cake with brandy before eating – but this is optional. You can make
it up to five weeks ahead of time and feed it every week or so.

BASIC FRUIT CAKE

FOR THE CAKE

50g mixed dried fruit, such as sultanas, raisins and currants

50g dried cranberries

50g pitted soft prunes

50g pitted soft-dried dates

50g dried figs

50ml brandy, plus optional extra to 'feed' the cake

Finely grated zest and juice of ½ orange

50g mixed whole nuts

50g butter, softened

50g dark muscovado sugar

1 tbsp black treacle or date syrup (see directory, p.307), optional

1 egg (at room temperature)

50g self-raising flour

1 tbsp ground mixed spice

EQUIPMENT

10cm round, deep, loose-bottomed tin (pork-pie size), greased and fully lined or lined using the snip-snip method (see p.21) – extend the parchment above the rim to protect the cake during the long baking

Cocktail stick

Put the mixed dried fruit and cranberries in a bowl. Using kitchen scissors, snip the prunes, dates and figs into small pieces, removing any stalks, and drop into the bowl. Add the brandy and orange zest and juice, and stir well to combine. Cover the bowl with a shower cap, clingfilm or plate and leave to soak in a cool place for at least 12 hours or, even better, 2 days.

When you're ready to make the cake, preheat the oven to 180°C/160°C fan/gas 4. Spread the nuts on a baking tray and toast, checking frequently to be sure they don't burn, for 5–10 minutes or until fragrant (you can skip the toasting, but it really brings out their flavour). Cool, then chop the nuts – I like them relatively chunky to contrast with the fruit. Turn the oven down to 140°C/120°C fan/gas 1.

Using a hand-held electric whisk (it's tricky to beat this small quantity in a free-standing mixer), beat together the butter and sugar for 5–10 minutes or until very light and creamy. Beat in the treacle or syrup, if using. Break the egg into a mug or jug and beat it lightly with a fork. Gradually add the egg to the butter and sugar mixture, beating well after each addition.

Sift the flour and spice into the mixture and fold in. (If you're making one of the larger quantities – see the table opposite – fold in in several batches.) Finally, stir through the soaked fruit, with any liquid left in the bowl, and the chopped nuts. Spoon the mixture into your prepared tin and smooth the surface with the back of a spoon dipped in hot water. Bake for 1¼–1½ hours or until the cake is firm to the touch and a skewer pushed into the centre comes out clean.

Set the tin on a wire rack. If you want to 'feed' the cake, leave it to cool for about 15 minutes, then prick the top all over with a cocktail stick or skewer, going about 3cm deep. Brush over about 1 tablespoon of brandy. Leave to soak in while the cake is cooling. Once the cake is cold, remove from the tin and wrap in fresh baking parchment, if you like, and then in foil before storing in an airtight tin or container for at least 5 days before eating. You can repeat the feeding process weekly for up to 5 weeks.

TO FINISH

As this cake is packed with fruit and is baked in a pork-pie tin, it will be very deep and dense. Cover in traditional style with marzipan – you could use my Orange Blossom Marzipan (see p.286) to pick up on the orange in the cake – and fondant. Or use warmed apricot jam or marmalade to both glue and glaze a selection of nuts and dried or glacé fruit on the surface of your cake once baked.

TO MAKE DIFFERENT-SIZED FRUIT CAKES, USE THE TABLE OPPOSITE >>

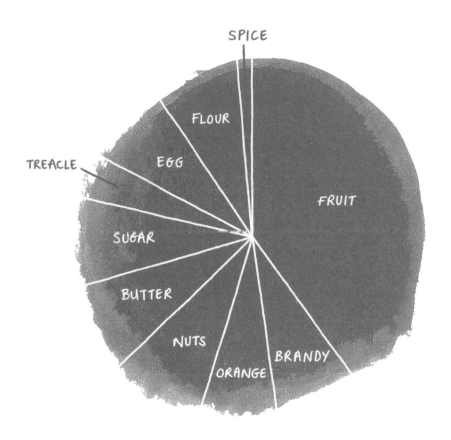

24-HOLE MINI-MUFFIN TIN	12-HOLE MUFFIN TIN	20CM SQUARE TIN	20CM ROUND DEEP TIN	900G (2LB) LOAF TIN	INGREDIENTS
50g	100g	100g	150g	100g	Equal quantities of each of the fruit listed opposite
50ml	100ml	100ml	150ml	100ml	Brandy (plus optional extra to feed the cake)
½ orange	1 orange	1 orange	1½ oranges	1 orange	Zest and juice of orange
50g	100g	100g	150g	100g	Mixed whole nuts
50g	100g	100g	150g	100g	Butter, softened
50g	100g	100g	150g	100g	Dark muscovado sugar
1 tbsp	2 tbsp	2 tbsp	3 tbsp	2 tbsp	Black treacle or date syrup
1	2	2	3	2	Egg(s)
50g	100g	100g	150g	100g	Self-raising flour
1 tbsp	2 tbsp	2 tbsp	3 tbsp	2 tbsp	Ground mixed spice
BAKE IN AN OVEN PREHEATED TO 140°C/120°C FAN/GAS 1					
for 25–30 minutes	for 50–60 minutes	for 1¼–1½ hours	for 2¼–2½ hours	for 1¾–2 hours	

CHRISTMAS PUDDING CUPCAKES

MAKES 12 CUPCAKES

FOR THE CAKE
100g mixed dried fruit

100g dried cranberries

100g pitted soft prunes, snipped into small pieces

100g pitted soft-dried dates, snipped into small pieces

100g dried figs, snipped into small pieces

100ml brandy, plus optional extra to 'feed' the cakes

Finely grated zest and juice of 1 orange

100g butter, softened

100g dark muscovado sugar

2 tbsp black treacle or date syrup (see directory, p.307), optional

2 eggs (at room temperature)

100g self-raising flour

2 tbsp ground mixed spice

100g mixed whole nuts, toasted and chopped (see p.148)

FOR THE GANACHE
150g white chocolate, chopped into small pieces

100ml double cream

TO DECORATE
24 dried cranberries

24 small holly leaves

EQUIPMENT
12-hole muffin tin

12 paper tulip muffin cases (you can use normal muffin cases but the sides of the cakes may be marked with ridges)

Cocktail stick

These give you both Christmas cake and Christmas pudding in one perfect portion. The cakes are topped with a decadent white chocolate ganache to represent custard. Cranberries appear both inside the cakes and on top as 'holly berries', and fresh holly tips finish them off with traditional rustic charm. You can also make mini Christmas puddings by scaling the mixture down and baking it in 24 mini-muffin cases (see the table on p.149).

Put all the dried fruit in a bowl. Add the brandy and orange zest and juice and stir to combine. Cover the bowl with a shower cap, clingfilm or plate and leave to soak in a cool place for at least 12 hours or, even better, 2 days. When you're ready to bake the cakes, preheat the oven to 140°C/120°C fan/gas 1. Line the muffin tin with the tulip cases.

Using a hand-held electric whisk, or in a free-standing mixer, beat the butter with the sugar for 5–10 minutes or until very light and creamy. Beat in the treacle or syrup, if using. Break the eggs into a mug or jug and beat lightly with a fork. Gradually add the egg to the butter and sugar mixture, beating well after each addition. Sift the flour and spice into the bowl in a couple of batches, folding in each batch gently. Finally, stir through the soaked fruit, with any liquid left in the bowl, and the chopped nuts. Spoon the mixture into your cases and flatten the tops with a spoon dipped in hot water.

Bake for 50–60 minutes or until the cakes are firm to the touch and a skewer pushed into the centre comes out clean. Leave to cool in the tin for 5 minutes before transferring the cakes, in their cases, to a wire rack. If you want to 'feed' the cakes, prick the surface with a cocktail stick, going about 3cm deep, then brush about 1 teaspoon of brandy over each. Leave to soak in while the cakes finish cooling. Once cold, you can store them in an airtight tin for up to 5 days.

Make the ganache on the day you serve the cakes. Put the chocolate in a medium-sized heatproof bowl. Gently heat the cream in a small saucepan over a medium heat. When it's just coming to the boil, pour it over the chocolate and stir gently until smooth and shiny. Leave to cool – in the fridge, if necessary – until the ganache reaches a soft, thick custard consistency.

Remove the cakes from their cases and, if necessary, trim off any domed tops to create a flat surface (this will become the base). Turn each cake over and spoon the ganache on top, letting it drip down the sides a little – tilting the cake in your hand can help this process. Leave to set before finishing the cakes by placing the cranberries and holly leaves on top (be sure to remove the holly leaves before eating).

KNIT ONE, BAKE ONE CAKE

MAKES A 15CM CAKE;
SERVES 5–6

FOR THE CAKE

100g mixed dried fruit

100g dried cranberries

100g pitted soft prunes, snipped into small pieces

100g pitted soft-dried dates, snipped into small pieces

100g dried figs, snipped into small pieces

100ml brandy, plus optional extra to 'feed' the cake

Finely grated zest and juice of 1 orange

100g butter, softened

100g dark muscovado sugar

2 tbsp black treacle or date syrup (see directory, p.307), optional

2 eggs (at room temperature)

100g self-raising flour

2 tbsp ground mixed spice

100g mixed whole nuts, toasted and chopped (see p.148)

EQUIPMENT

15cm round, 7–8cm deep, loose-bottomed tin, greased and fully lined or lined with the snip-snip method (see p.21) – extend the parchment above the rim to protect the cake during the long baking

Cake smoother

Mini cutters, 1.5–2.5cm

Cocktail sticks

INGREDIENTS CONTINUED
OVERLEAF >>

Knit one, purl one: a whole haberdashery department of edible goodies can be used to decorate this cake, from my homemade marzipan balls of wool to biscuit toggles and buttons. Although a little time-consuming, the marzipan wool is surprisingly easy to make, tastes great and looks impressively like the yarn used in Aran jumpers! A tape measure is the essential finishing touch, making this the perfect gift or birthday cake for someone with nimble fingers. You only need about 300g each of marzipan and fondant to cover the cake, but you have to start with about 500g to enable you to roll it out and cut it to fit. The trimmings can be used for covering other cakes or to create extra balls of wool.

Place all the dried fruits in a bowl. Add the brandy and orange zest and juice and stir to combine. Cover the bowl with a shower cap, clingfilm or plate and leave to soak in a cool place for at least 12 hours or, even better, up to 2 days.

When you're ready to bake, preheat the oven to 140°C/120°C fan/gas 1.

Using a hand-held electric whisk, or in a free-standing mixer, beat the butter with the sugar for 5–10 minutes or until very light and creamy. Beat in the treacle or syrup, if using. Break the eggs into a mug or jug and beat lightly with a fork. Gradually add the egg to the butter and sugar mixture, beating well after each addition. Sift the flour and spice into the bowl in a couple of batches and fold in each batch gently. Finally, stir through the soaked fruit, with any liquid left in the bowl, and the chopped nuts.

Spoon the mixture into the prepared tin and smooth the surface with the back of a spoon dipped in hot water. Bake for about 2¼ hours or until the cake is firm to the touch and a skewer pushed into the centre comes out clean.

Set the tin on a wire rack. If you want to 'feed' the cake, prick the surface all over with a cocktail stick or skewer, going about 3cm deep. Brush over about 1 tablespoon of brandy. Leave to soak in while the cake finishes cooling.

Once the cake is cold, remove it from the tin and wrap in fresh baking parchment, if you like, and then in foil before storing in an airtight tin or container for at least 5 days before decorating. You can repeat the feeding process weekly for up to 5 weeks.

CONTINUED OVERLEAF >>

KNIT ONE, BAKE ONE CAKE (CONTINUED)

TO DECORATE

1–2 tbsp smooth apricot jam

Icing sugar, to dust

500g natural marzipan

500g white fondant icing

85g Raspberry Marzipan (see p.286)

75g Pistachio Marzipan (p.287)

65g Orange Blossom Marzipan (p.286)

25g Basic Gingerbread dough (p.238)

15g Basic Butter Biscuits dough (p.206)

Paper or fabric tape measure (see directory, p.310)

55cm ribbon/cotton

Haberdashery pins

Cocktail sticks and bamboo skewers

Gold and ivory sugar pearls

Ideally, cover your cake with marzipan at least a day before you ice it with fondant, or up to 5 days ahead. Take a piece of string and, holding one end at the base of the cake on one side, run it up that side, straight over the top and down the other side. Add another 10cm and cut the string to this length. The string will be a guide when you are rolling out the marzipan and fondant.

Heat the apricot jam gently with a splash of water in a small saucepan, or in a bowl in the microwave, until liquid. Brush the warm jam over the top and sides of the cake in a thin, even layer.

Dust your work surface and your natural marzipan with icing sugar. Roll out the marzipan to a circle about 5mm thick – the diameter should be the same as the length of your cut piece of string. Roll the marzipan around the rolling pin and unroll it over the cake. Use your hands to smooth the marzipan across the top and down the sides. Trim off the excess marzipan from the base of the cake using a small knife (keep this marzipan for making beads and buttons). Leave in a tin for a day or so to set.

When you are ready to cover your cake with fondant, first brush the marzipan with a little water or clear alcohol. Roll out the fondant on a sugar-dusted surface to a circle 5mm thick with a diameter the same as the length of the string. Repeat the process you used to cover the cake with marzipan, trimming off excess fondant. Use the cake smoother to work over the sides and top of the cake to flatten out any lumps and bumps and create a smooth, even surface.

Divide the raspberry, pistachio and orange blossom marzipans into two pieces each – one roughly a third and the other two-thirds. Take the larger pieces of each marzipan and roll into a ball: these will be the basis of the balls of wool. Roll the remaining marzipan into long, thin lengths to represent strands of wool. Wrap these around the marzipan balls.

To create your marzipan buttons, roll out a little of the marzipan trimmings between two sheets of baking parchment to about the thickness of a £1 coin. Cut out about five button shapes with the mini cutters. Use the tip of a cocktail stick to create holes in the buttons and to score lines.

For marzipan beads, roll tiny pieces of the remaining marzipan into mini balls and thread them on to a cocktail stick to create a hole through their centres. Put the marzipan buttons and beads on a plate or tray, cover with clingfilm and leave for a few hours, preferably overnight, to firm up. >>

To create your biscuit buttons, roll out the gingerbread and butter biscuit doughs between two sheets of baking parchment to the thickness of a £1 coin. Use the mini cutters to cut out five (or more) button shapes from each dough. Peel away the excess dough, then lift the biscuits, on the parchment, on to a baking tray. Mark holes and score lines in the biscuits in the same way as for the marzipan buttons. Chill for 15 minutes. Preheat the oven to 180°C/160°C fan/gas 4.

To create your toggles, roll 5g pieces of gingerbread dough into fat sausages, thicker in the middle than at the ends, and use a bamboo skewer or the end of a fine paintbrush to create the toggles' holes. Add the toggles to the baking tray. Bake the biscuit buttons for about 5 minutes, and the toggles for 12–15 minutes, or until golden brown. Leave to firm up on the tray for a few minutes, then transfer to a wire rack to cool.

To assemble the cake, lay the tape measure on top of the ribbon or cotton and wrap both around the circumference of the cake, trimming away the excess and securing in place with haberdashery pins.

Cut the tips off some of the cocktail sticks and cut the bamboo skewers down to size to create knitting needles of varying lengths. Arrange your 'balls of wool' on top of the cake and push the cocktail stick/skewer 'needles' into them – push the needles right through into the cake to secure the balls of wool. Roll little balls of marzipan for the knitting needle tips and press them into place. Arrange the buttons, beads, toggles and sugar pearls around the balls of wool, sticking them in place with some apricot jam or honey, if necessary.

VARIATION
A slightly smaller version of this cake, baked in a 10cm tin, makes a beautiful gift for someone crafty. Use the quantities given for the basic recipe on p.148.

FAIR ISLE FRUIT CAKE

MAKES A 20CM SQUARE CAKE;
SERVES 10–12

FOR THE CAKE

150g mixed dried fruit

150g dried cranberries

150g pitted soft prunes, snipped
into small pieces

150g pitted soft-dried dates,
snipped into small pieces

150g dried figs, snipped into
small pieces

150ml brandy, plus optional
extra to 'feed' the cake

Finely grated zest and juice of
1½ oranges

150g butter, softened

150g dark muscovado sugar

3 tbsp black treacle or date
syrup (see directory, p.307),
optional

3 eggs (at room temperature)

150g self-raising flour

3 tbsp ground mixed spice

150g mixed whole nuts, toasted
and chopped (see p.148)

EQUIPMENT

20cm square, 7–8cm deep,
loose-bottomed tin, greased
and fully lined or lined
using the snip-snip method
(see p.21) – extend the
parchment above the rim
to protect the cake during
the long baking

Cake smoother

Fine paintbrush

INGREDIENTS CONTINUED
OVERLEAF >>

Having studied textiles, I have always loved the striking, graphic designs found in knitting patterns – and it seems to me there's a very pleasing overlap between the cosiness of knitwear and the comforting nature of cake. You can now buy square chocolate chunks, which make it particularly easy to translate stitch patterns into edible form. This design takes inspiration from traditional Fair Isle patterns and there is a pattern overleaf to trace or photocopy – or you can base the design on a favourite of your own.

Place all the dried fruit in a bowl. Add the brandy and orange zest and juice and stir to combine. Cover the bowl with a shower cap, clingfilm or plate and leave to soak in a cool place for at least 12 hours or, even better, up to 2 days.

When ready to bake the cake, preheat the oven to 140°C/120°C fan/gas 1.

Using a hand-held electric whisk, or in a free-standing mixer, beat the butter with the sugar for 5–10 minutes or until very light and creamy. Beat in the treacle or syrup, if using. Break the eggs into a mug or jug and beat lightly with a fork. Gradually add the egg to the butter and sugar mixture, beating well after each addition. Sift the flour and spice into the bowl in two or three batches and fold in each batch gently. Finally, stir through the soaked fruit, with any liquid left in the bowl, and the chopped nuts.

Spoon the mixture into the prepared tin and smooth the surface with the back of a spoon dipped in hot water. Bake for about 2¼ hours or until the cake is firm to the touch and a skewer pushed into the centre comes out clean.

Set the tin on a wire rack. If you want to 'feed' the cake, prick the surface all over with a cocktail stick or skewer, going about 3cm deep. Brush over about 1 tablespoon of brandy. Leave to soak in while the cake finishes cooling.

Once the cake is cold, remove it from the tin and wrap in fresh baking parchment, if you like, and then in foil before storing in an airtight tin or container for at least 5 days before decorating. You can repeat the feeding process weekly for up to 5 weeks.

Ideally, cover your cake with marzipan at least a day before icing it, or up to 5 days ahead. Place the cake on a board. Heat the apricot jam gently with a splash of water in a small saucepan, or in a bowl in the microwave, until liquid. Brush the warm jam over the top of the cake in a thin, even layer.

CONTINUED OVERLEAF >>

FAIR ISLE FRUIT CAKE (CONTINUED)

TO DECORATE
1–2 tbsp smooth apricot jam
Icing sugar, to dust
500g natural marzipan
500g white fondant icing
100g dark chocolate chunks
(see directory, p.307)

Dust your work surface and your marzipan with icing sugar. Roll out the marzipan into a rough square 5mm thick. Using the cake tin as a guide, cut out a square slightly bigger than the cake. Place this marzipan square on top of the cake. Smooth the marzipan across the top with your hands. Trim away the excess marzipan using a ruler and small sharp knife to get a clean, sharp edge. Leave in a tin for a day or so to set.

When you are ready to cover your cake with fondant, first lightly brush the marzipan with a little water or clear alcohol. Repeat the process you used to cover your cake with marzipan, rolling the fondant 5mm thick. Use the cake smoother to flatten out any bumps and create a smooth, even surface. Trim off the excess fondant with a small sharp knife and ruler.

To create your Fair Isle pattern, photocopy or trace the design opposite, or use another design on squared paper. Place the pattern over the cake and use a needle or pin to prick through the paper at the centre of the design: this will be a guide for where your first chocolate square should be placed. Remove the paper and place it next to the cake. Working outwards from the pinprick and following the pattern, arrange the chunks, flat side down, on the fondant.

Once you have the pattern of chocolate chunks right, melt the remaining chunks in a microwave, or in a small heatproof bowl set over a pan of simmering water (bain-marie). Dab a bit of melted chocolate on to the underside of each chunk with the paintbrush, then replace the chunk – the chocolate will help the chunks stick to the fondant. Leave to set before cutting the cake into rectangular fingers or squares.

FOR THE CAKE

150g mixed dried fruit

150g dried cranberries

150g pitted soft prunes, snipped
into small pieces

150g pitted soft-dried dates,
snipped into small pieces

150g dried figs, snipped into
small pieces

150ml brandy, plus optional
extra to 'feed' the cake

Finely grated zest and juice
of 1½ oranges

150g butter, softened

150g dark muscovado sugar

3 tbsp black treacle or date
syrup (see directory, p.307),
optional

3 eggs (at room temperature)

150g self-raising flour

3 tbsp ground mixed spice

150g mixed whole nuts, toasted
and chopped (see p.148)

EQUIPMENT

20cm square, 7–8cm deep,
loose-bottomed tin, greased
and fully lined or lined
using the snip-snip method
(see p.21) – extend the
parchment above the rim
to protect the cake during
the long baking

Cake smoother

INGREDIENTS CONTINUED
OVERLEAF >>

FRUIT CAKE PARCELS

Wrapped up in a traditional double layer of marzipan and fondant, and
finished off with gingerbread biscuit labels, these parcels make perfect
presents. They're ideal for Christmas (so much more welcome than bubble
bath or a pair of socks!) but are wonderful to give at any time of year. Even
more joy can be rolled out via my gingerbread ribbon reels, which can
feature real ribbon or, to be completely edible, marzipan and fondant strips.

Place all the dried fruit in a bowl. Add the brandy and orange zest and juice,
and stir to combine. Cover the bowl with a shower cap, clingfilm or plate and
leave to soak in a cool place for at least 12 hours or, even better, 2 days.

When you're ready to bake, preheat the oven to 140°C/120°C fan/gas 1.

Using a hand-held electric whisk, or in a free-standing mixer, beat the butter
with the sugar for 5–10 minutes or until light and creamy. Beat in the treacle
or syrup, if using. Break the eggs into a mug or jug and beat lightly with a fork.
Gradually add the egg to the butter and sugar mixture, beating well after each
addition. Sift the flour and spice into the bowl in two to three batches and fold
in each batch gently. Finally, stir through the soaked fruit, with any liquid left
in the bowl, and the chopped nuts.

Spoon the mixture into the prepared tin and smooth the surface with the back
of a spoon dipped in hot water. Bake for about 2¼ hours or until the cake is
firm to the touch and a skewer pushed into the centre comes out clean.

Set the tin on a wire rack. If you want to 'feed' the cake, prick the surface all
over with a cocktail stick or skewer, going about 3cm deep. Brush over about
1 tablespoon of brandy. Leave to soak in while the cake finishes cooling.

Once the cake is cold, remove it from the tin and wrap in fresh baking
parchment, if you like, and then in foil before storing in an airtight tin or
container for at least 5 days before decorating. You can repeat the feeding
process weekly for up to 5 weeks.

Ideally, cover the cake with marzipan at least a day before icing, or up to 5 days
ahead. Cut the cake into three pieces: first cut a large rectangle 12 x 20cm.
Then cut the remaining piece into two pieces: one an 8 x 12cm rectangle and
the other an 8 x 8cm square. Place all three cakes on a board or a tray lined
with baking parchment.

CONTINUED OVERLEAF >>

FRUIT CAKE PARCELS (CONTINUED)

TO DECORATE

3 tbsp smooth apricot jam

Icing sugar, to dust

1kg natural marzipan

1kg white fondant icing

Ribbons and trimmings for wrapping the cakes

3 Gingerbread Gift Tags (see p.302)

3 Gingerbread Ribbon Reels (p.303)

Heat the apricot jam gently with a splash of water in a small saucepan, or in a bowl in the microwave, until liquid. Brush the warm jam over the top and sides of each cake in a thin, even layer.

Dust your work surface and your marzipan with icing sugar. Start with the largest cake. Roll out half the marzipan to a rough 25 x 30cm rectangle, 5mm thick. Roll the marzipan around the rolling pin and unroll it over the cake, smoothing it across the top and down the sides with your hands. Tuck the edges of the marzipan under the cake with the help of a smoother or ruler.

Repeat to cover the other rectangular cake, rolling out half the remainder of the marzipan to a rough 20 x 25cm rectangle. Finally, cover the square cake, rolling out the rest of the marzipan to a rough 20 x 20cm square. (You will be left with marzipan trimmings, which can be kept in a sealed food bag – use them to cover other cakes or to make decorations.) Leave the cakes in tins for a day or so to set the marzipan. >>

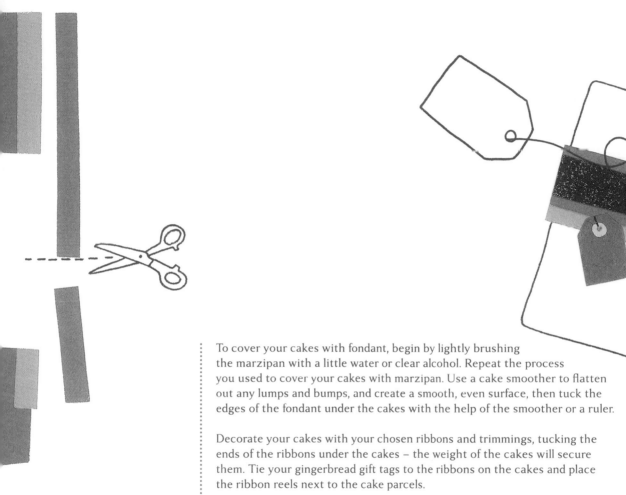

To cover your cakes with fondant, begin by lightly brushing the marzipan with a little water or clear alcohol. Repeat the process you used to cover your cakes with marzipan. Use a cake smoother to flatten out any lumps and bumps, and create a smooth, even surface, then tuck the edges of the fondant under the cakes with the help of the smoother or a ruler.

Decorate your cakes with your chosen ribbons and trimmings, tucking the ends of the ribbons under the cakes – the weight of the cakes will secure them. Tie your gingerbread gift tags to the ribbons on the cakes and place the ribbon reels next to the cake parcels.

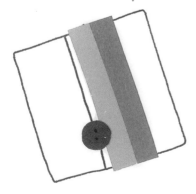

BROWNIES

• •

Created in one saucepan, these brownies are very easy to make and ultra-chocolatey. To ensure a great flavour, use a good-quality dark chocolate with at least 60 per cent cocoa solids – or, if you prefer your brownie less dark and rich, a good milk chocolate (at least 37 per cent cocoa solids). You can also use a mix of dark and milk. In my recipe, the unconventional inclusion of golden syrup gives the brownies an extra fudgy taste and texture. Judging the point at which a brownie is perfectly cooked – firm and risen, but with a little squidgy 'give' still in the centre – comes with practice. However, the skewer test is pretty reliable. When inserted into the centre of the cooked brownie, the skewer should come out with a little bit of moist mixture adhering to it – a herald of the fudgy delights to come.

BASIC BROWNIES

FOR THE BROWNIES
50g butter, roughly chopped
1 tbsp golden syrup
100g golden caster sugar
100g dark chocolate, chopped
    into small pieces
1 tsp vanilla extract
1 egg (at room temperature)
50g plain flour

EQUIPMENT
10cm round, deep, loose-
    bottomed tin (pork-pie size),
    greased and fully lined

Preheat the oven to 180°C/160°C fan/gas 4.

Put the butter, syrup and sugar into a saucepan. Set it over a medium heat and warm, stirring occasionally, until the butter has melted and the sugar has dissolved. Remove from the heat and add the chopped chocolate and the vanilla extract. Leave for a few minutes so the chocolate can soften and melt, then stir the chocolatey mixture until smooth and combined. I find it helpful to use a silicone spatula to combine the mix and fold in all the sugary syrup from the base and sides of the pan.

Use a hand-held electric whisk to beat the egg into the warm chocolatey mixture in the pan until thick and velvety. Sift over the flour and fold it in gently but firmly until just combined.

Pour into the prepared tin. Bake for 20–25 minutes or until the brownie has risen and is firm to the touch; a skewer inserted into the centre should come out a little sticky. Leave to cool completely in the tin – the brownie will firm up as it cools. If you like a really fudgy brownie, refrigerate before cutting or decorating (chilling the brownie also makes it easier to cut).

TO FINISH
As this is baked in a pork-pie tin, the brownie is extra thick and fudgy, perfect to share as a pud. It is delectable served absolutely plain but you can also dish it up warm with ice cream or crème fraîche and fresh raspberries.

TO MAKE DIFFERENT-SIZED BROWNIES, USE THE TABLE OPPOSITE >>

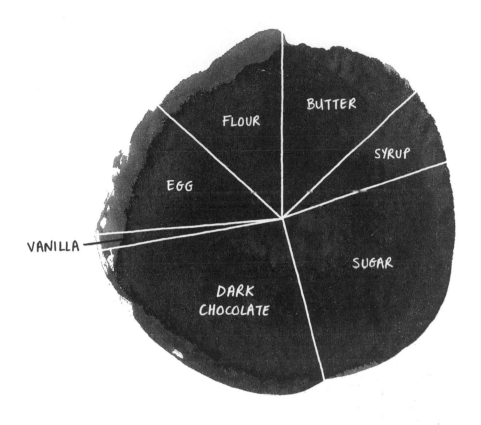

24-HOLE MINI-MUFFIN TIN	12-HOLE MUFFIN TIN	20CM ROUND TIN	20CM SQUARE TIN	INGREDIENTS
50g	150g	100g	150g	Butter, roughly chopped
1 tbsp	3 tbsp	2 tbsp	3 tbsp	Golden syrup
100g	300g	200g	300g	Golden caster sugar
100g	300g	200g	300g	Dark chocolate, chopped into small pieces
1 tsp	3 tsp	2 tsp	3 tsp	Vanilla extract
1	3	2	3	Egg(s)
50g	150g	100g	150g	Plain flour

BAKE IN AN OVEN PREHEATED TO 180°C/160°C FAN/GAS 4				
for 10–12 minutes	for 20–25 minutes	for 20–25 minutes	for 25–30 minutes	

FOR THE BROWNIES

24 caramel-filled chocolates,
    such as Rolos (a 126g pack)
50g butter, roughly chopped
1 tbsp golden syrup
100g golden caster sugar
100g dark chocolate, chopped
    into small pieces
1 tsp vanilla extract
1 egg (at room temperature)
50g plain flour

FOR THE GANACHE

50g dark chocolate, chopped
    into small pieces
½ tbsp golden syrup
½ tsp vanilla extract
50ml double cream

TO DECORATE

Edible gold glitter

EQUIPMENT

24-hole mini-muffin tin
24 mini-muffin cases
Small star stencil (see below)
Mini sieve

STAR STENCIL

BROWNIE POINTS

Combine bite-sized brownies with gold stars and you get your very own edible brownie points. Hidden inside each one is a reward, in the shape of a caramel-filled chocolate centre. Serve these individually to those who deserve them, or give them away en masse as favours – you'll certainly be earning the favour of anyone who receives one!

Preheat the oven to 180°C/160°C fan/gas 4. Line the muffin tin with the cases.

Place the pack of chocolates in the freezer. Put the butter, syrup and sugar into a saucepan. Set it over a medium heat and warm, stirring occasionally, until the butter has melted and the sugar has dissolved. Take the saucepan off the heat and add the chopped chocolate and the vanilla extract. Leave for a few minutes so the chocolate can soften and melt, then stir the chocolatey mixture until smooth and combined.

Use a hand-held electric whisk to beat the egg into the warm chocolately mixture in the pan until thick and velvety. Sift over the flour and fold it in gently until just combined. Spoon two-thirds of the mixture into the muffin cases, using a teaspoon and dividing the mixture evenly. Remove the chocolates from the freezer and place one in each partially filled case, with their narrower tops downwards. Spoon in the rest of the mixture to cover the chocolates completely.

Bake for 10–12 minutes or until the brownies have risen and are firm to the touch. Leave to cool completely in the tin – the brownies will firm up as they cool. If you like a really fudgy brownie, refrigerate before cutting (chilling also makes them easier to cut in half to reveal the hidden chocolate).

While the brownies are cooling, make the ganache. Put the chocolate in a medium-sized heatproof bowl with the golden syrup and vanilla. Gently heat the cream in a small saucepan over a medium heat. When it's just coming to the boil, pour it over the chocolate and stir gently until smooth and shiny. Leave the ganache to cool slightly but use it while still runny.

Use a teaspoon to spread the ganache over the brownies – tap the brownies on their bases to distribute the ganache evenly, if necessary. Leave to set.

Position the star stencil over one brownie (don't let the stencil touch the ganache-covered surface) and sprinkle with a little glitter, then carefully lift away the stencil. Repeat the process for the remaining brownies.

BROWNIE OWLS

FOR THE BROWNIES

24 round, cream-filled chocolate
    biscuits, such as Oreos
    (about 265g)
150g butter, roughly chopped
3 tbsp golden or maple syrup
300g golden caster sugar
300g dark chocolate, chopped
    into small pieces
1 tbsp vanilla extract
3 eggs (at room temperature)
150g plain flour

FOR THE GANACHE

100g dark chocolate, chopped
    into small pieces
1 tbsp golden syrup
1 tsp vanilla extract
150ml double cream

TO FINISH

24 giant milk chocolate buttons
    (about 100g)
24 small, round, dark chocolate
    chips
12 whole skin-on almonds
72 milk chocolate buttons
    (about 90g)
12 walnuts
12 pecans

EQUIPMENT

12-hole muffin tin
12 paper muffin cases
Fine paintbrush

These are a hoot – chocolate, biscuits and nuts all nestled together in a brownie cupcake. The recipe makes use of round, cream-filled chocolate biscuits, split in half. The cream-covered sides make up the owls' wise eyes; some of the other halves go to make crunchy bases for the cakes; and the remainder are broken up and stirred into the mix to give you a brownie with bite. If you want even more texture, add a handful of chopped nuts to the batter too: they'll make for a bake that's totally top of the tree!

Preheat the oven to 180°C/160°C fan/gas 4. Line the tin with the muffin cases.

Split the chocolate biscuits in half. Set the 24 cream-covered halves aside. Put 12 of the plain halves into your muffin cases, embossed side down. Put the remaining 12 plain halves in a sandwich bag encased in a tea towel and bash into large crumbs using a rolling pin. Set aside.

Put the butter, syrup and sugar into a saucepan. Set it over a medium heat and warm, stirring occasionally, until the butter has melted and the sugar has dissolved. Take the saucepan off the heat and add the chopped chocolate and the vanilla extract. Set aside for a few minutes to allow the chocolate to soften.

Stir the warm chocolatey mixture in the pan until smoothly combined, then use a hand-held electric whisk to beat in the eggs until the mixture is thick and velvety. Sift over the flour in a couple of batches, gently folding in each batch until just combined. Finally, fold in the broken-up biscuit pieces.

Spoon the mixture into the biscuit-based muffin cases, dividing it evenly. Bake for 20–25 minutes or until the brownies have risen and are firm to the touch; a skewer inserted into the centre should come out a little sticky.

Leave the brownies to cool completely in the tin – they will firm up as they cool. If you like a really fudgy brownie, refrigerate them before decorating.

CONTINUED OVERLEAF >>

BROWNIE OWLS (CONTINUED)

While the brownies are cooling, make the ganache. Put the chocolate in a medium-sized heatproof bowl with the golden syrup and vanilla extract. Gently heat the cream in a small saucepan over a medium heat. When it's just coming to the boil, pour it over the chocolate and stir gently until smooth and shiny. Leave the ganache to cool slightly but use it while still runny.

To make the owls' eyes, lay out the 24 cream-sided biscuit halves, cream side up. Using the paintbrush, carefully dab some of the chocolate ganache on to the centre of each biscuit, then stick a giant milk chocolate button on this. Carefully dab some more ganache on to the middle of each button and stick on a dark chocolate chip to create the pupil in the eye. To add even more personality and expression to your brownie owls, place the chocolate-chip pupils in varying positions on the buttons. Leave to set.

Leave the remaining ganache to cool further. You want it to reach a soft spreadable consistency for topping the brownies, so you may want to put it in the fridge to firm up a little. >>

Once the brownies have cooled,
remove them from their paper cases.
Cover each one with ganache. Place two
chocolate eyes on each cake and insert an
almond between them to represent a beak.
Press the milk chocolate buttons into the ganache
– six buttons per owl, in overlapping rows – to look like
feathers. Carefully cut the pecans and walnuts in half. Place the
pecans between the eyes to represent eyebrows, and the walnuts
either side of the chocolate buttons, as wings.

VARIATIONS

Using a coffee-flavoured chocolate, or coffee extract instead of vanilla,
will turn these brownies into night owls – sure to keep you wide awake!
For snowy owls, use white chocolate ganache and buttons.

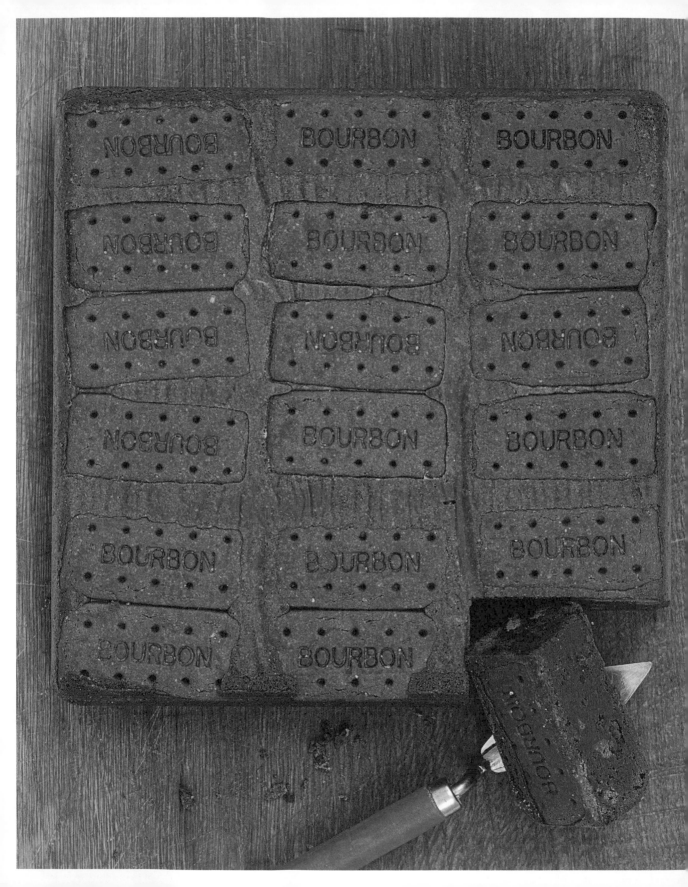

BOURBON BRICK BROWNIES

MAKES 18 BROWNIES

FOR THE BROWNIES
200g bourbon biscuits
100g butter, roughly chopped
2 tbsp barley malt extract (see directory, p.307)
200g golden caster sugar
200g dark chocolate, chopped into small pieces
2 tsp vanilla extract
2 eggs (at room temperature)
100g plain flour
2 tbsp bourbon whiskey, optional

EQUIPMENT
20cm square, loose-bottomed tin, greased and lined with seatbelt straps (see p.21)

A celebration of a much-loved teatime treat, these bakes turn out looking like super-chocolatey bourbon biscuit bricks. Whether or not you choose to actually build them up into a wall once baked, they go amazingly well with a brew of builder's tea. To play on the name of the biscuits, you can add a generous glug of a very different kind of bourbon to the mix, which builds up the depth of flavour provided by the barley malt extract.

Preheat the oven to 180°C/160°C fan/gas 4.

Split the bourbon biscuits in half. Select 18 halves that are unbroken (and ideally with creamy filling) and lay them, filling side up, on the base of the tin. Arrange them neatly in three rows of six, leaving a small gap between each biscuit so you can cut the cake into bricks once baked. Chop or break up the remaining biscuits, or put them in a sandwich bag encased in a tea towel and bash into large crumbs with a rolling pin. Set aside.

Put the butter, malt extract and sugar into a saucepan. Set it over a medium heat and warm, stirring occasionally, until the butter has melted and the sugar has dissolved. Take the saucepan off the heat and add the chopped chocolate and the vanilla extract. Set aside for a few minutes to allow the chocolate to soften and melt.

Stir the chocolatey mixture in the pan until smooth, then use a hand-held electric whisk to beat in the eggs until thick and velvety. Sift over the flour in a couple of batches, gently folding in each batch until just combined. Finally, fold in the broken-up biscuit pieces and the bourbon whiskey, if using.

Pour the mixture carefully over the bourbon biscuits in the tin, trying not to move them around on the base. Bake for 20–25 minutes or until the brownie has risen and is firm to the touch; a skewer inserted into the centre should come out a little sticky. Leave to cool completely in the tin – the brownie will firm up as it cools. It is then best refrigerated for a few hours, ideally overnight, to make cutting into bricks easier.

Remove the brownie from the tin with the help of the seatbelt straps. Place a board on top of the brownie and carefully flip over. Peel off the parchment. Don't worry if some of the biscuits have moved out of line, or are partly covered by the brownie mix because, once cut, they will look more even. Using a small sharp knife, trim off the outer edges around the biscuits, then cut the brownies into bricks following the lines of the biscuits.

MINT-CHOC BROWNIES

FOR THE BROWNIES

150g butter, roughly chopped

3 tbsp golden syrup

300g golden caster sugar

300g mint-flavoured dark
chocolate, chopped into
small pieces

1 tbsp vanilla extract

100g dark chocolate-mint crisps,
such as Matchmaker sticks or
Elizabeth Shaw Discs

3 eggs (at room temperature)

150g plain flour

TO DECORATE

25 sprigs of fresh mint

EQUIPMENT

20cm square, loose-bottomed
tin, lined with seatbelt straps
(see p.21)

Cocktail stick

Fine paintbrush

The moist crumb and crackled surface of a brownie reminds me of sweet, dark earth – and that's the inspiration behind these bite-sized mint-choc squares. Sprinkled with chocolate 'topsoil' and 'planted' with a sprig of mint, they look uncannily like little seed plugs, bursting with new life.

Preheat the oven to 180°C/160°C fan/gas 4.

Put the butter, syrup and sugar into a saucepan. Set it over a medium heat and warm, stirring occasionally, until the butter has melted and the sugar has dissolved. Take the saucepan off the heat and add the chopped chocolate and the vanilla extract. Set aside for a few minutes to allow the chocolate to soften.

Meanwhile, chop the chocolate-mint crisps into soil-like crumbs using a sharp knife. Set aside 25g of these to top the brownies later.

Stir the chocolatey mixture in the pan until smoothly combined, then use a hand-held electric whisk to beat in the eggs until thick and velvety. Sift over the flour in a couple of batches, gently folding in each batch until just combined. Finally, fold in the 75g of chocolate-mint crisp pieces.

Transfer the mixture to the prepared tin and bake for 25–30 minutes or until the brownie has risen and is firm to the touch; a skewer inserted into the centre should come out a little sticky. Leave to cool completely in the tin – the brownie will firm up as it cools. If you like a really fudgy brownie, refrigerate before serving (this will also make the brownie easier to cut).

Remove the brownie from the tin with the help of the seatbelt straps. Using a sharp knife and a ruler, trim off 1cm from the edges all around. Break this offcut into crumbs and set aside. Cut the brownie into 3.5cm squares.

Make a hole in the centre of each brownie with the tip of the cocktail stick and insert a mint sprig (or if any cracks have appeared on the brownies' surface, push the mint sprigs into these). Melt half of the 25g chocolate-mint crumbs in a microwave, or a small heatproof bowl set over a pan of simmering water (bain-marie). Use the paintbrush to dab a little melted chocolate around the mint sprigs, then scatter the rest of the chocolate-mint crumbs and brownie crumbs around the mint, to look like topsoil.

VARIATION

If you're not using mint-flavoured dark chocolate, replace the vanilla with peppermint extract or for a more subtle mint flavour add ½ tablespoon of each.

TIFFIN

This marvellous mingling of chocolate, bashed-up biscuits and chewy treats is, for me, the choccie equivalent of Eton Mess – greater than the sum of its parts. And, of course, it couldn't be simpler to make. There's no baking, just melting and mixing. I vary my tiffins, using a pick 'n' mix of tastes and textures in the chocolate base, depending on the theme – but the rule is always to include something crunchy (nuts, sesame seed bars, pretzel sticks...) and something chewy (raisins, toffees, milk bottle sweets...) in the mix.

BASIC TIFFIN

FOR THE TIFFIN

50g butter, roughly chopped

1 tbsp golden syrup

100g dark chocolate, chopped
into small pieces

100g milk chocolate, chopped
into small pieces

50g biscuits, such as shortbread
or chocolate chip cookies

50g crunchy items, such
as peanuts, pretzels or
crunchy chocolate-covered
honeycomb balls, such as
Maltesers

50g chewy items, such as raisins
or toffees

EQUIPMENT

15cm round, loose-bottomed
tin, greased and fully lined

Put the butter and golden syrup in a large, heavy-based saucepan. Set over
a gentle heat and warm, stirring occasionally, until the butter has melted.
Add all the chopped chocolate and stir the mixture until it is smooth and
combined. Remove the pan from the heat.

Place your biscuits and crunchy items in a large bowl and break them up by
pounding them with the end of a rolling pin, as if you were using a large pestle
in a mortar. Alternatively, chop the ingredients with a sharp knife. Aim to
create a mix of crumbs and larger bits, which will give your tiffin a good
texture. Also chop up the chewy items if they are large.

Stir the crushed/chopped biscuits and crunchy items plus your chewy items
into the chocolatey mixture. I find it helpful to use a silicone spatula to
combine the mix, taking all the chocolatey syrup from the sides of the pan.

Pour into the prepared tin and press out evenly. Refrigerate until set, preferably
overnight. Once set, you can store the tiffin at cool room temperature. To serve,
remove from the tin and cut into slices.

TO FINISH

This basic tiffin can be dusted with icing sugar, cocoa powder or a mix of the
two. A light dusting of edible glitter can also be sprinkled on top to make the
tiffin extra special. Alternatively, I sometimes scatter extra crushed biscuits,
crunchy items and chewy items on top before the chocolate has set –
homemade Honeycomb (see p.285) or popping candy works a treat.

TO MAKE DIFFERENT-SIZED TIFFIN, USE THE TABLE OPPOSITE >>

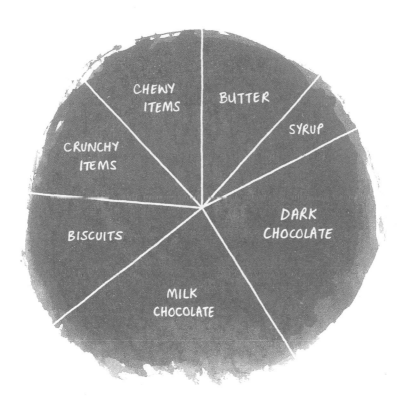

24-HOLE MINI-MUFFIN TIN	12-HOLE MUFFIN TIN	20CM ROUND TIN	20CM SQUARE TIN	INGREDIENTS
50g	100g	100g	150g	Butter, roughly chopped
1 tbsp	2 tbsp	2 tbsp	3 tbsp	Golden syrup
100g	200g	200g	300g	Dark chocolate, chopped into small pieces
100g	200g	200g	300g	Milk chocolate, chopped into small pieces
50g	100g	100g	150g	Biscuits, such as shortbread or chocolate chip cookies
50g	100g	100g	150g	Crunchy items, such as peanuts or pretzels
50g	100g	100g	150g	Chewy items, such as raisins or toffees
REFRIGERATE, PREFERABLY OVERNIGHT				
for 1 hour	for 2 hours	for 2 hours	for 3 hours	

MALTED MILK & COOKIES

MAKES 15 TIFFIN BISCUITS

FOR THE TIFFIN

100g butter, roughly chopped

2 tbsp barley malt extract (see directory, p.307)

200g dark chocolate, chopped into small pieces

200g milk chocolate, chopped into small pieces

200g malted milk biscuits

100g chocolate chip cookies

100g crunchy chocolate-covered honeycomb balls, such as Maltesers

100g milk bottle sweets

EQUIPMENT

23cm square tin, greased and lined with seatbelt straps (see p.21)

I've crammed a lot of malty deliciousness into these tiffin slabs, in the form of classic malted milk biscuits and malt extract. And, in a nostalgic nod to many comforting milk-and-cookie snacks, I've scattered in a good helping of chewy milk bottle sweets too. If you can, choose the kind dusted in icing sugar and made with real milk: the flavour is much more 'milky'.

Put the butter and barley malt extract in a heavy-based saucepan. Set over a gentle heat and warm, stirring occasionally, until the butter has melted. Add all the chopped chocolate and stir until smooth and combined. Remove the pan from the heat.

Reserve 15 malted milk biscuits and put the rest in a large bowl. Add the cookies and chocolate-coated honeycomb balls. Break up the biscuits and chocolates by pounding them with the end of a rolling pin – as if you were using a large pestle and mortar. Aim to create a mix of crumbs and larger chunks to give your tiffin a good texture.

Use scissors to snip up the milk bottle sweets into about five pieces each and add to the bowl containing the bashed-up mixture.

Add the dry ingredients to the melted chocolate mixture and stir together, combining everything thoroughly. Transfer the mixture to the lined tin. Level the surface with a cranked palette knife, spatula or the back of a spoon.

Arrange the reserved malted milk biscuits over the top in three neat rows of five, leaving a slight gap between each to make the tiffin easier to cut later. Firmly press them on to the top to be sure they stick.

Refrigerate until set, preferably overnight. To serve, remove from the tin using the parchment straps to help, and cut into portions, following the lines of the malted milk biscuits.

SEEDLINGS

These potting-shed-inspired tiffins are quite literally crammed with seeds, and finished off with edible chocolate topsoil and a butter biscuit plant label. Each tiffin is planted into an actual seedling cell (easy to find at garden centres). As well as the seeds, I've added sesame seed bars to the mixture for maximum crunch, while raisins supply a satisfying chew.

Line the base of each seed tray cell with a square of baking parchment. Put the seeds in a dry frying pan and toast them lightly over a medium heat, tossing frequently, for a few minutes. Leave to cool.

Put the butter and honey in a heavy-based saucepan. Set over a gentle heat and warm, stirring occasionally, until the butter has melted. Add all of the chopped chocolate and stir until smooth and combined. Remove the pan from the heat. Add the seeds, chopped sesame seed bars and raisins and stir to mix everything thoroughly.

Divide the mixture evenly among the lined seed tray cells using a teaspoon. Level off the mixture in each cell with the back of the spoon.

Put the extra 50g dark chocolate into a food processor and blitz to form chocolate crumbs, or chop with a sharp knife. Scatter this 'topsoil' over the surface of the tiffin mix in the trays while it is still warm (but not too hot or it might melt the chocolate). Refrigerate until set, preferably overnight.

To create your biscuit plant labels, roll out the butter biscuit dough between two sheets of baking parchment to the thickness of a £1 coin – if the dough seems very sticky, dust the dough and the parchment lightly with a little flour. Peel off the top sheet of parchment and cut the dough into label shapes using the plant label as a template. Make a hole in each label with the end of the paintbrush. Peel back the dough trimmings and lift the plant labels, on their parchment, on to a baking tray, then chill for 15 minutes.

Preheat the oven to 180°C/160°C fan/gas 4. If you like, stamp your chosen letters into the chilled dough using plunger cutters. Bake the biscuit labels for 5–10 minutes or until the edges turn slightly golden brown. Leave the biscuits to cool on the baking tray.

Serve the seedling tiffins, in the seed tray, with the biscuit plant labels. If you dunk the pointed end of a biscuit label into a cup of hot tea or coffee, you can secure it into the 'topsoil' before both label and seedling are devoured.

FOR THE TIFFIN

50g mixed seeds, such as pumpkin, sunflower, linseed and sesame

50g butter, roughly chopped

1 tbsp honey

100g dark chocolate, chopped into small pieces, plus 50g extra for decorating

100g milk chocolate, chopped into small pieces

50g crisp sesame seed bars, such as Sesame Snaps, chopped

50g raisins

FOR THE PLANT LABELS

About 165g Basic Butter Biscuits dough (about ¼ quantity; see p.206)

EQUIPMENT

10 seed tray cells, 5cm deep and 3.5cm wide at the top, cut down from a larger tray

Plant label, 10–12cm long and 1.3cm wide, to use as a template

Fine paintbrush

Letter plunger cutters (see directory, p.308), optional

LOLLI-POPCORN POPS

FOR THE TIFFIN

50g butter, roughly chopped

1 tbsp golden syrup

100g dark chocolate, chopped into small pieces

100g milk chocolate, chopped into small pieces

50g toffee popcorn, such as Joe and Seph's salted caramel popcorn

50g chocolate-covered toffee sweets, such as Poppets

50g puffed rice cereal, such as Rice Krispies

TO DECORATE

100g dark chocolate, chopped into small pieces

25g popping candy (see directory, p.307)

Edible gold glitter

EQUIPMENT

24-hole mini-muffin tin

24 paper mini-muffin cases

24 wooden latte stirrers

Cake pop stand or block of polystyrene

Medium paintbrush

These are definitely top of the pops and will tease your tastebuds with a host of different textures: toffee popcorn, puffed rice, chewy toffees and popping candy. They make impressive treats to hand around at a party, or you could wrap the pop tops loosely in cellophane for a take-home gift.

Line the mini-muffin tin with the muffin cases.

Put the butter and golden syrup in a large heavy-based saucepan. Set over a gentle heat and warm, stirring occasionally, until the butter has melted. Add all the chopped chocolate for the tiffin and stir the mixture until smooth and combined. Remove the pan from the heat.

Set aside 24 of the best pieces of toffee popcorn, then cut the remaining popcorn pieces and the chewy chocolate-toffee sweets into pieces. Stir these into the chocolate mixture along with the puffed rice, combining everything thoroughly. Divide among the mini-muffin cases.

Melt 10g of the chocolate for decoration in a microwave or a small heatproof bowl set over a pan of simmering water (bain-marie).

If your latte stirrers are very long, cut a quarter of the length off one with scissors. Coat the cut end of each longer piece in the melted chocolate before pushing it, chocolate end first, into the middle of a tiffin pop. Refrigerate until set, preferably overnight.

Carefully peel the mini-muffin cases away from the pops. Turn them the right way up, then push their sticks into either a cake pop stand or a block of polystyrene to hold them upright, or lay them on a sheet of foil.

Melt the remaining chocolate for decoration, then use the paintbrush to coat each pop with chocolate. Before it sets, sprinkle with popping candy and gold glitter. Finally, top each pop with a piece of toffee popcorn and leave to set. To play on the popcorn theme, the set pops can be displayed in a popcorn container, filled with extra popcorn to support them.

FOR THE TIFFIN

100g butter, roughly chopped

2 tbsp golden syrup

200g dark chocolate, chopped into small pieces

200g milk chocolate, chopped into small pieces

100g large shredded wheat cereal biscuits

100g salted pretzel sticks

100g desiccated coconut

TO DECORATE

50g dark chocolate, chopped into small pieces

Assortment of foil-wrapped chocolate eggs

Extra pretzel sticks

Extra chocolate-covered biscuit sticks, such as Mikado; chocolate sticks, such as Matchmakers; or chocolate flutes, such as Elizabeth Shaw's

EQUIPMENT

20cm frying pan

Medium paintbrush

SALTY & TWEET NEST

This is like a giant, gorgeous version of the little chocolate nests I used to make as a child. But the addition of salty pretzel sticks along with the sweet chocolate makes it much more delicious: a real tweet treat for Easter – or any other time of year. You could make the nest a feature of an Easter Egg hunt – every discovered egg must be brought back to the nest, and then everyone can dive in! As well as using plain foil-wrapped eggs, I sometimes unwrap larger, branded chocolate eggs and re-cover them with coloured foil.

Take a piece of baking parchment and scrunch it up in your hands, then smooth it out (this makes it easier to manipulate). Use the parchment to line the frying pan.

Put the butter and golden syrup in a large heavy-based saucepan. Set over a gentle heat and warm, stirring occasionally, until the butter has melted. Add all the chopped chocolate for the tiffin and stir the mixture until smooth and combined. Remove the pan from the heat.

Set aside one of the shredded wheat biscuits. Break up the remaining shredded wheat and the pretzel sticks and add these to the saucepan, along with the desiccated coconut. Combine everything gently but thoroughly. Transfer the mixture to the lined frying pan, pressing it up the sides with your fingers to produce a hollow nest shape. Refrigerate until set, preferably overnight.

Remove the nest from the fridge and allow it to return to room temperature. Melt the extra chocolate for decorating in a microwave or a heatproof bowl set over a pan of simmering water (bain-marie). Break up the reserved shredded wheat biscuit in a bowl. Remove the nest from the frying pan, keeping it on the parchment. Using the paintbrush or a pastry brush, paint the melted chocolate over the nest. Scatter over the shreds of shredded wheat and press them on to the surface of the nest so they adhere to the melted chocolate – apply more chocolate if any shredded wheat fails to stick. Leave to set before filling the nest with an assortment of chocolate eggs.

VARIATION

If you don't like coconut, you can use a mixture of salted peanuts and raisins instead. To create an even more realistic-looking nest and provide even more sweet tweets to nibble on, sit the nest in a bed of 'twigs' made from extra broken-up pretzel sticks and chocolate sticks or flutes.

FLAPJACKS

These are one of the simplest bakes you can make. You can weigh the ingredients directly into a saucepan set on digital scales and there's no whisking to worry about: just melt, mix and bake. It's very easy to add variety and interest to the essential flapjack by stirring extra ingredients into the mix itself, by baking the flapjacks in different forms, or by decorating them in different ways. The best kind of oats to use are standard porridge oats, rather than big 'jumbo' oats that don't stick together so well.

MAKES A 15CM ROUND FLAPJACK; SERVES 4

FOR THE FLAPJACKS
50g butter, roughly chopped
50g golden caster sugar
1 tbsp golden syrup
100g porridge oats

EQUIPMENT
15cm round, loose-bottomed tin, greased and base-lined

BASIC FLAPJACKS

Preheat the oven to 180°C/160°C fan/gas 4.

Put the butter, sugar and golden syrup in a saucepan. Set it over a medium heat and warm, stirring occasionally, until the butter has melted and the sugar has dissolved. Take the saucepan off the heat and stir in the oats, combining everything thoroughly.

Pour the mixture into the prepared tin and spread out evenly – a dough scraper is handy for this if you're pressing into a square tin, or you can simply use your fingers. Bake for 12–15 minutes or until golden brown around the edges. Leave to cool in the tin.

TO FINISH
Although they are delicious on their own, flapjacks needn't be plain. I enjoy them coated with chocolate. In fact, this 15cm round one can be made into something like a giant HobNob! Just cover it in 50g melted chocolate and use a palette knife to create biscuit markings on top. I also love citrus zest in my flapjacks to give a really fruity flavour, and often substitute marmalade or honey for the golden syrup. You can also finish off a flapjack with adornments such as my marzipan bees (see Honey Bee Bites, p.194).

TO MAKE DIFFERENT-SIZED FLAPJACKS, USE THE TABLE OPPOSITE >>

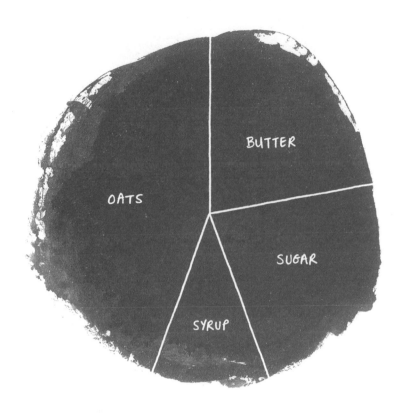

24-HOLE MINI-MUFFIN TIN	12-HOLE MUFFIN TIN	20CM ROUND TIN	20CM SQUARE TIN	INGREDIENTS
50g	100g	100g	150g	Butter, roughly chopped
50g	100g	100g	150g	Golden caster sugar
1 tbsp	2 tbsp	2 tbsp	3 tbsp	Golden syrup
100g	200g	200g	300g	Porridge oats

BAKE IN AN OVEN PREHEATED TO 180°C/160°C FAN/GAS 4				
for 8–10 minutes	for 12–15 minutes	for 20–25 minutes	for 25–30 minutes	

HONEY BEE BITES

MAKES 24 MINI BITES

FOR THE MARZIPAN
1 egg yolk (at room
    temperature)
Finely grated zest of 2 oranges
1 tsp orange blossom water
1 tsp orange blossom honey
100g icing sugar, sifted
100g ground almonds

FOR THE FLAPJACKS
100g butter, roughly chopped
100g golden caster sugar
Finely grated zest of 1 lemon
2 tbsp orange blossom honey
200g porridge oats

TO FINISH THE BEES
50g dark chocolate, chopped
    into small pieces
1 tsp orange blossom honey
100g toasted flaked almonds
    (you only need 48 but it's
    best to have a whole pack so
    you can pick the best ones)

EQUIPMENT
24-hole mini-muffin tin, lined
    with seatbelt straps
    (see p.21)
Piping bag fitted with a small
    plain nozzle
Cocktail stick or fine paintbrush

Lemon and honey is a classic combination that works brilliantly in these extra-deep flapjack bites. With an orange-flavoured marzipan bee on top, they're a citrussy bee-light! I like to use orange blossom honey in both the flapjack and the marzipan to run a lovely, floral, bee-friendly flavour right through the bake. Start the marzipan the day before, if you can, so the orange colour and flavour can develop.

To make the marzipan, place the egg yolk, orange zest, orange blossom water and honey in a medium bowl and mix into a paste. Stir in the icing sugar and ground almonds and bring together into a ball. Wrap in clingfilm or a small freezer bag and chill for a few hours, ideally overnight.

When you're ready to bake, preheat the oven to 180°C/160°C fan/gas 4.

Put the butter, sugar, lemon zest and honey in a medium saucepan. Set it over a medium heat and warm, stirring occasionally, until the butter has melted and the sugar has dissolved. Take the saucepan off the heat and stir in the oats, combining everything thoroughly.

Spoon the mixture into the lined mini-muffin tin, dividing equally. Press the surface of each mini flapjack with the back of a teaspoon or the lid/base of a small container, such as a bottle top, to level it. Bake for 10–12 minutes or until lightly golden brown around the edges.

Allow the flapjacks to cool completely in the tin before removing them with the help of the parchment straps.

Meanwhile, make the bees. Break off 24 pieces of chilled marzipan, each weighing about 5g. (You will have some marzipan left over, which you can keep in the fridge to use in other recipes, such as for the decorations in the Knit One, Bake One Cake on p.152.) Roll each ball into an oval bee-shape. Arrange the bees in neat lines on a sheet of baking parchment.

CONTINUED OVERLEAF >>

HONEY BEE BITES (CONTINUED)

Put the dark chocolate for finishing the bees in a heatproof bowl and melt in a microwave or over a pan of simmering water (bain-marie). Stir through the honey (this honey sweetens the chocolate and ensures it doesn't crack when applied to the bees).

Transfer the chocolate to the piping bag fitted with a small plain nozzle. Pipe three chocolate stripes across each bee – if they're lined up neatly, you should be able to drizzle the chocolate across several bees at once. Alternatively, you can paint on the chocolate lines with a fine paintbrush.

Select 48 unbroken toasted flaked almonds and carefully insert two into each marzipan bee to create wings. Using a cocktail stick or fine paintbrush, make dots of dark chocolate on the bees to resemble eyes. Leave to set. >>

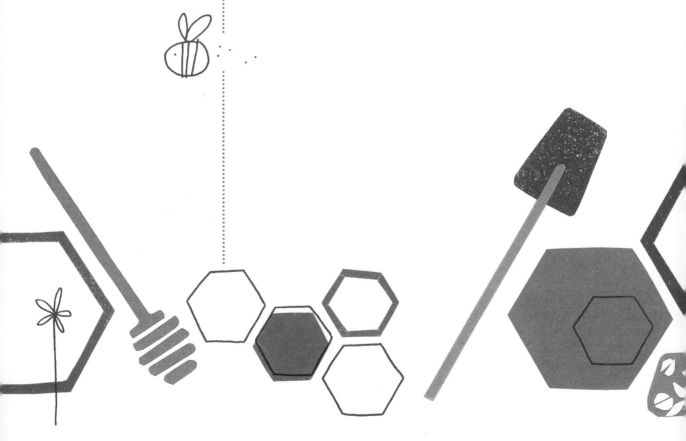

Turn the flapjacks over so the tops become their bases, creating a beehive shape for the marzipan bees to sit on. Apply a dab of chocolate to the top of each flapjack and carefully sit a marzipan bee on this. Allow the chocolate to set before serving.

VARIATIONS

For extra nutty flapjacks, toss in some toasted flaked almonds (use what is left from the pack after you've selected the 48 to use as wings), adding them with the oats. You could also use orange zest rather than lemon in the mix, to carry through the orange theme.

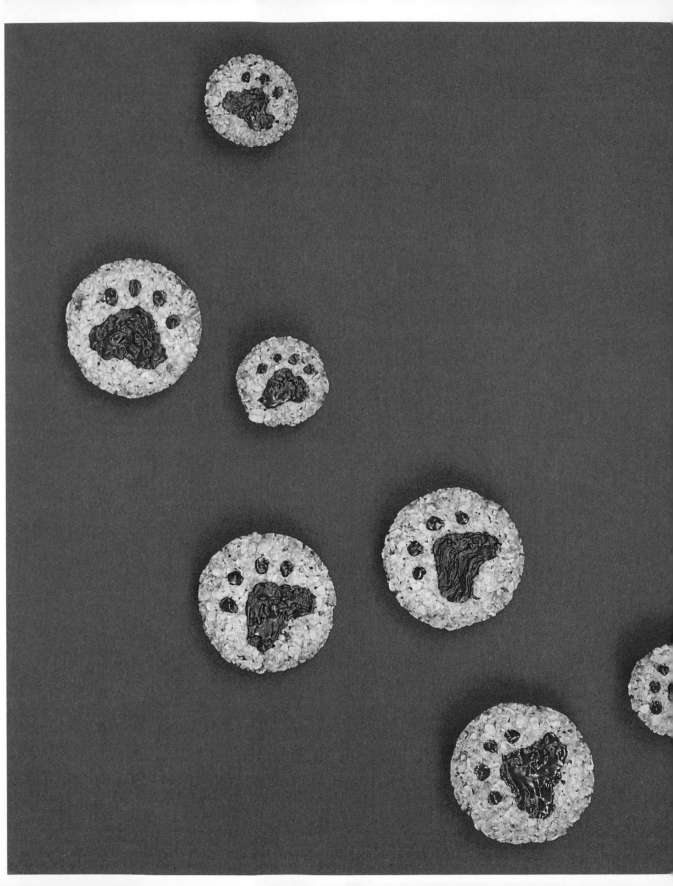

MARMALADE
CAT-FLAPJACKS

MAKES 12 FLAPJACK ROUNDS

FOR THE FLAPJACKS
100g butter, roughly chopped
100g golden caster sugar
Finely grated zest of 1 orange
2 tbsp marmalade, ideally
 fine-cut or shredless
200g porridge oats

TO DECORATE
20g dark chocolate – orange-
 flavoured if you like, broken
 into small pieces

EQUIPMENT
12-hole muffin tin, each hole
 lined with seatbelt straps
 (see p.21)
Medium paintbrush

Orlando may have had a thing or two to do with these flapjacks. Orange zest and marmalade make a purrfect pair of flavourings – and the tangy citrus note goes so well with the chocolate of the cat's pawprint (I sometimes use an orange-flavoured chocolate for this). You can create mini cat-flapjacks by baking the mixture in a 24-hole mini-muffin tin, or split your mixture and make both little and large cat-flapjacks. If you want to create a giant pawprint, fit for a lion king, bake your flapjack in a 20cm round tin (for different-sized bakes, see table on p.193).

Preheat the oven to 180°C/160°C fan/gas 4.

Put the butter, sugar, orange zest and marmalade in a medium saucepan. Set it over a medium heat and warm, stirring occasionally, until the butter has melted and the sugar has dissolved. Take the saucepan off the heat and stir in the oats, combining everything thoroughly.

Spoon the mixture into your lined muffin tin – you'll need about 37g mixture in each hole (or about 18g if you're creating mini flapjacks), which will mean each hole is just under half full. I set my tin on a set of digital scales to fill it, but you could weigh the precise quantity into one hole and fill the rest by eye.

Level the mixture with the back of a teaspoon or the base of a small glass or spice jar. Bake for 12–15 minutes or until golden brown around the edges. If you are baking mini flapjacks, they'll take 8–10 minutes.

Allow the flapjacks to cool completely in the tin before removing them with the help of the parchment straps.

Melt the dark chocolate for decorating in a microwave or a heatproof bowl set over a pan of simmering water (bain-marie). Use the paintbrush to paint a chocolate pawprint on the top of each flapjack. I usually do this free-hand; the shapes don't need to be too perfect as they're supposed to represent muddy pawprints. Leave to set before serving.

FLAPJACK & THE BEAN STALK

MAKES 24 MINI BITES

FOR THE FLAPJACKS
100g butter, roughly chopped
100g golden caster sugar
2 tbsp golden syrup
200g porridge oats
24 salted peanuts (about 25g)

FOR THE 'TOPSOIL'
50g dark chocolate, chopped
    into small pieces
100g crunchy peanut butter
1 tsp golden syrup

TO DECORATE
24 gold-wrapped chocolate
    coins, about 3cm diameter
24 sprigs of fresh mint
24 mini chocolate eggs,
    wrapped in gold foil
24 salted peanuts (about 25g)

EQUIPMENT
24-hole mini-muffin tin, lined
    with seatbelt straps
    (see p.21)
Fine paintbrush
Cocktail stick

These take inspiration from the Jack and the Beanstalk fairytale, and from my love of salted peanuts. Hidden within each deep mini flapjack, and made visible once it is sliced open, is a peanut that represents Jack's magic bean. A sprig of mint suggests the growing bean stalk, and the golden coins and goose eggs can be found on top and underneath each flapjack – fixed in place with a chocolate and peanut butter 'topsoil'. If you have difficulty finding gold-covered chocolate coins, just leave them out. You can make golden eggs by wrapping gold foil around mini chocolate eggs (the foil from some bars of chocolate works a treat).

Preheat the oven to 180°C/160°C fan/gas 4.

Put the butter, sugar and golden syrup in a medium saucepan. Set it over a medium heat and warm, stirring occasionally, until the butter has melted and the sugar has dissolved. Take the saucepan off the heat and stir in the oats, combining everything thoroughly.

Spoon enough of the mixture into the lined mini-muffin tin to half fill the holes. Place a peanut in the centre of each, then cover with the remainder of the mixture, levelling it with the back of a teaspoon. Bake for 10–12 minutes or until lightly golden brown around the edges. Allow the flapjacks to cool in the tin before removing them with the help of the parchment straps.

Melt the chocolate for the 'topsoil' in a microwave or a heatproof bowl set over a pan of simmering water (bain-marie). When melted, remove the bowl from the pan and stir in the peanut butter and golden syrup until combined.

Peel off one side only of the foil wrapping on each gold coin. With the paintbrush, spread some of the chocolate 'topsoil' on the chocolate side of each coin (avoid the peanuts if possible so the coin will lie flat), then press it on to the base of a flapjack. Leave to set while the remainder of the chocolate 'topsoil' firms up slightly.

Once the chocolate 'topsoil' has reached a dollop-able consistency (you can chill it in the fridge to speed up the process, if necessary), spread some over the top of each flapjack. Using the cocktail stick, make a hole in each mound of 'topsoil' and insert a mint sprig (don't do this until just before serving the flapjacks or the mint will wilt). Carefully place the golden eggs and remaining peanuts on top of the flapjacks around the mint sprig.

UNION FLAPJACK

FOR THE FLAPJACK

200g butter, roughly chopped
200g golden caster sugar
4 tbsp golden syrup
Finely grated zest of 2 lemons
400g porridge oats
80g dried cranberries

TO DECORATE

200g white chocolate, chopped
   into small pieces
200g fresh raspberries
200g fresh blueberries
20g dried cranberries

EQUIPMENT

20 x 27cm brownie tin, greased
   and lined with seatbelt straps
   (see p.21)
Cocktail stick, optional

It seems very fitting to use one of the nation's favourite traybakes as the base for our national flag, brought to life with fruit and a fanfare of chocolate. Complementing and cutting through the sweetness of the flapjack base and the white chocolate 'canvas' are zingy lemon zest and tangy dried cranberries, creating a truly triumphant range of textures and tastes.

Preheat the oven to 180°C/160°C fan/gas 4.

Put the butter, sugar, syrup and lemon zest in a medium saucepan. Set it over a medium heat and warm, stirring occasionally, until the butter has melted and the sugar has dissolved. Take the saucepan off the heat and stir in the oats and cranberries, combining everything thoroughly.

Transfer the mix to your lined tin. Smooth the surface level using a cranked palette knife or dough scraper. Bake for 30–35 minutes or until lightly golden brown around the edges. Once out of the oven, it's a good idea to use the palette knife to gently pat down and even out the edges of the flapjack, which can tend to rise at the sides of the tin.

Allow the flapjack to cool fully in the tin before removing it with the help of the parchment straps. Place the flapjack on a chopping board.

Melt the white chocolate in a microwave or a heatproof bowl set over a pan of simmering water (bain-marie). Pour the chocolate over the flapjack and spread with a palette knife to create a smooth, even surface. Allow the chocolate to cool and firm up slightly before creating your Union Jack design.

You can, if you like, lightly score guidelines on the white chocolate with the end of a cocktail stick. Start by creating the central raspberry cross, two raspberries (about 4cm) wide, placing the raspberries rounded end upwards on the chocolate. Once you've created your cross, carefully cut the remaining raspberries into pieces to fill in any gaps so no white chocolate is visible through the cross. Next create the blueberry sections. After the main shapes have been created, cut the remaining blueberries into pieces with a sharp knife and fill in the gaps, like a majestic mosaic. Finally, place the cranberries in diagonal lines as shown in the photograph, inserting the dried fruit into the chocolate so that they stick up and are level with the raspberries and blueberries, rather than lying flat. Leave to set before serving.

BUTTER BISCUITS

This is one of my standby recipes – I always like to have some butter biscuit dough to hand. The smallest batch I make, using one egg, still makes enough dough for a lot of biscuits, so I usually halve or quarter the dough and refrigerate or freeze some (the dough benefits from overnight chilling anyway). If you do the same, you'll be able to turn out these edible designs very easily indeed.

As with my shortbread dough, top-quality butter is essential. I like to use a slightly salted one to enhance the flavours in the biscuit, but unsalted is fine too. You can use golden or white caster sugar: golden gives a slightly fuller flavour, crunchier texture and richer colour.

FOR THE BISCUITS

150g butter, softened

150g golden or white caster
sugar

1 egg (at room temperature)

1 tbsp vanilla extract

300g plain flour

BASIC BUTTER BISCUITS

Using a hand-held electric whisk, or in a free-standing mixer, beat the butter and sugar together for 3–5 minutes or until smooth and creamy. Break the egg into a mug or jug, add the vanilla extract and beat with a fork. Gradually add the egg to the creamed mixture, beating well after each addition. Sift the flour into the mixture in two or three batches, mixing in each batch gently, to make a soft dough.

Halve the dough and pat each piece into a rough disc (this makes it easier to roll out later). Put into two food bags, or wrap in clingfilm. Refrigerate for several hours, preferably overnight, to firm up. If you don't want to use both portions of dough now (it's hard to make a smaller batch as that would mean halving an egg), keep the remainder in the fridge and use within a week, or freeze it in usable batches.

Remove the dough from the fridge 15–30 minutes before rolling it so it can soften slightly. Preheat the oven to 180°C/160°C fan/gas 4.

Roll out the dough between two sheets of baking parchment to the thickness of a £1 coin (or as specified in your recipe) – if the dough seems very sticky, dust it and the parchment lightly with a little flour. Peel off the top parchment sheet, then cut out your desired shapes. Pull up the surrounding dough, then lift the biscuits, on their parchment, on to a baking tray. Chill for 15 minutes.

Bake the biscuits for 5–15 minutes, depending on their size – see the table opposite – until they are lightly golden brown around the edges (or as specified in the recipe). Leave them to firm up for a few minutes on the baking tray, then transfer, still on the parchment, to a wire rack to cool.

TO FINISH

This simple biscuit recipe is richly flavoured with vanilla, but to intensify the effect, I sometimes use vanilla sugar. Other ingredients can be added on top of the vanilla extract, or substituted for it, to create a variety of tastes – try spicing with 1 tablespoon of ground cinnamon or cardamom; floral flavours such as 1 tablespoon of orange blossom water or rose water; or combinations such as the grated zest of 1 lemon with 1 tablespoon of poppy seeds. Sandwich the biscuits together with Ganache (see p.279) or Buttercream (p.276) for a special treat.

TO SEE HOW MANY BISCUITS YOU CAN MAKE, USE THE TABLE OPPOSITE >>

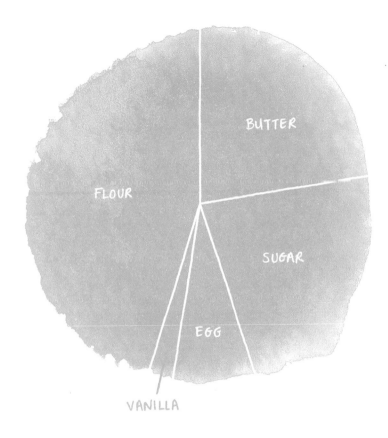

BUTTER

FLOUR

SUGAR

EGG

VANILLA

APPROX NUMBER OF SMALL BISCUITS (ABOUT 3.5CM) YOU CAN MAKE	APPROX NUMBER OF MEDIUM BISCUITS (ABOUT 7.5CM) YOU CAN MAKE	APPROX NUMBER OF LARGE BISCUITS (ABOUT 15CM) YOU CAN MAKE	QUANTITY OF DOUGH ROLLED OUT TO £1 COIN THICKNESS
120	30	10	Full quantity (660g)
60	15	5	½ quantity (330g)
40	10	3	⅓ quantity (220g)
30	6	2	¼ quantity (165g)
15	3	1	⅛ quantity (80g)

BAKE IN AN OVEN PREHEATED TO 180°C/160°C FAN/GAS 4			
for 5–8 minutes	for 8–12 minutes	for 12–15 minutes	

FOR THE BISCUITS
150g butter, softened
150g caster sugar
1 egg (at room temperature)
1 tbsp vanilla extract
300g plain flour

TO DECORATE
25g chilli-flavoured chocolate,
chopped into small pieces

EQUIPMENT
A match (about 2mm thick)
to use as a guide
Matchboxes, to serve

BISCUIT MATCHES

These little biscuits are nothing if not striking! They make a fantastic gift – especially if packaged up inside matchboxes. I finish off the matches with chilli chocolate tips to add a fitting burst of heat – but you can use plain chocolate if you prefer. Or you can add more spice to the bake with 1 tablespoon of ground ginger as well as the vanilla extract.

Using a hand-held electric whisk, or in a free-standing mixer, beat the butter and sugar together for 3–5 minutes or until smooth and creamy. Beat the egg with the vanilla in a mug with a fork. Gradually add to the creamed mixture, beating well after each addition. Sift the flour into the mixture in two or three batches, mixing in each batch gently, to make a soft dough. Quarter the dough and put into four food bags, or wrap in clingfilm. Chill for several hours, preferably overnight, to firm up. You'll only need one of the pieces of dough for this recipe. Keep the rest in the fridge and use within a week, or freeze.

Remove your piece of dough from the fridge 15–30 minutes before rolling so that it can soften slightly. Roll out the dough between two sheets of baking parchment to the thickness of a real match. If the dough seems very sticky, lightly dust it and the parchment with a little flour. Peel off the top parchment sheet, then use a pizza cutter or small sharp knife and a ruler to cut the dough into strips 2mm wide and 12cm long (you'll cut the strips into match lengths once baked). Running the cutter through some flour first will help to prevent sticking. Pick up the strips and lay them back on the parchment so there are a few millimetres between them. Re-roll the trimmings and cut out more strips. Lift them, on the parchment, on to baking trays and refrigerate for 15 minutes.

Preheat the oven to 180°C/160°C fan/gas 4 while the biscuits are chilling.

Bake for about 5 minutes or until only very lightly golden (to look authentic, you want them to hardly colour at all). Carefully slide the parchment on to a chopping board and, while still warm, cut the strips across into 5cm lengths (use an actual match as a guide). Leave the matches to cool on the parchment – they'll crisp up as they cool.

Melt the chocolate in a microwave or a heatproof bowl set over a pan of simmering water (bain-marie). Dip the ends of the matches in the chocolate, then leave to set on clean baking parchment. If you want to create matches with blackened ends that look like they've been used, don't dip them in chocolate but light them with an actual match just to char, then blow it out.

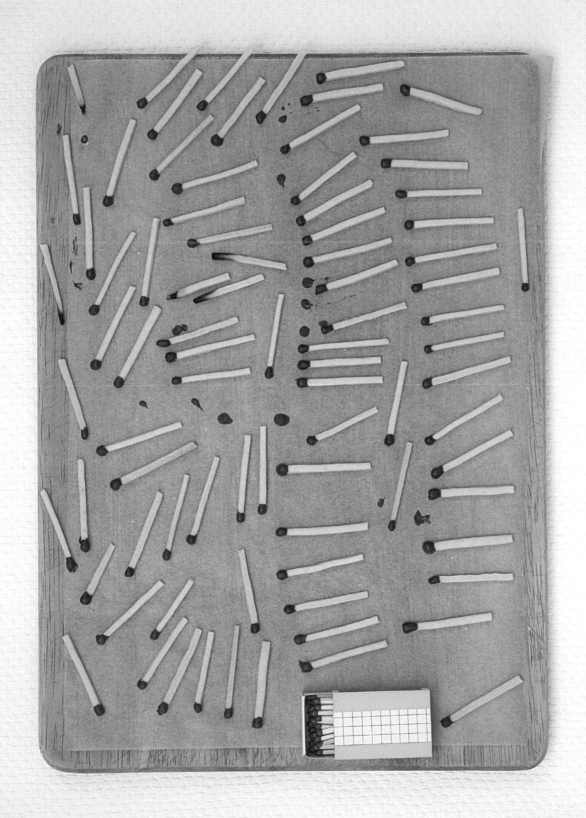

CLOUD CUT-OUTS

FOR THE BISCUITS

150g butter, softened

150g caster sugar or vanilla
sugar

1 egg (at room temperature)

1 tbsp vanilla extract

300g plain flour

1 large gold-wrapped chocolate
coin (about 4.5cm diameter)
per cloud, plus a few extra
for melting

EQUIPMENT

14.5 x 9cm cloud template
(see overleaf or make
your own)

Small shape, letter and/or
number cutters (see
directory, p.308)

Fine paintbrush

These simple biscuits, almost like edible greeting cards, are great to give
as a birthday present or to celebrate any other happy occasion. I like the
simplicity and playful nature of the 'Cloud 9' design but you can stamp out
any message you like using letter or number cutters. However, the cut-out
9 works especially well with the addition of a gold-wrapped chocolate coin
stuck to the back of the cloud, making reference to 'pennies from heaven'.
I like to present the biscuit in an envelope with a homemade silver-foil lining
– every cloud should have one – and it also protects the envelope from the
biscuit's butteriness.

Using a hand-held electric whisk, or in a free standing mixer, beat the butter
and sugar together for 3–5 minutes or until smooth and creamy. Beat the egg
with the vanilla extract in a mug with a fork. Gradually add to the creamed
mixture, beating well after each addition. Sift the flour into the mixture in
two or three batches, mixing in each batch gently, to make a soft dough.

Halve the dough and pat each piece into a rough disc (this makes it easier
to roll out later). Put into two food bags, or wrap in clingfilm. Refrigerate for
several hours, preferably overnight, to firm up. You'll only need one of the
pieces of dough for this recipe – less if you want to make just one or two
clouds. Keep the second piece in the fridge and use within a week, or freeze.

Remove your piece of dough from the fridge 15–30 minutes before rolling, so
that it can soften slightly. Roll out the dough between two sheets of baking
parchment to the thickness of a £1 coin. (If you want to make just one cloud,
roll out a 65–75g piece of dough.) If the dough seems very sticky, lightly dust
it and the parchment with a little flour. Peel off the top sheet of parchment.
Using the cloud template, cut out two or three clouds (or just one), going
around the template with a small, sharp knife. Pull up the dough trimmings and
re-roll them between fresh parchment to cut more clouds, if you like. Peel away
the excess dough.

Lift the clouds, on their parchment, on to a baking tray (or trays) and chill
for 15 minutes.

With your choice of cutters, cut out your message or design. If you are creating
Cloud 9 biscuits, cut out the 9 from near the top of each cloud and place the
cut-out piece, including the 'hole' from the middle of the 9, next to the cloud.
Refrigerate for 15 minutes.

CONTINUED OVERLEAF >>

CLOUD CUT-OUTS (CONTINUED)

Preheat the oven to 180°C/160°C fan/gas 4 while the biscuits are chilling.

Bake for about 5 minutes or until the cut-out numbers are lightly golden brown around the edges. (Keep an eye on the 'holes' and remove them early if they are browning too much.) Carefully lift the cut-out numbers from the tray with a palette knife and transfer to a wire rack to cool. Return the cloud biscuits to the oven to continue baking for 5–10 minutes or until lightly golden brown around the edges. Leave to firm up on the baking tray for a few minutes before transferring them, on the parchment, to the wire rack to cool.

To create the 'pennies from heaven' finish, remove the foil from one side of a large chocolate coin or coins – use one coin per cloud. Melt a few extra chocolate coins in a microwave or a heatproof bowl set over a pan of simmering water (bain-marie). >>

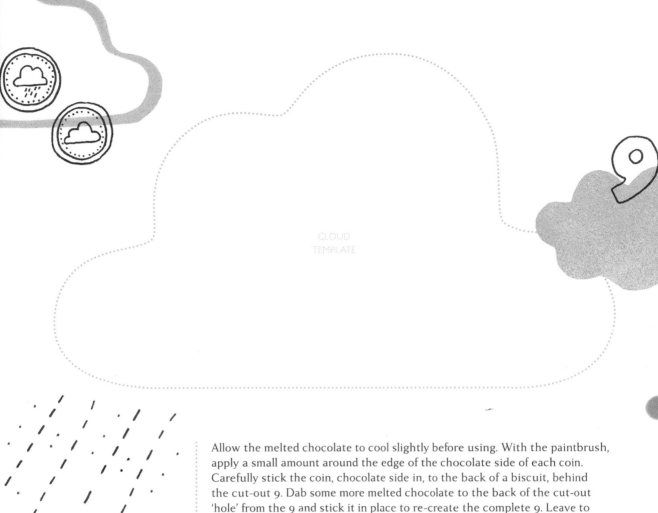

CLOUD
TEMPLATE

Allow the melted chocolate to cool slightly before using. With the paintbrush, apply a small amount around the edge of the chocolate side of each coin. Carefully stick the coin, chocolate side in, to the back of a biscuit, behind the cut-out 9. Dab some more melted chocolate to the back of the cut-out 'hole' from the 9 and stick it in place to re-create the complete 9. Leave to set. You can put the little cut-out 9 in the envelope with the biscuit, along with some extra chocolate coins.

Display the clouds in a silver-foil-lined envelope or box, or carefully wrapped up in silver-foil parcels.

VARIATION

Another idea is to create cloud 'dodgers', sandwiching together two cloud biscuits – one whole and one with cut-outs – with a Ganache (see p.279), chocolate hazelnut spread, or a 'cloud' of Buttercream (p.276) and jam filling.

SWEET BOMBAY MIX

150g butter, softened
150g caster sugar or vanilla
    sugar
1 egg (at room temperature)
1 tbsp vanilla extract
300g plain flour
1 tbsp ground cardamom,
    optional

FOR THE MIX
Cinnamon, to dust, optional
100g pistachios
100g blanched, toasted
    hazelnuts
100g cashews
100g peanuts
100g toasted coconut flakes
(Or replace the nuts and
    coconut above with
    a 500g bag of mixed nuts)

EQUIPMENT
Biscuit maker (see directory,
    p.308)

I love salty, spicy Bombay mix as a savoury snack, and I couldn't resist creating a sweet version. It makes a great party nibble or a fitting treat after a spicy meal. It's based on my butter biscuit dough, which, while still soft, can be pumped through the nozzle of a biscuit maker to form little strands. I like to add ground cardamom to the dough, and to dust the biscuits with cinnamon to underline the Indian theme. A selection of mixed nuts make up the remainder of the mix. You can use whichever nuts you like – honey-roasted nuts are particularly delicious – but try to include hazelnuts and pistachios, which look just like the chickpeas and split peas in the authentic, savoury Bombay mix.

Preheat the oven to 180°C/160°C fan/gas 4.

Using a hand-held electric whisk, or in a free-standing mixer, beat the butter and sugar together for 3–5 minutes or until smooth and creamy. Beat the egg with the vanilla extract in a mug with a fork. Gradually add to the creamed mixture, beating well after each addition. Sift the flour (and the cardamom, if using) into the mixture in two or three batches, mixing in each batch gently, to make a soft dough.

Divide the dough into thirds. Put one portion into the biscuit maker fitted with the round cutter disc with 11 holes, each 5mm diameter. Press out through the disc to make strands of dough 5–7cm long – use scissors or the tips of your fingers to break off the strands – allowing them to fall on to sheets of baking parchment. Move the biscuit maker so the strands are spread out in a single layer on the parchment. They will naturally taper, which helps to create a curled shape. Refill the biscuit maker with the rest of the dough, in two batches, and press out more strands on to parchment sheets.

Slide the parchment on to baking trays (bake in rotation, depending on the number of baking trays you have, but be sure to cool the trays between batches – I sometimes set them on a cold surface outside to speed up the cooling). Bake the strands for 7–10 minutes or until light golden brown. Dust some or all of the biscuit strands lightly with cinnamon while still warm, if you like. Leave to firm up on the tray for a few minutes before transferring, on the parchment, to a wire rack to cool.

Meanwhile, carefully cut the pistachios across in half to mimic split peas. Mix all the nuts and coconut together, stirring the cooled biscuits in too. Serve in bowls, or present in cellophane bags or tins as a gift (the mix will keep for 5–7 days in an airtight container).

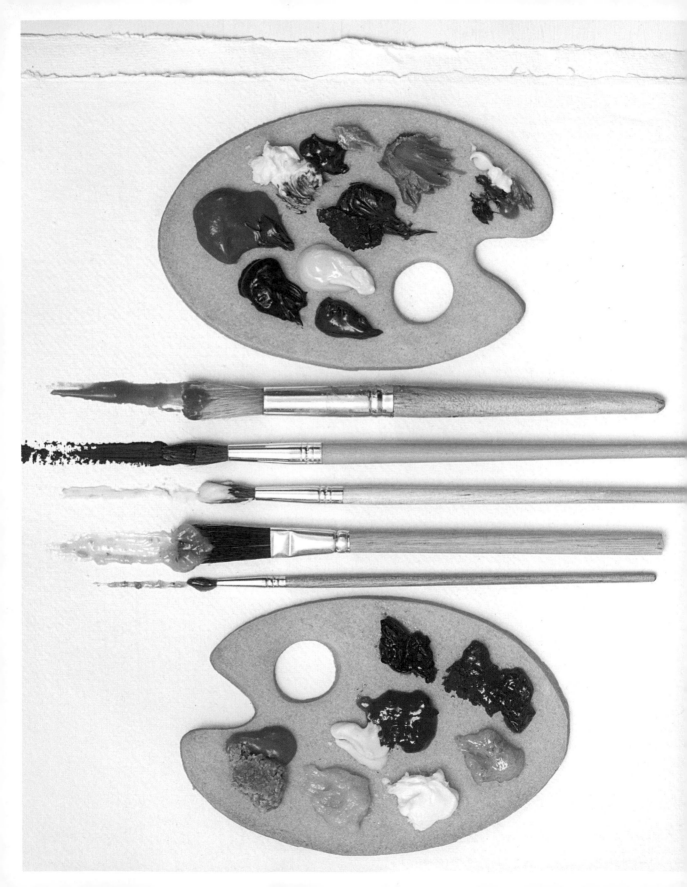

PAINTER'S PALETTE

150g butter, softened
150g caster sugar or vanilla
   sugar
1 egg (at room temperature)
1 tbsp vanilla extract
300g plain flour

Choose from homemade or
   shop-bought:
   Ganache (see p.279)
   Melted chocolate
   Nut butters (see directory,
      p.307)
   Caramel (p.284)
   Jams (p.272)
   Curds (p.273)
   Marzipan (p.286)

Paint palette template (see
   overleaf)
2.5cm round cutter
Medium paintbrush or wooden
   latte stirrer

From gouache to ganache, here's a crisp biscuit artist's palette of edible paints to mix to your own taste palate. It's a fun and flavoursome way of creating edible art, and you can mix up a whole host of colours, from peanut butter burnt ochre to lemon curd cadmium yellow! Using a paintbrush or a pastry brush, you can even use the colours to paint on to a blank canvas of cake or rice paper to create your very own munch-able masterpieces.

Using a hand-held electric whisk, or in a free-standing mixer, beat the butter and sugar together for 3–5 minutes or until smooth and creamy. Beat the egg with the vanilla extract in a mug with a fork. Gradually add to the creamed mixture, beating well after each addition. Sift the flour into the mixture in two or three batches, mixing in each batch gently, to make a soft dough.

Halve the dough and put into two food bags, or wrap in clingfilm. Refrigerate for several hours, preferably overnight, to firm up. You'll only need one of the pieces of dough for this recipe. Keep the second one in the fridge and use within a week, or freeze it.

Remove your piece of dough from the fridge 15–30 minutes before rolling so that it can soften slightly. Halve the piece of dough. Take one half and roll it out between two sheets of baking parchment to the thickness of a £1 coin. If the dough seems very sticky, lightly dust it and the parchment with a little flour. Using the paint palette template, cut out two palette shapes from the dough. Peel away the excess dough (keep these trimmings). Create the thumb hole using the cutter, or cut it out with a knife.

Roll out the other half of the dough and cut two more palette shapes in the same way. Peel away excess dough. Gather all the dough trimmings, re-roll between sheets of parchment and cut out another palette. Lift the palettes, on the parchment, on to baking trays and refrigerate for 15 minutes.

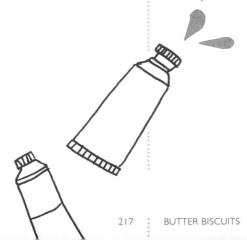

CONTINUED OVERLEAF >>

PAINTER'S PALETTE (CONTINUED)

Preheat the oven to 180°C/160°C fan/gas 4 while the biscuits are chilling.

Bake for 12–15 minutes or until lightly golden brown around the edges. Leave to firm up on the tray for a few minutes before transferring, on the parchment, to a wire rack to cool.

Spread, dab or spoon your choice of edible 'paints' on to the palette using the paintbrush or wooden latte stirrer. You'll need ½–1 teaspoon of each 'paint' per palette. Chocolate can be melted in a microwave or a heatproof bowl set over a pan of simmering water (bain-marie); ganache that has set in the fridge can be softened in the same way. Dab and smear them in a painterly fashion to create varying textures.

If you are going to decorate with jams or curds, I'd advise eating the palette sooner than if you are using chocolate and ganache, as jams and curds tend to soften the biscuit more quickly.

PALETTE
TEMPLATE

SHORTBREAD

This, to my mind, is the bread and butter of baking. A classic biscuit, super simple to put together, it's a delicious treat on its own. But it also makes a fantastic building block in a whole medley of edible designs. It goes without saying that top-quality butter is essential here as it's one of only three ingredients, and crucial to the flavour of the finished shortbread. I love using a slightly salted butter to enhance the flavour of the finished biscuit, but you can use unsalted butter and add a pinch of salt instead – or leave out the salt entirely, if you prefer. When it comes to the sugar, you can use golden or white caster, or even a flavoured sugar such as lavender. I like to ring the changes: golden caster sugar gives a slightly fuller flavour and crunchier texture than the very pure, fine white variety.

BASIC SHORTBREAD

FOR THE SHORTBREAD
50g caster sugar
100g butter, softened
150g plain flour

EQUIPMENT
15cm round, loose-bottomed
tin (for petticoat tails)

Using a hand-held electric whisk, or in a free-standing mixer, beat the sugar and butter together for 3–5 minutes or until smooth and creamy. Sift the flour into the mixture in two batches, mixing in each batch until just combined. Use your hands to bring the mix together into a dough, but try not to overwork it – just like pastry, too much mixing or kneading will mean the baked shortbread won't be 'short' and crumbly.

To make petticoat tails, press the dough into the tin, using your fingers to spread it out gently in a smooth, even layer. Press a fork around the edge of the dough round to create a crimped pattern, then score into eight wedges using a sharp knife. Chill for 15 minutes – this will help the shortbread to keep its shape during baking, so is particularly important when you are making cut-out shapes and biscuits.

Preheat the oven to 170°C/150°C fan/gas 3 while the shortbread is chilling.

Bake for 25–30 minutes or until lightly golden brown around the edges. Leave to cool in the tin for 15 minutes before carefully removing and placing on a wire rack. Once completely cold, cut into pieces following the scored lines, using a small, sharp, serrated knife.

TO FINISH

Before baking, you can sprinkle your shortbread with sugar to add extra crunch. I also like to decorate baked biscuits with both icing sugar and cocoa powder, dusted through stencils such as lettersets and doilys, to create striking patterns. Drizzling or dousing your shortbread with melted chocolate is delicious too. A scattering of chopped nuts or freeze-dried fruit will add to the finish – dark chocolate with pistachios, and white chocolate with raspberries are two of my favourites.

Shortbread fingers have always reminded me of the wooden blocks in a game of Jenga, and you can 'play' on this by building up the shortbread fingers into a tower on a plate or board. It will make teatime a lot more fun.

If you have any baked trimmings of shortbread left over, they can be broken up, bagged and saved for a few weeks in an airtight container. Add them to Tiffin (see p.180) or use them to add textural interest to cake toppings and ice cream.

TO MAKE DIFFERENT-SIZED BISCUITS, USE THE TABLE OPPOSITE >>

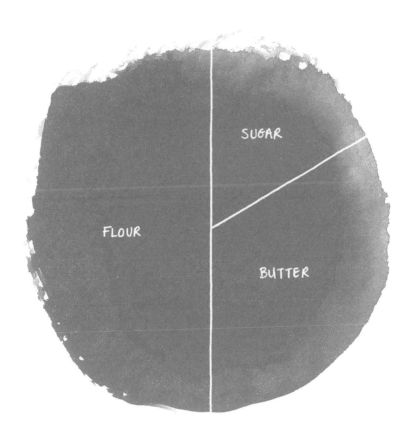

TO MAKE APPROX 25 SMALL BISCUITS (ABOUT 4CM)	20CM SQUARE TIN	23CM SQUARE TIN	INGREDIENTS
50g	100g	150g	Caster sugar
100g	200g	300g	Butter, softened
150g	300g	450g	Plain flour

BAKE IN AN OVEN PREHEATED TO 170°C/150°C FAN/GAS 3			
for 15–20 minutes	for 35–40 minutes	for 40–45 minutes	

STRAWBERRY HEARTS

FOR THE SHORTBREAD
50g caster sugar
100g butter, softened
150g plain flour

TO DECORATE
100g fresh strawberries (about
    5 medium-large
    strawberries)
25g white chocolate, broken
    into small pieces
5g freeze-dried strawberry
    pieces (not slices)

EQUIPMENT
4cm and 2.5cm heart-shaped
    cutters (see directory, p.308)
Medium paintbrush
Wooden latte stirrer

Spread a little love (and white chocolate) with these beautiful shortbread bites. They are perfect as wedding favours, for an engagement party, or on Valentine's Day. The dried strawberry decorations don't just look pretty: their intense berry flavour is also delicious with the chocolate and biscuit. Freeze-dried strawberry pieces are easy to find from baking suppliers. You can buy the whole dried strawberry slices too – but I prefer to make my own.

Using a hand-held electric whisk, or in a free-standing mixer, beat the sugar and butter together for 3–5 minutes or until smooth and creamy. Sift the flour into the mixture in two batches, mixing in each batch until just combined. Use your hands to bring the mix together into a dough, but take care not to overwork it.

Roll out the dough between two sheets of baking parchment to a 1cm thickness. (I snip off and discard the rounded end of a wooden lollipop stick or latte stirrer, then mark a 1cm measurement on the stick to use as a guide when rolling out the dough.) Peel off the top layer of parchment and use the 4cm cutter to cut out about 20 hearts. Pull up the dough trimmings and re-roll them between more parchment, then use the smaller cutter to cut out about 15 mini hearts. Peel away the excess dough.

Transfer the hearts, on their parchment, on to two baking trays – keep all the larger hearts on one tray and all the smaller ones on the other, as they have different baking times. Chill the biscuits for 15 minutes.

Preheat the oven to 170°C/150°C fan/gas 3 while the biscuits are chilling.

Bake the mini hearts for 10–15 minutes and the larger ones for 15–20 minutes, or until lightly golden around the edges. Leave to firm up on the trays for a few minutes before transferring to a wire rack to cool.

Turn the oven down to 120°C/100°C fan/gas ½ for the dried strawberry slices.

Lay some double layers of kitchen paper on your work surface. Hull the berries, then cut them into slices the thickness of a £1 coin. Place them on the kitchen paper. Lay more paper on top and press down gently to blot any excess juice.

CONTINUED OVERLEAF >>

STRAWBERRY HEARTS (CONTINUED)

While your strawberry slices are draining, line a rimless baking tray with baking parchment. Carefully transfer the slices to the lined tray, then use the tray to help you slide the parchment directly on to the oven shelf.

Dry out the strawberries for 1–1¼ hours or until slightly shrunken and a little deeper in colour – drying time will depend on the size of your slices and how juicy your strawberries were to begin with. Near the end of the drying time, carefully peel back the slices and flip them over so they can dry on the other side. (If you have a dehydrator you can dry the strawberries in this instead; see directory, p.309.) Remove the strawberry slices from the oven and snip into the top of each with scissors to create an even more pronounced heart shape.

To assemble the biscuits, melt the white chocolate in a microwave or in a heatproof bowl set over a pan of simmering water (bain-marie). Use the paintbrush to dab a little white chocolate on to the centre of the larger heart biscuits, then stick on a dried strawberry slice. Cover the central area of the smaller hearts with white chocolate, then sprinkle with the freeze-dried strawberry pieces. To create another variation, place just a few freeze-dried strawberry pieces in a tight cluster on the chocolate-covered mini hearts. Leave to set before serving.

FOR THE WHITE KEYS
100g caster sugar
200g butter, softened
300g plain flour

FOR THE BLACK KEYS
50g caster sugar
100g butter, softened
1 tsp vanilla extract
125g plain flour
25g cocoa powder

TO DECORATE
150g white chocolate, chopped
    into pieces
50g dark chocolate, chopped
    into pieces
1 tsp golden syrup

EQUIPMENT
20cm square, loose-bottomed
    tin
900g (2lb) straight-sided loaf tin
    (about 21 x 11cm), greased
    and lined with seatbelt straps
    (see p.21)

PIANO KEYS

Sometimes it's good to play with your food! You can eat these shortbread keys note by note, or devour them in a crescendo of crunching (harmonious, of course). The chocolate on top of the keys adds sheen and sweetness. But, for more of a stripped-back look and sound, you can display the shortbread unadorned. To create an even bigger keyboard, just double the recipe.

To make the plain shortbread dough for the white keys, use a hand-held electric whisk, or a free-standing mixer, to beat the sugar and butter together for 3–5 minutes or until smooth and creamy. Sift the flour into the mixture in two batches, mixing in each batch until just combined. Use your hands to bring the mix together into a dough, but take care not to overwork it.

Transfer the dough to the square tin and press it out into an even layer, smoothing the surface with the back of a spoon and your fingers. Prick the dough all over with a fork, just indenting the surface rather than going all the way through. Refrigerate while you prepare the chocolate shortbread dough for your black keys.

Using a hand-held electric whisk, or in a free-standing mixer, beat the sugar, butter and vanilla extract together for 3–5 minutes or until smooth and creamy. Sift the flour and cocoa powder into the mixture in two batches, mixing in each batch until just combined. Use your hands to bring the mix together into a dough, but be careful not to overwork it.

Transfer the dough to the loaf tin and press it out into an even layer, smoothing the surface with the back of a spoon. Prick the dough all over with a fork, just indenting the surface rather than going all the way through. Put into the fridge with the plain shortbread and chill for 15 minutes.

Preheat the oven to 170°C/150°C fan/gas 3 while the shortbread is chilling.

Bake the plain shortbread for 35–40 minutes or until lightly golden brown and firm to the touch; the chocolate shortbread needs only 30–35 minutes. Leave both shortbreads to cool in their tins, set on a wire rack.

Remove the plain shortbread from its tin and lay it squarely in front of you on the work surface. Using a ruler and small serrated knife, score a line 1cm in from the left and right edges of the shortbread. Cut through these scored lines and remove the trimmings. Next score the shortbread in half horizontally, to create two 10cm-wide strips.

CONTINUED OVERLEAF >>

PIANO KEYS (CONTINUED)

With a ruler (I use a 2.5cm-wide metal ruler, found at a DIY/art & craft shop, which is perfect for dividing up this bake), score seven 2.5cm-wide keys down the full width of each shortbread half. Carefully cut through these scored lines to create 14 shortbread keys.

Remove the chocolate shortbread from the loaf tin with the help of the parchment straps and lay the rectangle vertically on the work surface in front of you. Trim a few millimetres from each short end of the shortbread to create a neat, straight edge. Now trim off a 3cm-wide strip from one of the longer sides (you can use this to cut extra keys from, or simply cut into squares to snack on), leaving you with a 6.5cm-wide block of shortbread. With a ruler, score this across into 10 keys, each just under 2cm wide.

To decorate the keys, melt the white chocolate in a microwave or a heatproof bowl set over a pan of simmering water (bain-marie), then cool slightly. Place the larger, plain shortbread keys close together in two blocks of seven on a sheet of baking parchment or foil. Pour on the white chocolate and spread it carefully with a palette knife. Try not to let too much drip down the sides. Leave the chocolate to set almost fully before running a sharp knife between the keys to separate them again. Leave to set before cleaning up the edges with a sharp knife.

Melt the dark chocolate with the golden syrup (this adds a sheen and prevents the chocolate from cracking too much when cut later on). Repeat the coating process with the chocolate shortbread keys.

Once all the chocolate-coated keys have set, you can assemble your keyboard, ready to play and eat! Place the white chocolate keys in a line, almost flush against each other, then arrange the dark chocolate keys on top, following the arrangement shown in the illustration below.

If you're skipping the chocolate coating, flip the shortbread pieces over so that their flat bases become their tops, producing a smoother, more uniform finish.

GIANT STRAWBERRY DODGER

MAKES I GIANT 23CM BISCUIT;
SERVES 12–15

FOR THE SHORTBREAD
200g caster sugar
400g butter, softened
600g plain flour

FOR THE BUTTERCREAM
100g butter, softened
200g icing sugar
1 tbsp whole milk
1 tsp vanilla extract

TO DECORATE
200g strawberry jam –
    homemade (see p.272) or
    shop-bought
¼ tsp golden linseeds
Icing sugar, to dust

EQUIPMENT
23cm loose-bottomed, fluted
    tart tin (or use 2 tins if you
    have them)
10cm heart-shaped cutter (see
    directory, p.308)
4cm leaf plunger cutter (see
    directory, p.309)
Piping bag with optional 1.5cm
    round nozzle

I've increased the appeal of a much-loved biscuit by rendering it giant-sized. Rather than the tooth-sticking stuff you find inside conventional jammy dodgers, this one is filled with luscious buttercream and tender jam. The heart-shaped cut-out at the centre, adorned with biscuit leaves and golden linseeds, becomes a big strawberry, fit to burst.

Using a hand-held electric whisk, or in a free-standing mixer, beat 100g of the sugar and 200g of the butter together for 3–5 minutes or until smooth and creamy. Sift 300g of the flour into the mixture in several batches, mixing in each batch until just combined. Use your hands to bring the mix together into a dough, taking care not to overwork it.

Cut off 25g of this dough, wrap it in clingfilm and chill it for later (to make the strawberry stalks and leaves). Transfer the rest of the dough to the fluted tart tin and press it out into an even layer, smoothing the surface with the back of a spoon. Prick the dough all over with a fork, just indenting the surface rather than going all the way through. Refrigerate for 15 minutes.

Preheat the oven to 170°C/150°C fan/gas 3 while the dough is chilling.

Bake the shortbread for 35–40 minutes or until lightly golden brown and firm. Remove from the oven and, while still hot, press the heart-shaped cutter into the shortbread, just below the centre (when the leaves are added later, the whole thing will look completely central). Leave the cutter in the shortbread. Set the tin on a wire rack and leave to cool for 15 minutes, then carefully remove the sides of the tin and slide the shortbread off the base back on to the wire rack. Take out the cutter now, but leave the scored shortbread heart in place. Leave to cool completely.

Wash the tin. Repeat the whole process with the remaining sugar, butter and flour to make a second disc of shortbread, not forgetting to cut off 25g dough before putting the remainder into the tin. Don't cut out a heart from this second baked disc, as it will form the base of the jammy dodger. (If you have two tart tins you can, of course, make both discs of shortbread at the same time.) Leave the oven on for the shortbread leaves and stalk.

CONTINUED OVERLEAF >>

GIANT STRAWBERRY DODGER (CONTINUED)

Take the two reserved 25g portions of dough out of the fridge and bring them to room temperature, then work them gently together. Roll out between two sheets of baking parchment to the thickness of a £1 coin. Using the leaf plunger cutter or a knife, cut out leaf shapes about 4cm long, plus a strawberry stalk about the same length. Cut as many leaves and stalks as possible so that you can choose the best ones once baked.

Peel away the excess shortbread dough and lift the cut-out shapes, on their parchment, on to a baking tray. Chill for about 15 minutes, then bake for about 5 minutes or until lightly golden. Leave to firm up on the tray for a few minutes before transferring to a wire rack to cool.

Next make the vanilla buttercream. If you have a free-standing mixer, put all the ingredients into the bowl, cover the bowl with a tea towel to prevent a cloud of sugar from escaping and start beating slowly. Increase the speed and beat until the mixture is fluffy, creamy and almost white, stopping a few times to scrape down the sides of the bowl. I beat for up to 10 minutes at full speed to create a really light finish. If you are using a hand-held electric whisk, beat the butter in a medium bowl until soft and pale, then sift the icing sugar into the bowl in batches, working in the sugar with a spoon before adding the milk and vanilla. Beat at full speed until the buttercream is really light and fluffy.

Transfer the buttercream to the piping bag fitted with the 1.5cm nozzle; if you are using a disposable piping bag, you can just snip off a similar-sized opening from the tip.

To assemble the dodger, place the shortbread biscuit without the cut-out on a plate or cake stand, pricked-side up. Place the heart cutter at its centre to match the position of the heart-shaped hole in the other biscuit. Starting close to the edge of the heart cutter, pipe on the buttercream in a spiral, working your way outwards to the edge of the biscuit and leaving a 1cm border clear at the outer edge: the buttercream will spread out into this gap when the shortbread is sandwiched together. Remove the cutter, then spoon half the strawberry jam into the heart-shaped space so it's surrounded by buttercream. >>

Remove the shortbread heart shape from the second biscuit and set it aside. Gently flip the biscuit over so that it is pricked-side down and, using a cake paddle, carefully place it on top of the buttercream and jam layer. Fill up the heart-shaped centre with the remaining jam, so it comes almost level with the top of the biscuit. Holding the reserved heart biscuit over the jam so it does not get covered, dust the surface of the shortbread with sifted icing sugar.

Dab a little buttercream or jam on the back of your three best strawberry leaves and the best stalk, and stick them at the top of the strawberry jam heart. Using tweezers, or your fingertips, carefully place individual linseeds on the jam heart to look like strawberry seeds.

Enjoy your jammy dodger in slices, giant or genteel. And, if you have a heart, give away the extra shortbread heart biscuit with or without a smudge of leftover buttercream and jam.

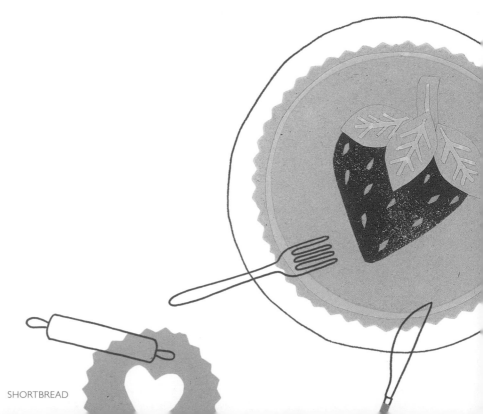

MILLIONAIRE'S SHORTCHANGE

FOR THE SHORTBREAD
50g caster sugar
100g butter, softened
150g plain flour

FOR THE CARAMEL
50g golden syrup
50g caster sugar
25ml double cream
Pinch of salt, optional

TO DECORATE
24 gold-wrapped chocolate
coins, about 4cm diameter

EQUIPMENT
24-hole mini-muffin tin, greased
and lined with seatbelt straps
(see p.21)

Based on the classic biscuit-caramel-chocolate layer known as millionaire's shortbread, these gold coin-topped bites take the concept to a whole new level. I like to make my own rich caramel for the middle layer as a softer version of the shop-bought toffee pennies that I loved as a child – and still do today.

Preheat the oven to 170°C/150°C fan/gas 3.

Using a hand-held electric whisk, or in a free-standing mixer, beat the sugar and butter together for 3–5 minutes or until smooth and creamy. Sift the flour into the mixture in two batches, mixing in each batch until just combined. Use your hands to bring the mix together into a dough without overworking it.

Transfer the dough to the muffin tin, putting about 12g dough into each hole. Level off each mini shortbread with your fingertips or the back of a teaspoon, then prick the surface with a fork, just indenting rather than going right through. Bake for 15–20 minutes or until lightly golden brown and firm. Leave to cool in the tin.

Next make the caramel. Weigh the golden syrup into a small/medium saucepan. Sprinkle the sugar over the surface of the syrup, then set the pan over a medium heat and stir with a wooden spoon or silicone spatula until the sugar has dissolved. Cook gently, swirling the caramel around in the pan, until it reaches a rich amber colour. Remove the pan from the heat and set it on your digital scales. Pour and weigh in the cream. Stir as the caramel bubbles until everything is fully combined and smooth. Stir in the salt, if using. Pour the caramel into a small bowl and leave to cool.

Now remove your shortbread bases from the tin. Pull off a piece of caramel (about 4g), roll into a ball and flatten on top of a shortbread round (like a soft toffee penny). It helps to slightly dampen your fingertips and palms of your hands, to prevent the caramel from sticking while creating your pennies. Peel off the foil from one side of a chocolate coin. Place it, chocolate side down, on top of the caramel layer, pressing gently but firmly to make it stick.

Continue assembling the remaining shortchanges in the same way. Leave them to set before serving.

GINGERBREAD

Although it has a definite association with Christmas, I could quite
happily eat gingerbread all year round – and create myriad designs
with it too. My biscuit baubles have a festive feel, but the rest of the
ideas that follow can be used at any time of year. For me, gingerbread
has got to have a bit of a kick, so I like to use plenty of ground ginger
in the mix, and a spoonful of ground mixed spice too for good
measure. If you prefer your gingerbread a little milder, just reduce
the quantity of spice you put in. I use muscovado sugars for their
lovely, rich flavour, which goes so well with the spice.

BASIC GINGERBREAD

50g light muscovado sugar
50g dark muscovado sugar
50g golden syrup
150g butter, roughly chopped
1 egg (at room temperature)
300g plain flour
1 tbsp ground ginger
1 tbsp ground mixed spice

Put both types of sugar, the golden syrup and the butter in a heavy-based saucepan. Set it over a medium heat and warm, stirring occasionally, until the butter has melted and the sugars have dissolved. Transfer the mixture to a large bowl and leave to cool for about 5 minutes.

Beat the egg into the mixture. Sift the flour and spices into the bowl in two batches, mixing in each batch gently, to make a soft dough.

Halve the dough and transfer to two food bags, or wrap in clingfilm. Chill for several hours, preferably overnight, to firm up – this makes the dough easier to roll out. If you don't want to use both portions of dough now (it's hard to make a smaller batch as that would mean halving an egg), keep the remainder in the fridge and use within a week, or freeze.

Remove the dough from the fridge 15–30 minutes before rolling it so it can soften slightly.

Roll out the dough between two sheets of baking parchment to the thickness of a £1 coin (or according to the recipe instructions). If the dough seems very sticky, dust it and the parchment lightly with a little flour.

Peel off the top sheet of parchment and cut out your desired shapes. Peel away the excess dough, then lift the gingerbread shapes, on their parchment, on to a baking tray. Chill for 15 minutes. Preheat the oven to 180°C/160°C fan/gas 4 while the gingerbread shapes are chilling.

Bake for 5–15 minutes, depending on the size of the biscuits – see the table opposite – until golden brown around the edges. Leave to firm up on the tray for 5–10 minutes, then transfer the biscuits, still on the parchment, to a wire rack to cool completely.

TO FINISH

Dipping in chocolate, or sandwiching together with Ganache (see p.279) or Cream Cheese Buttercream (p.277), are just a few ways to elevate your gingerbread biscuits to sublime heights. Trimmings can also be baked, then broken up and used in Tiffin (p.180) or scattered over creamy-topped cakes and bowls of ice cream to add a spicy sweet snap.

TO SEE HOW MANY BISCUITS YOU CAN MAKE, USE THE TABLE OPPOSITE >>

GINGER SPICE

SUGAR

SYRUP

FLOUR

BUTTER

EGG

APPROX NUMBER OF SMALL BISCUITS (ABOUT 3.5CM) YOU CAN MAKE	APPROX NUMBER OF MEDIUM BISCUITS (ABOUT 7.5CM) YOU CAN MAKE	APPROX NUMBER OF LARGE BISCUITS (ABOUT 15CM) YOU CAN MAKE	QUANTITY OF DOUGH ROLLED OUT TO £1 COIN THICKNESS
120	30	10	Full quantity (660g)
60	15	5	½ quantity (330g)
40	10	3	⅓ quantity (220g)
30	6	2	¼ quantity (165g)
15	3	1	⅛ quantity (80g)

BAKE IN AN OVEN PREHEATED TO 180°C/160°C FAN/GAS 4		
for 5–8 minutes	for 8–12 minutes	for 12–15 minutes

150g white chocolate (without
   vanilla seeds), chopped into
   small pieces
100g full-fat cream cheese

50g light muscovado sugar
50g dark muscovado sugar
50g golden syrup
150g butter, roughly chopped
1 egg (at room temperature)
300g plain flour
1 tbsp ground ginger
1 tbsp ground mixed spice

100g butter, softened
200g icing sugar, sifted
1 tbsp lemon juice
1 tsp lemon extract
150g full-fat cream cheese

50g white chocolate (without
   vanilla seeds)
50g white chocolate mice

10cm round, deep, loose-
   bottomed tin (pork-pie size)
20cm round, loose-bottomed
   sandwich tin
Round piping nozzle or straw,
   for cutting small holes,
3cm round, crimped/fluted
   cutter, to create
   'bite marks', optional
Paintbrush
Wooden Camembert box
   (250g), optional

CHEESE BISCUITS

I like to serve these treats at the end of a meal instead of savoury cheese and biscuits – but still on a cheeseboard (see directory, p.310). The ginger biscuits look like wedge-shaped slivers of cheese, while chunks of white chocolate represent firm, crumbly Cheddar or Lancashire. I add white mice for a novel tweak as well as a box of sweet 'Camembert' and a buttercream 'cream cheese'. These soft cheeses can also be used to sandwich the biscuits together. Make the 'Camembert' the night before so it has time to set.

Start with the 'Camembert'. Put the white chocolate and cream cheese in a heatproof bowl and melt in a microwave or set over a pan of simmering water (bain-marie). When melted, stir to combine, then remove from the heat. Take a 20cm square piece of white baking parchment and crumple it up, then open it out again (this makes it easier to manipulate). Use it to line the 10cm tin, pressing the paper over the base and up the sides. Pour the white chocolate mixture into the lined tin and gently press it down with a spoon to cover the base evenly. Refrigerate overnight.

For the gingerbread biscuits, put both types of sugar, the golden syrup and the butter in a heavy-based saucepan. Set it over a medium heat and warm, stirring occasionally, until the butter has melted and the sugars have dissolved. Transfer the mixture to a large bowl and leave to cool for about 5 minutes before beating in the egg. Sift over the flour and spices in two batches, mixing in each batch gently, to make a soft dough.

Halve the dough and transfer to two food bags, or wrap in clingfilm. Chill for several hours, preferably overnight, to firm up – this makes the dough easier to roll out. Using the full batch of dough will give you 32 biscuits; if you want to make a smaller batch, you can keep the remaining dough in the fridge for up to a week or freeze for later use.

Now make the cream cheese buttercream to cover your sweet 'Camembert'. If you have a free-standing mixer, put the butter, icing sugar, lemon juice and lemon extract into the bowl, cover the bowl with a tea towel to prevent a cloud of sugar from escaping and start beating slowly. Increase the speed and beat until the mixture is fluffy, creamy and almost white, stopping a few times to scrape down the sides of the bowl. I beat for up to 10 minutes at full speed to create a really light finish. Finally, beat in the cream cheese for another minute (not much more – if you overbeat at this stage, the cream cheese can 'split' and loosen the buttercream; if this happens, chill it to firm up slightly).

CONTINUED OVERLEAF >>

Alternatively, if you are using a hand-held electric whisk, beat the butter in a medium bowl until soft and pale, then sift the icing sugar into the bowl in batches, working in the sugar with a spoon before adding the lemon juice and extract. Beat at full speed until the buttercream is really light and fluffy before beating in the cream cheese for no more than 1 minute.

Remove your sweet 'Camembert' from the fridge and take it out of the tin. Peel back the paper from around the side of the 'cheese'. You can either use a piece of kitchen paper to clean away any ganache still sticking to the parchment and then use this parchment again, or crumple up a fresh piece of white parchment and carefully transfer your cheese on to it.

With a small palette knife, smooth 1–2 tablespoons of the buttercream over the surface of the 'Camembert' and another 1–2 tablespoons around the sides. Press a sieve over the buttercream surface to create a 'cheesecloth' finish. Return to the fridge, on the parchment, so the buttercream can set. Set the remaining buttercream aside.

About 15–30 minutes before you're ready to bake, remove the dough from the fridge so it can soften slightly. Roll out one half of the dough between two sheets of baking parchment to the thickness of a £1 coin. If the dough is very sticky, lightly dust it and the parchment with a little flour.

Peel off the top layer of parchment. Use the base of the 20cm tin (or other 20cm round template) to mark a circle on the dough. Cut out the circle, then cut it into eight wedges using a sharp knife or pizza cutter. Re-roll the trimmings between fresh parchment and repeat to create more wedge-shaped biscuits. Repeat with the other half of the dough. Lift the biscuits, on their parchment, on to baking trays and refrigerate for 15 minutes.

Preheat the oven to 180°C/160°C fan/gas 4 while the biscuits are chilling.

Use a palette knife to separate the biscuits on the baking trays so they are not touching each other. With the tip of the nozzle or straw, stamp out holes from the biscuits, to represent the holes in a piece of cheese. To create biscuits with extra 'bite', use the crimped cutter to cut out pieces from the edges of some of the biscuit wedges to look like bite marks. >>

Bake the biscuits for 8–12 minutes or until golden. Leave them to firm up on their trays for a few minutes before transferring them, on the parchment, to a wire rack to cool completely.

While the biscuits are baking, remove your partly covered sweet 'Camembert' from the fridge and carefully turn it over to reveal the uncovered base. Either place it on a fresh 20cm square of crumpled-up white parchment, or clean up the previously used parchment square by wiping it with kitchen paper.

If your remaining buttercream has stiffened up, beat it for a few minutes to return it to a creamy, spreadable consistency. Spread 1–2 tablespoons of the buttercream over the uncovered surface of the 'Camembert'. Again, press a sieve over the buttercream to create a cheesecloth finish, then return the 'Camembert' to the fridge, on the paper, to set. Put the remainder of the cream cheese buttercream in an empty, cleaned-out 250–300g cream cheese tub or a small serving bowl.

Once the biscuits have cooled, break the 50g of white chocolate into chunks. If you like, carve or chip the chunks a little to make them look more like pieces of cheese. You could also melt a few of the chunks in a microwave or a heatproof bowl set over a pan of simmering water (bain-marie) and use the melted chocolate to stick a few chocolate mice and chocolate 'cheese' chunks on to some of the biscuits. Leave to set.

To finish the sweet 'Camembert', carefully place it in an empty wooden Camembert box, still on the parchment, so the paper overhangs the sides of the box. To create authentic Camembert markings, use a sharp knife or tip of a small palette knife to score diagonal lines over the set buttercream surface on top of the 'cheese'. As with the real cheese, this sweet 'Camembert' is best enjoyed at room temperature, but can be kept in the fridge for up to a week.

Serve the biscuits on a cheeseboard with the chunks of white chocolate 'cheese', white mice, the box of sweet 'Camembert' and the spreadable buttercream 'cream cheese'.

GINGERBREAD BAUBLES

MAKES ABOUT 15 BISCUITS

FOR THE GINGERBREAD

50g light muscovado sugar
50g dark muscovado sugar
50g golden syrup
150g butter, roughly chopped
1 egg (at room temperature)
300g plain flour
1 tbsp ground ginger
1 tbsp ground mixed spice

TO DECORATE

50g hard sweets, such as Fox's Glacier Mints, Murray Mints or buttermints, or hard toffees, such as Werther's Originals
4m string or embroidery thread
15g dark or milk chocolate, chopped into small pieces
10 Reese's Mini Peanut Butter Cups or other mini chocolates

EQUIPMENT

6, 7 and 7.5cm plain round cutters (or use just one size)
4cm star cutter (see directory, p.309)
Fine paintbrush or cocktail stick

I have an affection for Reese's Mini Peanut Butter Cups. Their shape reminds me of the fixing on top of a Christmas bauble, which is how the idea for these biscuits was born. The gingerbread baubles are also adorned with a 'stained glass' star, made using melted mints and toffees. You can leave out this element if you prefer, and create simple star cut-outs. I like to use three sizes of cutter to produce a mix of baubles, but you can cut out just one size. The edible baubles make great gifts and lovely decorations to hang on the tree.

Put both types of sugar, the golden syrup and the butter in a heavy-based saucepan. Set it over a medium heat and warm, stirring occasionally, until the butter has melted and the sugars have dissolved. Transfer the mixture to a large bowl and leave to cool for about 5 minutes before beating in the egg. Sift over the flour and spices in two batches, mixing in each batch gently, to make a soft dough.

Halve the dough and transfer to two food bags, or wrap in clingfilm. Chill for several hours, preferably overnight, to firm up – this makes the dough easier to roll out. You'll only need one portion of dough for this recipe. Keep the other one in the fridge and use within a week, or freeze.

Remove the dough from the fridge 15–30 minutes before rolling so it can soften slightly. Split the dough in half and roll out one piece between two sheets of baking parchment to the thickness of a £1 coin. If you think the dough is very sticky, lightly dust it and the parchment with a little flour.

Peel off the top sheet of parchment. Using the round cutters – either just one size or a variety – cut out discs. For each bauble, you need to cut a 1.5 x 2cm strip of dough as well (it's easiest to cut these from one long 2cm-wide piece of dough). Peel away the excess dough and re-roll the trimmings between fresh parchment to cut more discs. Repeat with the other piece of dough.

Lift up the edge of a disc and slip the end of a strip of dough under it; press gently so the strip adheres to the underside of the disc – about 1cm of the strip should protrude from the bauble (this will be the hanging fixture). Use the end of the paintbrush handle or a cocktail stick to make a hole near the top of the protruding strip (you can thread this with string once the biscuit is baked). Repeat with the remaining discs and strips. Make sure there is a little space between the baubles, then lift them, on their sheets of parchment, on to baking trays and refrigerate for 15 minutes.

CONTINUED OVERLEAF >>

GINGERBREAD BAUBLES (CONTINUED)

Preheat the oven to 180°C/160°C fan/gas 4 while the biscuits are chilling.

Meanwhile, put the hard sweets, in their wrappers, in separate sandwich bags encased in a tea towel (to prevent the sweets from flying loose). Crush the sweets with a rolling pin. Discard the wrappers.

Remove the baubles from the fridge and use the star cutter to stamp out a star shape from the centre of each. Carefully remove these stars and lay them on a separate parchment-lined baking tray.

Carefully put the crushed-up pieces of sweets inside the cut-out star shapes (don't mix the sweets together). Bake the biscuits for 8–12 minutes or until the sweets have melted and the biscuits are deep golden around the edges. Bake the cut-out stars separately for about 5 minutes (or, if you have asbestos fingers, like me, bake them all on the same tray and carefully remove the stars halfway through the baubles' cooking time). You can eat these stars as they are or give them away with the biscuit baubles as a gift. >>

While still warm, check the holes in the strips – if they have closed during baking, open them up with the end of the paintbrush handle or cocktail stick. Leave the biscuits to firm up on their trays until the melted sweets have set before transferring, on the parchment, to a wire rack to cool.

Thread string or cotton through the hole in each bauble, using the end of a cocktail stick or a needle to help feed it through. Tie into loops for hanging.

Melt the chocolate in a microwave or a heatproof bowl set over a pan of simmering water (bain-marie), then leave to cool a little. Carefully cut the mini chocolates in half (you need only 15 halves, but it's worth having a few spare in case of damage). Use the paintbrush to dab melted chocolate on to the protruding strip at the top of each bauble and press on a mini chocolate half, which should just conceal the hole and cover the thread. Leave to set.

GINGER SNAP CARDS

FOR THE BISCUITS
50g light muscovado sugar
50g dark muscovado sugar
50g golden syrup or honey
150g butter, roughly chopped
1 egg (at room temperature)
300g plain flour
1 tbsp ground ginger
1 tbsp ground mixed spice

EQUIPMENT
Standard playing card, about
    8.75 x 5.75cm, to use as a
    guide
Wooden latte stirrer
2–2.5 x 3–3.5cm shaped cutters
    – numbers, letters, shapes
    such as hearts and clubs, etc.
    (see directory, p.308)

You can use a variety of cutters to make the designs on these buttery biscuit snap cards: use alphabet cutters to spell out the names of friends and family or to mark out slogans or sayings, or opt for numbers to create key dates, such as birthdays, or even help teach little ones their times tables! Deal out these snappy snacks at home, or present them in a box as a fun edible gift. Either way, while the rules shouldn't be broken, the biscuits most definitely should – a line scored in the dough before baking enables you to snap the finished biscuits cleanly in half.

Put both types of sugar, the golden syrup or honey and the butter in a heavy-based saucepan. Set it over a medium heat and warm, stirring occasionally, until the butter has melted and the sugars have dissolved. Transfer the mixture to a large bowl and leave to cool for about 5 minutes before beating in the egg. Sift over the flour and spices in two batches, mixing in each batch gently, until you have a soft dough.

Halve the dough and transfer to two food bags, or wrap in clingfilm. Chill for several hours, preferably overnight, to firm up – this makes the dough easier to roll out.

Remove the dough from the fridge 15–30 minutes before rolling so it can soften slightly. Split one portion of dough in half and roll out one piece between two sheets of baking parchment to the thickness of a £1 coin. If the dough is very sticky, lightly dust it and the parchment with a little flour. Peel off the top layer of parchment and use a pizza cutter and a ruler to cut out cards, using the playing card as a guide. Peel away the excess dough. Lift the biscuits, on the parchment, on to a baking tray. Repeat with all the remaining dough, and any trimmings, to cut more cards. Refrigerate for 15 minutes.

Preheat the oven to 180°C/160°C fan/gas 4 while the biscuits are chilling.

Score a line across the centre of each card by pressing with the latte stirrer or the blunt side of a knife blade, without going right through – this will enable you to easily snap the baked biscuits in two before eating. Cut out shapes from either side of the scored lines, making lots of different patterns. Remove these shapes and place them on a separate parchment-lined baking tray.

Bake the biscuits for 8–12 minutes, and the cut-outs for 5 minutes, or until golden. Leave to firm up on the trays for a few minutes before transferring, on the parchment, to a wire rack to cool.

GINGER NUTS & BOLTS

SERVES 5–6

FOR THE BISCUITS
50g light muscovado sugar
50g dark muscovado sugar
50g golden syrup
150g butter, roughly chopped
1 egg (at room temperature)
300g plain flour
1 tbsp ground ginger
1 tbsp ground mixed spice

TO DECORATE
25g dark chocolate, chopped
    into small pieces
Mixed nuts – roasted and salted,
    if you like

EQUIPMENT
Hexagonal lid of a cocktail
    stick container or a small
    hexagonal cutter
2.75cm, 1.75cm and 1.5cm
    plain round cutters – or
    piping nozzles
Cocktail stick
Wooden latte stirrer
Fine paintbrush

I love the play on words here between the classic ginger biscuits, the hardware items and actual nuts. These nibblesome nuts and bolts won't hold anything together, but you can still construct a very appealing centrepiece – which will soon be dismantled! Make a few tasty tools to serve with this eye-catching ironmongery using the second portion of dough, or some spare butter biscuit dough (see p.206), and a 12cm spanner-shaped cutter (see directory, p.308).

Put both types of sugar, the golden syrup and the butter in a heavy-based saucepan. Set it over a medium heat and warm, stirring occasionally, until the butter has melted and the sugars have dissolved. Transfer the mixture to a large bowl and leave to cool for about 5 minutes before beating in the egg. Sift over the flour and spices in two batches, mixing in each batch gently, to make a soft dough.

Halve the dough and transfer to two food bags, or wrap in clingfilm. Chill for several hours, preferably overnight, to firm up – this makes the dough easier to roll out. You'll only need one half of the dough for this recipe. Keep the remainder in the fridge and use within a week, or freeze.

Remove the dough from the fridge 15–30 minutes before rolling so it can soften slightly. Roll out between two sheets of baking parchment to a 5mm thickness. If the dough is very sticky, lightly dust it and the parchment with a little flour. Peel off the top layer of parchment and use the hexagonal container lid or cutter to cut out about 25 (or more) 'nuts'. Peel away the dough trimmings and set aside to roll out later.

With the 1.75cm cutter (or the 1.75cm-diameter wider end of a round piping nozzle), cut out holes from the centre of 10 of the hexagonal biscuits. Use the cocktail stick poked into the centre to remove these little discs of dough and put them on a separate baking tray lined with baking parchment – these will become your bolt heads. Cut the end off the latte stirrer (a pair of scissors works a treat) to make a straight edge, then use this to indent a cross in the centre of each bolt head, using the cocktail-stick hole as a marker.

CONTINUED OVERLEAF >>

Use the 1.5cm cutter (or the 1.5cm-diameter wider end of a round piping nozzle) to cut out a hole from the centre of each of the remaining hexagonal biscuits. Remove the little discs of dough as before and put them on the baking tray with the other bolt heads. With your latte stirrer, or the cocktail stick on its side, press down straight across the middle of each disc to create a different bolt-head pattern.

Re-roll the dough trimmings between more parchment to the thickness of a 50-pence piece. Using the 1.5cm cutter, cut out mini circles to create your 3D bolts. You will need nine circles for each of the larger bolt heads.

Roll out the dough trimmings to the thickness of a 50-pence piece and use the 2.75cm cutter (or the 2.75cm-diameter wider end of a 1cm piping nozzle) to cut out circles. Then use the 1.75cm cutter to cut out holes from these to create 'washers'. (You can add the cut-out holes to the other 'bolt heads'.) Peel away the excess dough. Refrigerate all the biscuits for 15 minutes.

Preheat the oven to 180°C/160°C fan/gas 4 while the biscuits are chilling.

Bake the thin mini circles and washers for 3–5 minutes, and the nuts and bolt heads for 10–12 minutes, or until golden. The mini circles and washers can colour quite quickly, so check often. Leave the biscuits to firm up on their trays for a few minutes before transferring, on the parchment, to a wire rack to cool. >>

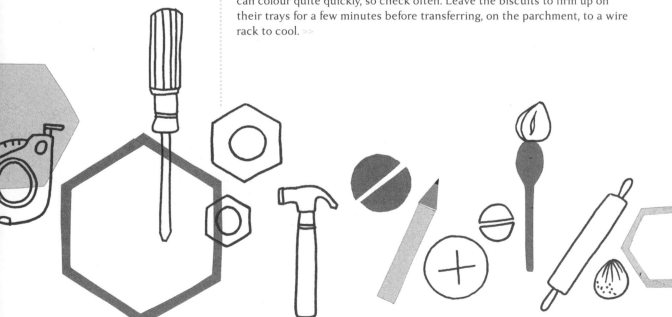

When the biscuits are completely cooled, you can assemble your bolts. Melt the chocolate in a microwave or a heatproof bowl set over a pan of simmering water (bain-marie). Using the paintbrush, carefully dab melted chocolate on to the mini circles. Sandwich them together in threes, then sandwich the sets of threes into lengths of nine. When sticking the sets of three together I lay them in a mini foil 'gutter', created by moulding a doubled sheet of foil over a pen and then turning it over – the foil gutter keeps the circles in place, resulting in a less wonky bolt!

Once your stacks of mini circles are set, dab some chocolate on to the centre of the back of each larger bolt head (those marked with crosses), then place a stack of circles on it. Hold in place with your finger until it is set enough to let go. Leave to set completely.

Serve the bolts with the rest of the biscuit nuts, washers and bolt heads together with your selection of mixed nuts. (If using plain nuts, I'd recommend roasting them for 5 minutes – at the same oven temperature as the biscuits – to enhance their flavour.) To complete the look, serve everything in empty food tins or in a tool box.

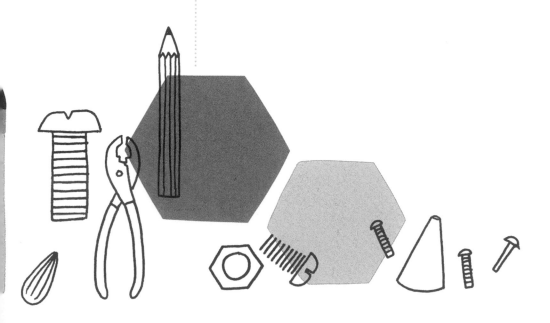

MERINGUES

· ·

The sweet and sculptural properties of meringue make it a key baking medium. Don't be afraid of this marvellously flexible, glossy white stuff – it's not hard to make. The secret is in whipping the egg whites and sugar to a state of static stiffness, which is easily achieved with a mixer or hand-held electric whisk. Do ensure your bowl and whisk are spotless, as any grease or other residues can stop the whites whipping up nicely. Metal or ceramic bowls are best, as plastic ones can sometimes harbour traces of grease – a good tip is to wipe the inside of your bowl with half a lemon to clean it before you begin. Once you've got that billowy, snowy bowlful of meringue, you can pipe, spoon or splodge it into intricate edible masterpieces or more relaxed peaks and puffs. A long, low bake is very important – you're barely cooking the meringue at all, more just drying it out.

BASIC MERINGUE

FOR THE MERINGUE
50g caster sugar
1 egg white (at room
    temperature)

EQUIPMENT
10cm round tin – or another
    10cm-diameter round object
    to use as a template

Preheat the oven to 120°C/100°C fan/gas ½. Using the tin (or similar-sized round object) as a guide, draw two circles on a sheet of baking parchment. The drawn lines need to be visible on the other side of the parchment too.

Weigh your sugar into a bowl. Put the egg white into a large metal or ceramic bowl. (You could use a free-standing mixer but this small, one-egg-white quantity can get a bit lost in it. I find it's easiest to use a hand-held electric whisk here.) Begin by whisking the egg white on a slow-to-medium speed for about 20 seconds to break it up. Then increase the speed to medium and whisk until the white forms stiff peaks and the bowl can be turned upside down without the egg slipping out.

Now increase the speed further and gradually add the sugar, a teaspoon at a time. Keep whisking until all the sugar is incorporated and the meringue is thick and shiny.

Put a few little dabs of meringue in the corners of the sheet of parchment (on the marked side), then turn it over and lay it meringue-side down on a baking tray (the meringue will help to stick the paper to your tray). Spoon the meringue on to the tray, inside the marked circles – or in whatever shape you wish or that the recipe specifies.

Bake for 1–1¼ hours or until the meringues have a crisp outer shell and you are able to peel them off the parchment without them sticking. Turn off the oven but leave the meringues inside until they are completely cold. I often bake my meringues in the evening, so I can leave them to cool in the oven overnight.

TO FINISH

The basic meringue mix can be given a more marshmallowy texture, as for a classic pavlova, by adding some lemon juice. Fill pavlovas and meringue nests with whipped cream, or a mix of cream and mascarpone, swirled with jam or curd. Meringue kisses are all the sweeter sandwiched with a Ganache (see p.279). And broken-up, left-over meringue can be used to make Eton Mess. Meringue will always leave you with spare egg yolks. There are lots of uses for them: in my Orange Blossom Marzipan (p.286) or custard for Banoffee Tumbler Trifles (p.52). Or whisk up a batch of Lemon Curd (p.273) and add a couple of spoonfuls through the creamy filling for Midsummer Night's Dream on p.258.

TO MAKE DIFFERENT-SIZED MERINGUES, USE THE TABLE OPPOSITE >>

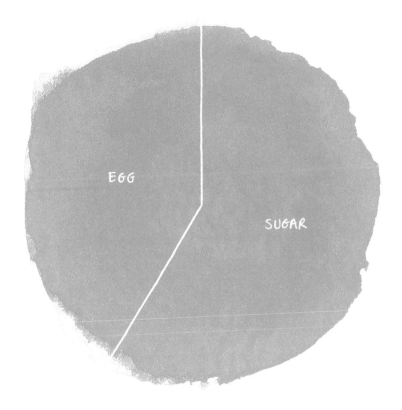

EGG

SUGAR

TO MAKE 12 MINI-MERINGUE KISSES (ABOUT 3.5CM WIDE)	TO MAKE A 15CM MERINGUE NEST	TO MAKE A 20CM MERINGUE NEST	TO MAKE A 23CM MERINGUE NEST	INGREDIENTS
50g	100g	150g	200g	Caster sugar
1	2	3	4	Egg white(s)

BAKE IN AN OVEN PREHEATED TO 120°C /100°C FAN/GAS ½; COOL IN THE TURNED-OFF OVEN OVERNIGHT

for 1–1½ hours	for 1½–2 hours	for 2–2½ hours	for 2½–3 hours	

MIDSUMMER NIGHT'S DREAM

MAKES A 23CM MERINGUE
DESSERT; SERVES 8

FOR THE MERINGUE
200g caster sugar
4 egg whites (at room
    temperature)
2 tsp lemon juice

TO DECORATE
400ml double cream
4 tbsp limoncello, optional
Raspberries
Strawberries
Cherries
Blueberries
Selection of fresh flowers
    (unsprayed)
Fresh mint

EQUIPMENT
23cm round cake tin – or
    another 23cm-diameter
    round object you can use
    as a template

This *Midsummer Night's Dream*-inspired meringue celebrates Shakespeare and my love of all things natural. The play itself involves three plots, and this dessert contains three different textures, thanks to the meringue and its filling: crispy, chewy and creamy. A display of fresh fruit and flowers on top, meanwhile, makes a dramatic flourish. I've included limoncello in the cream filling to give a touch of lemon-meringue flavour, and also as a reference to the intoxication and enchantment within Shakespeare's play. Use elderflower cordial instead of limoncello, if you prefer: the dessert will still be as dreamy. I like to serve the meringue on a tree-trunk board (see directory, p.309).

Preheat the oven to 120°C/100°C fan/gas ½. Draw around the cake tin, or other object, on a sheet of silicone-coated paper or baking parchment. The drawn line needs to be visible on the other side of the parchment.

Weigh your sugar. Put the egg whites into a large metal or ceramic bowl (if you are using a hand-held electric whisk) or in the bowl of a free-standing mixer. Whisk the whites on a slow-to-medium speed for about 20 seconds, then increase the speed to medium and whisk until the whites form stiff peaks and the bowl can be turned upside down without them slipping out.

Now increase the speed further and gradually add the sugar, a teaspoon at a time. Keep whisking until all the sugar is incorporated and the meringue is thick and shiny. Whisk in the lemon juice.

Dab a little of the meringue on the corners of the sheet of baking parchment (marked side up), to act as glue. Turn the sheet over meringue-side down and lay it on a large baking tray. Using a small palette knife or round-ended knife, spread the rest of the meringue inside the circle drawn on the parchment, smoothing it into shape and making a hollow in the centre.

Bake for 2½–3 hours or until the meringue will peel easily from the parchment. Turn off the oven and leave the meringue inside to cool and crisp up for several hours, ideally overnight.

When you are ready to assemble the meringue, whip the double cream in a large bowl, with the limoncello if using, until it forms soft peaks.

Peel the parchment away from the meringue and place it on a plate, cake stand or board. Fill the hollow with the cream and add the fresh fruit, flowers and mint. Remove the flowers (if non-edible) before eating.

MINI SWAN LAKES

FOR THE MERINGUE

50g caster sugar
1 egg white (at room
    temperature)

TO DECORATE

1 egg white (at room
    temperature)
25g desiccated coconut
12 clear mints, such as Fox's
    Glacier Mints
Edible silver glitter, to dust
5g dark chocolate
75ml double cream

EQUIPMENT

Swan template (see below)
2 piping bags and a 5mm plain
    round nozzle
Fine paintbrush
Cocktail stick

SWAN
TEMPLATE

Meringue swans have always had a retro feel, so I thought I'd go with the flow and pair them up with some rather retro clear mint sweets. These can be melted in the oven to form organic-looking mini mint 'lakes' for the swans to float on. Coconut feathers add both taste and texture to the swans' wings, and pair perfectly with the mint.

Preheat the oven to 120°C/100°C fan/gas ½.

Lay out two sheets of baking parchment. Using the template, draw at least 12 swan heads/necks and at least 24 wings on the parchment to act as a guide when you come to pipe your meringue (you'll be making 12 swans, but it's worth having a few extra pieces to play with). The drawn lines need to be visible on the other side of the parchment too.

Weigh your sugar. Put the egg white into a large metal or ceramic bowl. Whisk the white with a hand-held electric whisk on a slow-to-medium speed for about 20 seconds. Increase the speed to medium and whisk until the white forms stiff peaks and the bowl can be turned upside down without the white slipping out. Now increase the speed further and gradually add the sugar, a teaspoon at a time. Keep whisking until the meringue is thick and shiny.

Spoon most of the meringue into a piping bag fitted with the 5mm round nozzle. Dab the remaining meringue from the bowl on the corners of the parchment sheets (on the marked side), then turn them over and lay them on two large baking trays.

Pipe 12 swan heads/necks and 24 wings on to the parchment, using your drawn markings as a guide. You should have enough meringue to pipe a few extras so you can choose the best ones once baked. Bake for 1–1½ hours or until you can peel the meringues away from the parchment without them sticking. Remove the baking trays and set them on a heatproof surface. Turn off the oven and open the oven door to cool down quickly.

Very lightly beat the egg white for decoration to break it up a little, then carefully paint a thin layer over each swan wing – this will act as glue. Sprinkle coconut over the wings to look like feathers. Return the trays to the oven (it is important that the oven has hardly any heat left in it, otherwise you risk the coconut toasting slightly – producing less than white swans). Leave the meringues in the turned-off oven for several hours, ideally overnight.

CONTINUED OVERLEAF >>

MINI SWAN LAKES (CONTINUED)

Once the meringues are ready, you can make your clear mint lakes.

Preheat the oven to 180°C/160°C fan/gas 4. Unwrap the clear mints and spread them out, spaced well apart, on a baking tray lined with baking parchment. Heat in the oven for about 5 minutes or until completely melted. Remove the tray from the oven and tip it this way and that to encourage the melted mints to form 12 organic-looking lakes. While still warm, sprinkle over some edible silver glitter, then leave the lakes to set on the parchment.

To finish the swan heads, melt the chocolate in a microwave or in a small heatproof bowl set over a pan of simmering water (bain-marie). Dip the (cleaned) paintbrush in the melted chocolate and paint on to the tip of each swan head to resemble a beak. Use the cocktail stick to add eyes. Leave to set.

To assemble, arrange your mint lakes on a board, flat plate, glass cake stand or even a mirror. Whip the cream until it holds soft-to-medium peaks – don't make it too stiff because it will thicken up further when piped. Spoon the cream into a disposable piping bag and snip off the tip to make a 1cm opening. Pipe a little cream on to the flat, non-coconut side of a swan wing and sandwich with a second wing. Repeat with all the wings, then place these swan bodies on the mint lakes. Gently push the swan necks into the cream.

ANNA PAVLOVA'S BALLET SHOES

MAKES A PAIR OF 'BALLET'
SHOES; SERVES 4–6

FOR THE MERINGUE
100g caster sugar
2 egg whites (at room
    temperature)
1 tbsp beetroot juice (from
    a vacuum pack of plain
    cooked beetroot)
1 tsp lemon juice
Few drops of rose water

TO DECORATE
150ml double cream
150g raspberries
1 tsp freeze-dried raspberries
Rose petals, optional
Pink embroidery thread
Pink satin ribbon

EQUIPMENT
Large disposable piping bag
Fine paintbrush

The pavlova has been a classic pud for decades. The precise date of its invention is a matter of some dispute but it's certain that it was named in honour of the Russian ballerina Anna Pavlova. Here I've brought the dessert and Anna's ballet shoes together with a secret ingredient that Anna was believed to be partial to – beetroot. As well as colouring the meringues pink, the beetroot references the ballerina's love of borscht, a soup popular in Russia. It's vital to mix lemon juice with the beetroot juice – apart from providing the pavlova with its soft marshmallowy centre, the acid keeps the beetroot and meringue pink rather than purple. Fresh berries decorate the creamy filling, and rose water adds a floral note that duets perfectly with the fruit. Fresh rose petals can be scattered around the finished bake to highlight the rose flavouring, and to represent the flowers tossed on stage at the end of a ballerina's performance, or you could create the rose petal effect with my dried Beetroot Hearts (see p.292) to continue the beetroot theme.

Preheat the oven to 120°C/100°C fan/gas ½. Draw the outline of two ballet shoes, about 23cm long, 7.5cm wide at the broadest part of the toe and 5cm wide at the heel, on a sheet of baking parchment. The drawn lines need to be visible on the other side of the parchment too.

Weigh your sugar into a bowl. Put the egg whites into a large metal or ceramic bowl (if you are using a hand-held electric whisk) or the bowl of a free-standing mixer. Whisk the whites on a slow-to-medium speed for about 20 seconds, then increase the speed to medium and whisk until the whites form stiff peaks and the bowl can be turned upside down without them slipping out. Now increase the speed further and gradually add the sugar, a teaspoonful at a time. Keep whisking until all the sugar is incorporated and the meringue is thick and shiny. Mix together the beetroot juice, lemon juice and rose water, then fold through the meringue to colour evenly.

Transfer the meringue to the piping bag. Dab a little of the remaining meringue from the side of the bowl on the corners of the baking parchment (the marked side), to act as glue, then turn the sheet over, meringue-side down, and lay it on a large baking tray.

Cut a 2.5cm opening from the tip of the piping bag, then pipe the meringue into the ballet shoe shapes you have drawn on the parchment. Smooth the meringue into shape with a small palette knife, making a slight hollow to mark the inside of each shoe (you'll fill this with cream later).

CONTINUED OVERLEAF >>

ANNA PAVLOVA'S BALLET SHOES (CONTINUED)

Bake for 1½–2 hours or until the meringues can be peeled off the parchment without sticking. Turn off the oven. Leave the meringues in the oven to cool and crisp up for several hours, ideally overnight.

When you're ready to assemble the shoes, whip the cream until it holds soft peaks. Peel the parchment paper away from the meringues and place them on a plate or cake stand.

Carefully fill the hollows of the shoes with the cream, using a spoon and palette knife. Scatter some of the fresh and freeze-dried raspberries over the cream and place the remainder around the meringue shoes, together with any rose petals, if using.

Tie two bows with short lengths of embroidery thread and stick these to the front of the shoes – the cream within the shoes will help to keep the bows in place. Finally, tuck in the pink ribbons on either side of the shoes in true Pavlova style. For a truly showstopping dessert, serve these ballet shoes alongside my Mini Swan Lakes meringues (see p.260).

MIDNIGHT MUNCHIES & HIDDEN GEM STARS

MAKES 24 MERINGUE BITES

FOR THE SHORTBREAD
100g caster sugar
200g butter, softened
300g plain flour

FOR THE MERINGUE
100g caster sugar
2 egg whites (at room temperature)

TO DECORATE
12 milk chocolate-coated caramel and biscuit sweets, such as Munchies
12 milk chocolate stars, such as Milky Way Magic Stars, plus extra to decorate
Edible silver and gold glitter, optional
50g dark chocolate, chopped into small pieces

EQUIPMENT
5cm and 6cm round, crimped cutters
Large piping bag fitted with a large star nozzle (see directory, p.309)
Fine paintbrush

I have always had a soft spot for Iced Gems and they have inspired these mini meringue-and-biscuit mouthfuls – but these stars provide extra cosmic chocolate delight, as I've hidden small chocolate treats inside. Whether you enjoy these gems indoors, as part of a midnight feast, or graze as you gaze at the real night sky, I defy you not to munch your way through the lot.

Begin by making your shortbread. Using a hand-held electric whisk, or in a free-standing mixer, beat the sugar and butter together until smooth and creamy. Sift the flour into the mixture in two batches, mixing in each batch until just combined, then use your hands to bring the mix together into a dough without overworking it.

Roll out the dough between two sheets of baking parchment to a 1cm thickness. Peel off the top layer of parchment and, using the 5cm crimped cutter, cut out 12 shortbread rounds. Re-roll the trimmings between fresh parchment and use the 6cm cutter to cut out 12 more rounds. You can cut out extra rounds with the trimmings.

Lift the shortbread rounds, on the parchment, on to two baking trays. Prick the centre of each round with a fork, then chill for 15 minutes.

Preheat the oven to 180°C/160°C fan/gas 4 while the biscuits are chilling.

Bake the biscuits for 15–20 minutes or until lightly golden around the edges. Remove from the oven and turn it down to 120°C/100°C fan/gas ½. Leave the shortbread to firm up on the trays for a few minutes before transferring to a wire rack to cool. Once cold, keep in an airtight container until ready to use.

To make your meringues, weigh the sugar into a bowl. Put the egg whites into a large metal or ceramic bowl (if you are using a hand-held electric whisk) or the bowl of a free-standing mixer. Whisk the whites on a slow-to-medium speed for about 20 seconds, then increase the speed to medium and whisk until the whites form stiff peaks and the bowl can be turned upside down without them slipping out. Increase the speed and gradually add the sugar, a teaspoon at a time. Keep whisking until the meringue is thick and shiny.

Fill the piping bag with the meringue. Dab a little of the remaining meringue from the side of the bowl on to the corners of a sheet of baking parchment, to act like glue, then place it meringue-side down on a baking tray.

CONTINUED OVERLEAF >>

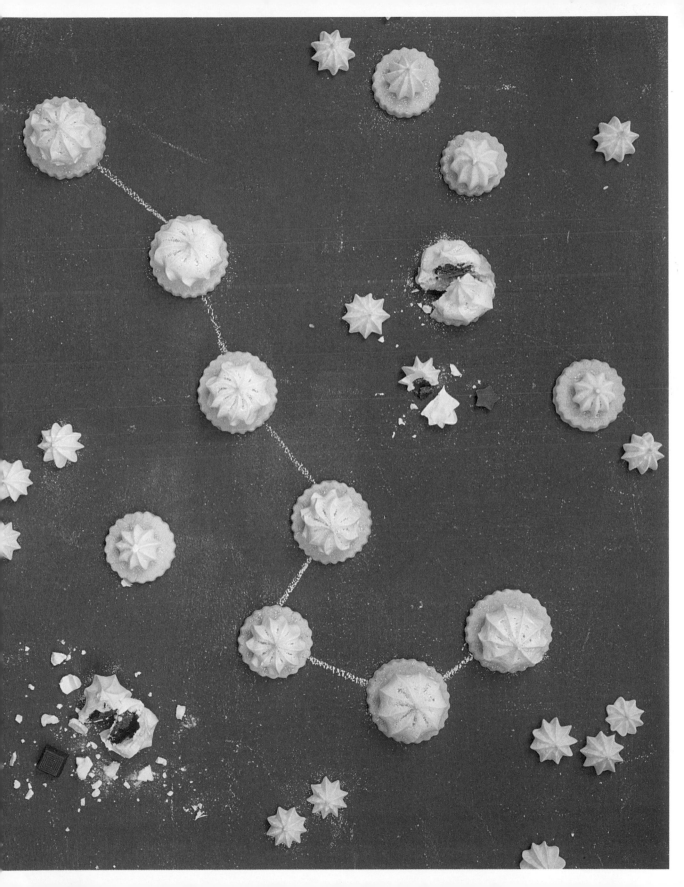

MIDNIGHT MUNCHIES
& HIDDEN GEM STARS (CONTINUED)

Use a little more leftover meringue to stick the 12 chocolate-coated caramel and biscuit sweets on to one half of the parchment-lined tray, evenly spaced. Hold the piping bag directly over a sweet and gently but firmly squeeze the bag to fully encase the sweet in meringue, pulling it up to a point as you lift the bag away. Repeat to cover all the sweets.

Use a little more leftover meringue to stick the 12 chocolate-coated stars on to the other half of the baking tray, flat side down and evenly spaced (depending on the size of your baking tray, you might need to use two). Repeat the piping process over the stars to cover all of them with meringue.

Lightly sprinkle your meringues with edible silver and gold glitter, if you like, so they sparkle. Bake for 1–1½ hours or until the meringues can be peeled off the parchment without sticking. Turn off the oven. Leave the meringues in the oven to cool and crisp up for several hours, ideally overnight. (Don't worry if any of the caramel from the sweets has leaked out during baking: once cooled, you can easily peel it off or wrap it back under the sweet.) >>

Melt the chocolate in a microwave or a heatproof bowl set over a pan of simmering water (bain-marie). Use the paintbrush to dab melted chocolate on to the centre of each shortbread round. Allow to cool slightly before placing the meringues on top – the smaller meringues on the smaller shortbread bases and the larger meringues on the larger bases. Leave to set.

I love to display these on a slate board with extra meringue stars placed amongst them. You can even use chalk to draw constellations on the slate, joining the meringues together.

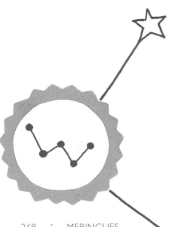

FILLINGS & TOPPINGS

● ● ● ● ● ● ● ◆ ● ● ● ● ◆ ● ● ◆ ● ◆ ● ● ● ● ● ● ● ● ◆ ● ● ● ● ● ● ● ● ● ● ● ●

I like to see these as the paints, gouaches and glazes that can elevate a plain canvas of cake or biscuit into a feast for the eyes and tastebuds. Berry-bright jams, velvety buttercreams and edible confetti toppings – the varying tones, tastes and textures can provide you and your bakes with a fabulous palette to play with. To customise your own bakes with the right quantities of buttercream, Chantilly cream, sweetened mascarpone cream or ganache, follow these guidelines:

10cm cake: 35–50g for filling, the same for topping
15cm cake: 100–150g for each
20cm round cake: 200–250g for each
20cm square cake: 250–300g for each
23cm cake: 250–300g for each
25cm cake: 300–350g for each
900g (2lb) loaf cake: 200–250g for topping
Mini muffin: 5–10g for topping
Muffin or cupcake: 25–50g for topping

STRAWBERRY JAM

MAKES ABOUT 375G

FOR THE JAM
250g strawberries
250g caster sugar
Juice of 1 lemon

This is a particularly fruity preserve. It includes the juice of a whole lemon, which helps set the jam and also lifts the flavour of the berries. You can replace some of the strawberries with raspberries for a 'very berry' jam, and you can even make the jam with frozen fruit. In the past, when jamming was a way to preserve large gluts of homegrown fruit, big batches were the norm. These days, when fresh berries can actually be very pricey, it's nice to be able to cook up a small quantity, which is what I've done here.

Hull your strawberries and cut them into small pieces. Put them in a large, deep, heavy-based saucepan. Add the sugar, then place a sieve over the pan, to catch any pips, and squeeze in the lemon juice. Stir everything together. Cover the pan and leave to macerate overnight. The next morning you will discover a pool of fruit and syrupy juice.

Sterilise your jam jar(s) by washing them in very hot, soapy water and drying in a low oven, or by putting them through a very hot dishwasher cycle. Keep the jar(s) warm.

Put a saucer in the fridge to chill (unless you are going to test for set with a sugar thermometer).

Stir the berry mixture again before setting the pan on a medium heat. Stir gently for about 2 minutes or until all the sugar has dissolved, then increase the heat and bring the mixture up to the boil. Boil rapidly for 8 minutes (don't stir during this time). Skim off any frothy scum from the surface of the jam. Remove from the heat.

Drip a little of the jam on to the cold saucer. Return it to the fridge and leave for a couple of minutes, then push the jam on the saucer with your finger: if the surface crinkles, the jam is ready. If it doesn't crinkle, return the pan of jam to the heat and boil for few more minutes before testing again. If you have a sugar thermometer, the setting point for jam is around 105°C.

When the jam is ready, pour it into your clean jar(s) and seal immediately. Leave to cool completely before labelling and storing in the fridge or a cool, dark place. Once opened, keep in the fridge for up to a month.

VARIATION

Raspberry jam Replace the strawberries with raspberries. Don't worry about chopping them, just combine with the sugar and lemon juice. Boil the jam for 5 minutes before taking it off the heat and testing for set.

LEMON CURD

MAKES ABOUT 350G

FOR THE CURD
100g caster sugar
100g butter, roughly chopped
2 lemons
4 egg yolks (at room
  temperature)

Made with egg yolks, not whole eggs, my curds have a vibrant colour and punchy citrus hit. The lack of egg white also reduces the risk of any little lumps being left in your mixture. Using equal quantities of butter and sugar produces a luxuriously rich and creamy base, which beautifully complements the sharpness of the citrus.

Sterilise your jam jar(s) by washing them in very hot, soapy water and drying in a low oven, or by putting them through a very hot dishwasher cycle. Keep the jar(s) warm.

Using a set of digital scales, weigh the sugar and butter into a large, heatproof glass bowl. Grate the zest from the lemons into the bowl, then place a sieve over it, to catch any pips, and squeeze in the juice of both lemons. Finally, add the egg yolks.

Set the bowl over a pan of simmering water. Using a balloon whisk, whisk the mixture for a few minutes until the butter has melted, then continue whisking for 5–7 minutes or until the curd has thickened slightly and looks like a thin custard – it will continue to thicken as it cools. Constant whisking helps lighten the finished curd, as well as keeping the mixture moving in the bowl, preventing overheating, which can lead to curdling.

Remove the bowl from the pan. Pour the curd into your warm jar(s) and seal immediately, then label. Store in the fridge and consume within 1–2 weeks.

VARIATION

Orange curd Use the grated zest of 2 oranges, the juice of 1 orange and the juice of 1 lemon (the lemon juice prevents the orange curd from tasting too sickly sweet). The curd will need a few more minutes on the heat to thicken.

BUTTERCREAM

MAKES ABOUT 300G:
ENOUGH TO FILL AND
TOP A 15CM ROUND CAKE
OR TO TOP 12 CUPCAKES

FOR THE BUTTERCREAM
100g butter, softened
200g icing sugar, sifted
1 tbsp whole milk
1 tsp vanilla extract

I see this as a sort of a creamy cement with which to build my bakes: it's so useful for sandwiching and securing cakes and biscuits, and you can easily create flavoured variations. I love it best of all as the foundation for my Cream Cheese Buttercream (see opposite).

If you have a free-standing mixer, put all the ingredients into the bowl. Cover the bowl with a tea towel to prevent a cloud of sugar from escaping and start beating slowly. Increase the speed and beat until the mixture is fluffy, creamy and almost white, stopping a few times to scrape down the sides of the bowl. I beat for up to 10 minutes at full speed to create a really light finish.

If you're using a hand-held electric whisk, beat the butter in a medium bowl until soft and pale, then sift the icing sugar into the bowl in batches, working in the sugar with a spoon. Add the milk and vanilla, and beat at full speed until the buttercream is really light and fluffy.

VARIATIONS

Lemon buttercream Instead of vanilla, add the finely grated zest of 1 lemon and 1 tablespoon of lemon juice. If you want a completely smooth buttercream, replace the zest with 1 teaspoon of lemon extract.

Orange buttercream Instead of vanilla, add the finely grated zest of 1 orange and 1 tablespoon of orange juice. For a completely smooth buttercream, replace the zest with 1 teaspoon of orange extract. As an optional extra, you could also add a few drops of orange blossom water.

Coffee buttercream Instead of vanilla, add 1 teaspoon of coffee extract, or 1 tablespoon of instant coffee dissolved in 1 tablespoon of hot water and cooled.

Fruity buttercream Instead of vanilla, add 1 tablespoon of lemon juice and 1 tablespoon of sifted freeze-dried fruit powder, such as raspberry. As an optional extra, you could also add a few drops of lavender extract, rose water or orange blossom water.

Chocolate buttercream Add 50g melted, cooled dark chocolate to the basic buttercream at the end. Or, for a really rich and indulgent chocolate buttercream, stir in 150g dark or milk chocolate Ganache (see p.279) – this should have a similar consistency to the finished buttercream. For a quick, chocolate hazelnut buttercream, stir in 150g chocolate hazelnut spread. >>

Cream cheese buttercream This is a fresher-tasting, less sweet alternative to classic buttercream. Essentially, you need to add about half the weight of full-fat cream cheese to whatever weight of basic buttercream you have made – i.e. 150g cream cheese for the 300g quantity of buttercream in this recipe – or, for a lighter, sharper, more loose-textured buttercream, add the same weight of cream cheese (i.e. 300g here). Beat the cream cheese into the buttercream at the end, and beat for another minute but not much more. If overworked, it can slacken and split, especially if you are making a 50:50 buttercream/cream cheese mix.

CHANTILLY CREAM

MAKES ABOUT 100G:
ENOUGH TO FILL AND
TOP A 10CM ROUND CAKE

FOR THE CREAM
100ml double cream
Few drops of vanilla extract
    (or another extract) or
    1 tbsp liqueur
1 tbsp icing sugar

This sweetened, vanilla-laced cream is a classic. Vanilla is the traditional flavouring but you can add other extracts or even liqueurs.

Place the cream and extract in a bowl and sift over the icing sugar. Whip with a hand-held electric whisk until the cream will hold soft peaks. It's important not to overbeat at this stage because the cream will stiffen further when it is spread or piped.

VARIATIONS
For creams with crunch, fold through a handful of broken meringue, chopped or ground caramelised nuts, smashed chocolate bars or biscuits once the cream has reached soft peak stage.

SWEETENED MASCARPONE CREAM

MAKES ABOUT 100G:
ENOUGH TO FILL AND
TOP A 10CM ROUND CAKE

FOR THE CREAM

100g mascarpone

Few drops of vanilla extract
(or another extract) or
1 tbsp liqueur

1 tbsp icing sugar

A splash of milk or cream,
if needed

Mascarpone makes a good topping or filling for a cake, being thicker than whipped cream and able to hold its shape for longer. Mixing mascarpone with double cream (to make what I like to call maschilly) gives you an even more luscious mix. And you can also combine mascarpone with jam, curd, caramel or ganache to create a whole medley of mascarpone variations.

Put the mascarpone and extract in a bowl and sift over the icing sugar. Whisk together with a hand-held electric whisk until the mixture holds soft peaks, adding just a splash of milk or cream to loosen if necessary. It's important not to overbeat as the mascarpone may slacken too much. If this happens, put the bowl in the fridge and leave to firm up.

VARIATIONS

Flavoured mascarpone cream A whole assortment of toppings and fillings can be created by combining mascarpone with jam, curd, caramel sauce or ganache. The formula is simple: just add half the weight of your chosen sweet treat to mascarpone – i.e. 50g raspberry jam or lemon curd to 100g mascarpone. Beat together until soft and creamy but avoid overbeating. If the mascarpone slackens too much, chill until it firms up. You can also add a few drops of an extract or flower water to enhance the flavour – rose water with raspberry jam and orange blossom water with orange curd are two of my favourites.

Maschilly cream This somewhat bilingual baking affair unites France's Chantilly cream and Italy's luxurious mascarpone in sweet harmony. The two together create a stable filling for cakes, where cream alone might split and collapse. Maschilly is also a handy accompaniment to puddings and sweet treats. Use 50g mascarpone and 50ml double cream with the vanilla and icing sugar, and follow the method above.

GANACHE

MAKES ABOUT 275G: ENOUGH
TO FILL AND TOP A 15CM
ROUND CAKE

FOR THE GANACHE
100g dark chocolate
1 tbsp golden syrup
1 tsp vanilla extract, optional
150ml double cream

Ganache is simply a combination of chocolate and cream (I add syrup too, for extra gloss). It can be poured over a cake when still liquid or left to thicken and then spread or piped as a topping. It can also be whipped to make a lighter mousse-like filling.

Chop the chocolate into small pieces. Place in a heatproof bowl with the golden syrup and vanilla extract, if using. Heat the cream in a saucepan over a medium heat. As soon as it starts coming to the boil, pour the hot cream over the chocolate and leave to soften and melt for a minute or two. Stir until the chocolate is completely melted and the mixture is smooth and shiny. If some of the chocolate is reluctant to melt, set the bowl over a pan of simmering water (bain-marie) or heat briefly in a microwave.

If you are using the ganache as a pourable glaze, it needs to be still warm and liquid. In this case, have the cake set on a wire rack over a sheet of foil or baking parchment so you can scrape up the excess ganache and re-use it. To ensure a really smooth finish, apply an initial, thin coating of ganache (or buttercream) to the cake and let it set completely before pouring on the ganache glaze – the coating will even out the cake's surface as well as trapping any crumbs that would spoil the finished glaze.

If you want the ganache to have a spreadable, truffle-like consistency, leave it to cool (you may need to let it firm up a little in the fridge).

VARIATIONS

Very dark chocolate ganache (extra bitter and firm) Reduce the cream to 100ml.

Semi-sweet milk chocolate ganache Replace the dark chocolate with 100g milk chocolate, omit the golden syrup and reduce the quantity of cream to 100ml.

Firm white or milk chocolate ganache Replace the dark chocolate with 150g white chocolate or milk chocolate, omit the golden syrup and reduce the quantity of cream to 100ml.

Creamy white or milk chocolate ganache Replace the dark chocolate with 100g white chocolate or milk chocolate, omit the golden syrup and reduce the quantity of cream to 100ml.

Chocolate orange, peppermint or coffee ganache Use an orange-, mint- or coffee-flavoured chocolate, or add orange, peppermint or coffee extract in addition to vanilla.

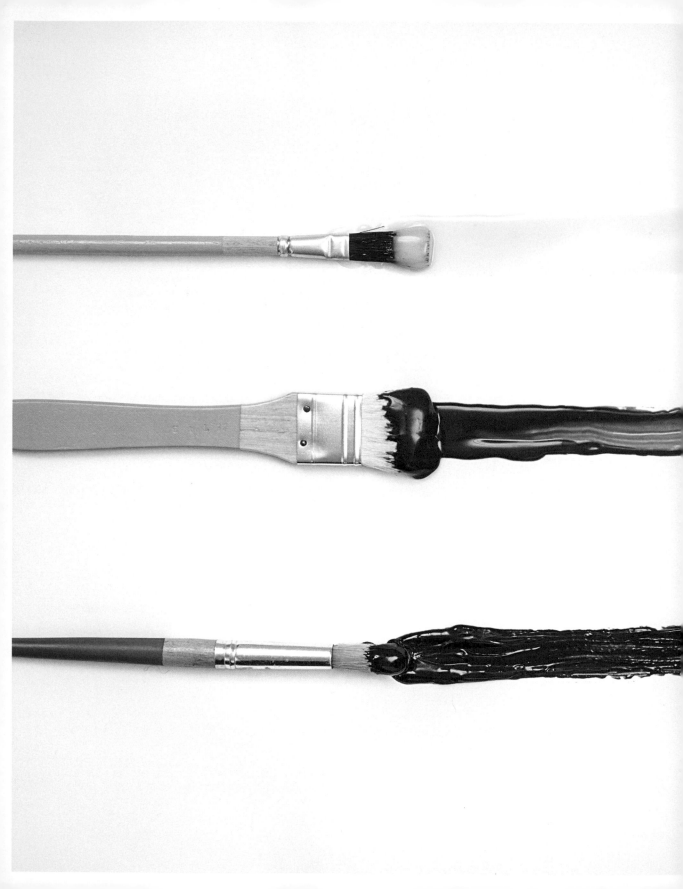

FLAVOURED SYRUP

MAKES ABOUT 200ML

FOR THE SYRUP

100g caster sugar

100ml liquid, such as water or juice (see variations)

1 tsp–1 tbsp flavouring, such as an extract or liqueur (see variations), optional

Flavoured sugar syrups are simple to make, and brushing them over a bake is a quick way to add extra flavour. Poured into attractive bottles or jars, they also make lovely gifts – like perfumes for the store cupboard. The syrups will keep for a couple of weeks if sealed and stored in the fridge.

Put the sugar and water or juice in a pan over a medium heat and bring to the boil, stirring to help dissolve the sugar. Reduce the heat and simmer gently for about 2 minutes or until the sugar has completely dissolved and you have a clear syrup. Remove from the heat and stir in the flavouring. Pour into a sterilised bottle or jar (see p.272) while still hot, then seal and leave to cool.

VARIATIONS

Vanilla syrup Stir 1 tablespoon of vanilla extract into the syrup.

Lemon syrup Use 100g caster sugar and 100ml lemon juice; stir in 1 tablespoon of limoncello at the end, if you like.

Lemon & lavender syrup Use 100g lavender sugar (or caster sugar) and 100ml lemon juice; stir in 1 teaspoon of lavender extract at the end if you haven't used lavender sugar, plus 1 tablespoon of limoncello, if you like.

Orange syrup Use 100g caster sugar and 100ml orange juice; stir in 1 tablespoon of Grand Marnier or orange blossom water at the end.

Coffee syrup Put 1 tablespoon of instant coffee in a pan and add 100ml boiling water. Stir to dissolve the coffee granules, then add 100g caster sugar. Set the pan on the heat and continue as the basic method above; stir in 1 tablespoon of Tia Maria at the end, if you like.

FLAVOURED SUGAR

Apart from adding more flavour, depth and interest to your bakes, jams and desserts, flavoured sugars are a perfect gift. They can be made in an instant, but are best kept for a month in an airtight jar before using, to allow the flavours time to develop. It helps to give the jars a shake every so often during this time to redistribute the contents. I use caster sugar – sometimes golden caster sugar – as the base.

Vanilla sugar Add 1 split-open vanilla pod to 500g caster or golden caster sugar.

Citrus sugar Add the finely grated zest of 1 orange or lemon or 2 limes to 500g caster sugar. Stir the zest through the sugar.

Lavender sugar Add 1 teaspoon of dried or 1 tablespoon of fresh lavender flowers to every 100g caster sugar. Stir well. When you come to use the sugar, you can sift out the lavender flowers, then use them to flavour more sugar. Lavender sugar is beautiful paired with raspberries when making jam, or with lemons for a fragrant Lemon Curd (see p.273).

Cinnamon sugar Add 1 teaspoon of ground cinnamon to every 100g caster or golden caster sugar. Stir well. I like to put a cinnamon stick into the jar as well to enhance and highlight the flavour. Cinnamon sugar makes a delicious alternative to plain white or golden caster in butter biscuits and shortbread (see p.206 and p.222).

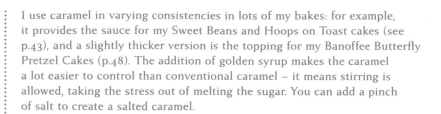

CARAMEL SAUCE

MAKES ABOUT 175ML

FOR THE CARAMEL
50g golden syrup
50g caster sugar
100ml double cream
Pinch of salt, optional

I use caramel in varying consistencies in lots of my bakes: for example, it provides the sauce for my Sweet Beans and Hoops on Toast cakes (see p.43), and a slightly thicker version is the topping for my Banoffee Butterfly Pretzel Cakes (p.48). The addition of golden syrup makes the caramel a lot easier to control than conventional caramel – it means stirring is allowed, taking the stress out of melting the sugar. You can add a pinch of salt to create a salted caramel.

Using digital scales, weigh the golden syrup into a medium saucepan. Sprinkle the sugar over the surface of the syrup. Set the pan over a medium heat and stir with a silicone spatula or wooden spoon until the sugar has dissolved, then simmer gently, stirring constantly, as the caramel bubbles.

When it reaches a rich amber colour, remove the pan from the heat and pour in the cream (be careful as it will steam and bubble). Stir until everything is fully combined and smooth. Stir in the salt if using. If you find there are bits of sugar that have formed into toffee pieces, set the pan back on the heat and stir to melt these into the sauce. Don't heat it for too long, though, or the caramel will thicken up.

Pour the caramel into a sterilised jar (see p.272) and leave to cool before sealing with a lid. It will keep for a few days at room temperature or for several weeks in the fridge. Before using, leave it at room temperature to regain a pouring consistency, or warm slightly in the microwave or by sitting the jar in a pan of hot water.

VARIATIONS

Spreadable caramel Use 50g golden syrup, 50g caster sugar and 50ml double cream, plus a pinch of salt, if using.

Chewy caramel Use 50g golden syrup, 50g caster sugar and 25ml double cream. Remove from the heat and stir through a pinch of salt, if using. Leave to cool.

HONEYCOMB

MAKES 125G

FOR THE HONEYCOMB
50g golden syrup or honey
100g caster sugar
1 tsp bicarbonate of soda

EQUIPMENT
15cm round tin

This is so simple to make and satisfyingly sweet to eat. You can stick to the traditional golden syrup or use honey instead, for a fully authentic 'honey'comb. Shards of honeycomb add texture and dimension to bakes or served alongside them, while splinters of meringue and honeycomb together are a delicious addition to many desserts. Dip shards of honeycomb into melted dark chocolate to make your own irresistible honeycomb bites that can be used in my Crunchie Cake (see p.132).

Take a 30cm square piece of baking parchment and crumple it up, then open it out again (this makes it easier to manipulate). Use it to line the tin, pressing the paper over the base and up the sides.

Using digital scales, measure the golden syrup or honey into a small saucepan. Add the sugar and stir to combine, then set the pan over a gentle heat and warm for a few minutes until the sugar has dissolved, stirring occasionally. Turn up the heat and gently swirl the syrup around in the pan until it bubbles to a golden amber colour.

Remove from the heat and whisk in the bicarbonate of soda – the syrup will billow and foam up into a frothy mass. Pour into the prepared tin and leave to set and harden. Once set, bash or break the honeycomb into shards.

FLAVOURED MARZIPAN

MAKES ABOUT 230G

FOR THE MARZIPAN

1 egg yolk (about 15g) or ½ egg
  white (about 17g), at room
  temperature
1 tsp extract or honey (see
  variations)
1 tsp flavouring, such as the juice
  of 1 lemon (see variations)
100g ground almonds or other
  nuts, or desiccated coconut
  (see variations)
100g icing sugar

If you think you don't like marzipan, please reconsider. My homemade version doesn't contain the traditional bitter almond extract (though of course you can add it if you like), so it has only a mild, sweetly nutty flavour, rather than a pungent 'amaretti biscuit' kick. Ground almonds are traditional but you can use a variety of other ground nuts, or even ground desiccated coconut (which produces a slightly less pliable marzipan). You'll need to grind other nuts or coconut finely, in batches, using a spice grinder, small food processor, mini chopper or Nutribullet to reach a similar consistency to ground almonds. I find that rolling out marzipan between two sheets of clingfilm or baking parchment works a dream and does away with the need for a surface dusted with extra icing sugar. A medium 60g egg gives about 15g yolk and 35g white (the rest of the weight is the shell).

Place the egg yolk or white in a medium bowl and add any wet ingredients, such as extracts or honey and flavouring. Then add any zest, fruit powder or spices (see below). Mix into a paste.

Sift in the ground almonds, or other nuts or coconut, and the icing sugar. Start mixing with a spoon, then bring the mix together into a ball with your hands. At the beginning, it may seem that the mixture is too dry, but keep going and it will draw together like pastry. You can use the marzipan straight away or keep it, wrapped in clingfilm or in a sandwich bag, in the fridge for 2–3 weeks.

VARIATIONS

Orange blossom marzipan This variation can be used to make marzipan bees that decorate my Honey Bee Bites (see p.194). Follow the basic method above, mixing 1 egg yolk with 1 teaspoon of orange blossom water, 1 teaspoon of orange blossom honey and the finely grated zest of 2 oranges to make a paste before sifting in 100g each of ground almonds and icing sugar. Makes about 230g.

Raspberry marzipan This can be used to make berry shapes or other decorations, such as balls of wool or buttons for my Knit One, Bake One Cake (see p.152). Follow the basic method above, mixing 1 egg yolk or ½ egg white with 3 tablespoons (15g) of sifted freeze-dried raspberry (or strawberry) powder, ½ teaspoon of lemon juice, ½ teaspoon of rose water and the finely grated zest of ½ lemon to make a paste, before sifting in 50g ground almonds or ground desiccated coconut and 50g icing sugar. Makes about 140g. >>

Pistachio marzipan I like to use this marzipan to create peas for my Fish & Chip Cakes (see p.34). It can also be used to make leaves: roll it out between two sheets of clingfilm to the thickness of a 50-pence piece and cut out leaves with a variety of cutters; let the leaves firm up slightly before using. Follow the basic method opposite, mixing 1 egg yolk or ½ egg white with 1 teaspoon of honey, 1 teaspoon of lime juice and the finely grated zest of 1 lime to make a paste, before sifting in 100g each of ground pistachios (see directory, p.307) and icing sugar. For a pure pistachio flavour, eliminate the zest. Makes about 230g.

Coconut marzipan A great alternative to traditional white fondant icing, I make snowballs, snowflakes and stars from this for my Winter Wonderland Cake (see p.124). Follow the basic method opposite, mixing ½ egg white with 2 teaspoons of lemon juice before sifting in 100g each of ground desiccated coconut and icing sugar. Coconut marzipan stiffens up more quickly than the almond version, so make the shapes as soon as it's mixed; if it does get too hard, warm it slightly in a microwave or by putting it in a sealed sandwich bag and immersing in a bowl of warm water. Makes about 230g.

Strawberry coconut marzipan I use this for the ears on my White Rabbit Cakes (see p.66). Follow the basic method opposite, mixing ½ egg white with 2 teaspoons of lemon juice and 1 teaspoon of sifted freeze-dried strawberry powder to make a paste, before sifting in 100g each of ground desiccated coconut and icing sugar. Makes about 230g.

Terracotta marzipan This marzipan is used to make the 'pot' in my Hidden Carrot Cake (see p.76). Follow the basic method opposite, mixing 1 egg yolk with 1 teaspoon of orange blossom water, 1 teaspoon of orange blossom honey, the finely grated zest of 1 orange, a dab of orange food colouring (such as Sugarflair tangerine/apricot colour paste; see directory, p.308) and 1 teaspoon of ground cinnamon to make a paste, before sifting in 100g each of ground almonds and icing sugar. To create a more orange marzipan, leave out the cinnamon. Makes about 230g.

PINEAPPLE FLOWERS

MAKES ABOUT 25 FLOWERS

FOR THE FLOWERS
1 large or medium pineapple

EQUIPMENT
1 regular or mini-muffin tin

These make gorgeous decorations for cakes – either individually on cupcakes or in a cluster on a celebration cake alongside marzipan bees and berries (see photograph on p.104). After storage, if you find your pineapple flowers (or other dried fruit or vegetable decorations) have returned to a slightly soft state, put them in the oven on a very low heat to dry out again.

Preheat the oven to 120°C/100°C fan/gas ½. Lay some doubled-up sheets of kitchen paper on your work surface.

Place the pineapple on its side on a chopping board and slice off the base and top. Stand it upright and, using a sharp serrated knife such as a bread knife, cut down all around it to slice off the rind. Remove the 'eyes' from the pineapple with the tip of a small sharp knife.

Lay the pineapple on its side again and cut it across into slices about 2mm thick. Spread these out on the kitchen paper. Place more kitchen paper on top of them and press down gently so the excess juice will be absorbed. You can repeat this blotting process with more kitchen paper if your pineapple is very juicy.

Line a baking tray with baking parchment. Lay five or six of the pineapple slices side by side on the tray, then slide them, still on the sheet of parchment, off the tray and directly on to the oven shelf. Repeat with the remaining pineapple slices on more parchment sheets.

Bake for about 1 hour or until dried out but not brittle, flipping the slices over after 30 minutes to prevent them from sticking to the parchment too much. Remove them from the oven while they are still flexible enough to bend and push them gently into the holes of a muffin tin to shape them into flowers. A regular muffin tin will produce more open-looking blooms; mini-muffin tins will create tighter flowerheads. If your slices are cut from a medium pineapple, they may fit best in a mini-muffin tin. Put them back in the oven and leave for 15–30 minutes to dry out fully and set into the flower shape. If you leave them in the oven overnight, with the oven door ajar, they will develop a really deep golden colour. Store in an airtight container for up to 5 days.

VARIATION

Pineapple sunflowers Once cooled, dab the centres of the dried flowers with honey to act as 'glue', then cover with poppy seeds.

STRAWBERRY HEARTS

MAKES ABOUT 25 HEARTS

FOR THE HEARTS
150g medium strawberries

These beautiful hearts are used to decorate my shortbread Strawberry Hearts (see p.224). Strawberries are best dried out at a low temperature, either in the oven or in a dehydrator (see directory, p.309). If the heat is too high, the colour and flavour of the fruit will be lost as the natural sugars caramelise.

Preheat the oven to 120°C/100°C fan/gas ½. Lay some doubled-up sheets of kitchen paper on your work surface.

Hull your strawberries and cut lengthways into slices the thickness of a £1 coin (you can dry the end bits too for mini hearts). Spread them out on the kitchen paper. Place more kitchen paper on top of the strawberry slices and press down gently so the excess juice will be absorbed.

Line a baking tray with baking parchment (one tray should be big enough). Lay the strawberry slices side by side on the tray, then slide them, still on the sheet of parchment, off the tray and directly on to the oven shelf. Dry out for 1–1¼ hours or until no longer damp. Near the end of the drying time, carefully release the strawberries from the parchment and flip them over to dry out the reverse surface.

Remove from the oven and leave to cool on the parchment, set back on the tray again. If you like, use a pair of scissors to snip into the top of each strawberry slice to give a more pronounced heart shape. Store in an airtight container in a cool, dark place for 2 weeks.

BEETROOT HEARTS

MAKES ABOUT 50 HEARTS

FOR THE HEARTS
150g vacuum-packed, plain
    cooked beetroot (without
    vinegar or other flavourings)
Icing sugar to dust, optional

EQUIPMENT
4cm heart-shaped cutter (see
    directory, p.308)

Beetroot has such incredible colour, and very thin, dried slices will add
a natural but striking finish to many bakes (as photographed on p.142). The
beetroot shade of purplish-red makes it perfect for heart shapes – which also
bear a resemblance to rose petals, thus ideal for Valentine and floral-themed
cakes. I use white parchment to line the baking tray because the stain from
the beetroot hearts creates a lovely pattern on the paper – this can then
be used as gift wrapping or to decorate bespoke cards. You can also use
a dehydrator, if you have one (see directory, p.309).

Preheat the oven to 120°C/100°C fan/gas ½. Lay some doubled-up sheets of
kitchen paper on your work surface.

Trim off the top and bottom of your beetroots to create flat ends. Next cut
each beetroot horizontally into two or three thick slices, depending on their
size. Use the cutter to cut a heart shape from each beetroot slice. (Keep the
beetroot trimmings to add to a salad, or use them to make the purée for my
Heart Beet Cake on p.142.) With a sharp knife or a mandoline, cut the hearts
into very thin slices (about 2mm).

Spread out the thin heart slices on the kitchen paper. Place more kitchen paper
on top and press down gently so the excess beetroot juice will be absorbed.
You can repeat this blotting process with more kitchen paper if necessary.

Line a large baking tray with baking parchment (one tray should be big
enough). Carefully peel back the top layer of kitchen paper from the beetroot
hearts. If you want them to be sweeter-tasting, lightly dust with sifted icing
sugar, then transfer them to the tray, laying them side by side. Slide them, still
on the sheet of parchment, directly on to the oven shelf. Dry out for 1–1¼ hours
or until crisp and slightly reduced in size. Near the end of the drying time,
carefully release the hearts from the parchment and flip over to dry out the
reverse surface.

Remove from the oven and leave the hearts to cool on the parchment, set on
the baking tray again. Store in an airtight container for up to a month.

VARIATION

Mango hearts These can be made in the same way as beetroot hearts. Choose
a not-too-ripe mango and peel it, then cut the flesh into 2cm-thick slabs or
cubes. Cut out heart shapes using a 4cm or 2.5cm cutter, then slice these
thinly. Continue with the method above, blotting the thin hearts and then
drying them (omit the optional dusting of icing sugar).

BANANA BUTTONS

MAKES ABOUT 50 BUTTONS

FOR THE BUTTONS
2 medium-sized, medium-ripe
   bananas

EQUIPMENT
2.5cm round cutter, or small
   cutters of other shapes,
   optional

I have always had an affection for banana chips – the hard, crunchy type –
and use them to add texture to my bakes. But I also love homemade buttons,
which are chewier and pure banana through and through, as used in my
Banana Button Bites (see p.55). I find it best to use medium-ripe bananas,
as these create a more toffee-coloured finish. When I say ripe, though,
I don't mean black. You want banana buttons with chew rather than goo!
An average small banana will create about 15 buttons, a medium banana
will give you 25 and a large one 30.

Preheat the oven to 120°C/100°C fan/gas ½. Line a baking tray with baking
parchment (one tray should be big enough).

Cut your bananas into slices about the thickness of a £1 coin and spread out
on the lined tray. If you want your buttons to be all the same size, cut out
circles from the banana slices using a small round cutter or the wider end
from a large metal piping nozzle. (If you are making these for snacking, you
can exert a little less banana discipline.) You could also cut the banana slices
into stars, hearts or squares.

Carefully slide the banana buttons, still on the parchment, off the baking tray
and directly on to the oven shelf. Dry out for 1¼–1½ hours or until slightly
reduced in size; they should be chewy, not brittle. Remove from the oven and
leave to cool on the parchment, set on the baking tray again, or cool in the
turned-off oven with the door ajar, which will increase their toffee colour.
Alternatively, you can use a dehydrator (see directory, p.309).

Once cooled, transfer the buttons to an airtight container and store
somewhere cool and dark. They will keep for up to a month.

DRIED RHUBARB

FOR THE RHUBARB SLICES

Well-coloured stalks of rhubarb
(each 5cm length – weighing
15–20g – will make about
15–20 slices)
Icing sugar to dust

Thin slices of dried rhubarb add a tart tang and rosy colour to my Edible Confetti for spring (see opposite). Use rhubarb that's as pink and as broad in diameter as possible because, once dried, the slices shrink significantly.

Preheat the oven to 120°C/100°C fan/gas ½. (You can also use a dehydrator, if you have one; see directory, p.309.)

Lay some doubled-up sheets of kitchen paper on your work surface and dust with icing sugar. Cut your rhubarb stalks into thin slices. Spread these out on the kitchen paper and dust with more icing sugar. Leave it to soak in.

Line a large baking tray with baking parchment. Transfer the rhubarb slices to the tray in one layer, then slide the parchment off the tray directly on to the oven shelf. Dry for 45 minutes–1 hour or until crisp to the touch. Remove from the oven and leave to cool on the parchment, or in the turned-off oven with the door ajar. Store in an airtight container somewhere cool for up to a month.

DRIED CITRUS ZEST

FOR THE CITRUS SLIVERS

Limes, lemons or oranges –
preferably unwaxed

Little slivers of zest add a sharp and mouthwatering zing to my Edible Confetti mixes (see opposite). They can also be added to citrus sugar for an extra layer of flavour (see p.283). If you have a dehydrator, you can use it to dry the zest (see directory, p.309).

Preheat the oven to 120°C/100°C fan/gas ½.

If not using unwaxed fruit, wash and dry the limes, lemons or oranges, then pare off the zest – without taking any of the white pith – using either a sharp knife or vegetable peeler. Line a baking tray with baking parchment. Spread out the zest on the tray, then slide the parchment off the tray directly on to the oven shelf. Bake for 45 minutes–1 hour or until fully dried out. Cool, then cut the zest into 1mm slivers with a sharp knife or scissors. Keep in an airtight container for up to a month.

EDIBLE CONFETTI

These natural hundreds and thousands add a striking and tasty touch to many bakes, such as my Confetti Cupcakes (see p.104) and Chocolate Forest Cake (p.135). They look equally beautiful in jars, and could be given as gifts. You can celebrate the seasons with the different colour and flavour combinations, from summery pistachio, raspberry and pineapple to autumnal apple, blackberry and hazelnut.

You can dry some of the fruit yourself (either in the oven or in a dehydrator if you have one; see directory, p.309) or buy it from a specialist supplier (see directory, p.307, for the freeze-dried berries and pineapple and apple crisp pieces). I have even been known to pull out the freeze-dried fruit from a box of granola! The nuts, seeds and other ingredients, such as crystallised ginger pieces, can be sourced from most supermarkets, healthfood shops and online stockists (see directory, p.307).

To give your confetti an extra special appearance, you can add touches of gold leaf. Use a fine paintbrush to paint a little golden syrup or honey on to the tips of a few of the nuts or seeds, then carefully press them on to some gold leaf. Leave your gilded ingredients to set before mixing into the medley.

The flavours and colours are at their best when the confetti is just made, although – depending on the mixture of fruit and their moisture content – it can be kept for up to a month in an airtight container. Because of this, I recommend making the confetti mixtures in small batches – for example, just enough to fill a 70ml Kilner jar.

MARZIPAN TEALIGHTS

MAKES 15 TEALIGHTS

FOR THE TEALIGHTS
500g natural marzipan
15 toasted flaked almonds
  or about 1 tsp desiccated
  coconut
Sheet of edible gold leaf (see
  directory, p.307)
Golden syrup or honey

EQUIPMENT
4cm round metal cutter,
  about 2cm deep
Fine paintbrush

Using shop-bought marzipan, these tealights are surprisingly quick and easy to create, and make unique cake decorations (see photograph on p.136) as well as edible gifts. I use a flaked almond to represent the flame (and give a nod to the main ingredient in marzipan). Alternatively, you can use a shred of desiccated coconut, toasted or untoasted, as a 'wick'. I sometimes do this and then place a handful of toasted, gold-flecked almond 'flames' alongside the tealights so people can 'light up' the confectionery candles themselves.

Roll out your marzipan to an even 1.75cm thickness, preferably between two sheets of baking parchment to prevent the marzipan from sticking. Peel off the top sheet of parchment and, using the cutter, cut out your marzipan discs. Pull up the surrounding marzipan and squash this up, then re-roll to cut a few more discs. Set the marzipan discs aside, on the parchment.

Lay the flaked almonds on a piece of foil or baking parchment and, with the paintbrush, apply a tiny dab of syrup or honey to the centre of each nut. Clean and dry your paintbrush, then use it to pick up gold leaf, a tiny bit at a time, and stick it on to the 'glue' on the almonds.

With the tip of a scalpel or sharp knife, press an indent a few millimetres deep into the centre of each marzipan disc and stick in your flaked almond (being carefully not to touch the gold leaf). Leave the marzipan to firm up before decorating or packaging up as a gift.

If you want to make coconut wicks instead, you can either toast the coconut lightly in a frying pan or leave it white. Choose six to ten of the longest coconut shreds. Using a cocktail stick, press an indent a few millimetres deep into the centre of each marzipan disc and stick in a coconut shred.

VARIATION
To add more sweetness and make your candles look very realistic, apply some melted white chocolate on top and down the sides of the tealights to create the appearance of melted wax.

WHITE CHOCOLATE CANDLES

MAKES 15 CANDLES

FOR THE CANDLES
50g white chocolate (without vanilla seeds), chopped into small pieces
About 1 tsp desiccated coconut

EQUIPMENT
Small disposable piping bag
5 drinking straws, 21cm long and ideally 7.5mm diameter, each cut into 3 equal pieces

These striking white candles are formed using ordinary plastic drinking straws as moulds (see photograph p.74). After lining the straws with baking parchment, you just fill up with melted white chocolate and leave to set, then push the 'candle' out of the straw. Coconut strands make very realistic-looking wicks. The straws I like best are straight, clear plastic ones, about 7.5mm in diameter; however, you can use other straws of larger diameters.

Boil the kettle. While waiting, put the white chocolate into the disposable piping bag and twist the end closed. Once the water has boiled, pour it into a jug and put the piping bag into it. Leave the chocolate to melt inside the bag. Once melted, remove the piping bag from the jug and wipe dry with a tea towel. Wait for the chocolate to firm up a little: you don't want to pipe it into the straws while it's still really runny or it will flood out again.

Meanwhile, line your cut-down drinking straws with baking parchment – the parchment will ensure that the candles can be pushed out of the straws without getting stuck. To line the straws, cut strips of parchment 10 x 7.5cm, then cut these down into 7.5 x 2.5cm strips. Wrap each strip around the end of a slim-handled paintbrush (or a drinking straw smaller in diameter than the ones you are using to create your candles) and slide inside a piece of straw. Gently pull out the paintbrush or smaller straw.

Once the chocolate has reached a paste-like consistency, snip the very tip off the piping bag so it will fit snugly inside your drinking straws. Pipe the chocolate into each piece of straw, filling it almost full. Lay flat to firm up.

While the candles are firming up, toast the desiccated coconut lightly in a frying pan (this makes the shreds look like wicks that have been alight). You can leave some of the coconut untoasted to create a mixture of candles.

Before the chocolate has fully set, carefully insert a coconut shred into the tip of each 'candle'. Leave the candles to set completely in the fridge. Remove them from the straws by pushing them out with the end of the paintbrush.

VARIATION
To add drips of 'melted wax', melt a little extra white chocolate and apply to the sides of the candles with a fine paintbrush or latte stirrer.

GINGERBREAD ACORNS

MAKES 40 ACORNS

FOR THE ACORNS
About 80g Basic Gingerbread
    dough (about ⅛ quantity;
    see p.238)
20 brazil nuts
50g dark chocolate, melted and
    cooled until thickened
    and not too runny

EQUIPMENT
Fine paintbrush

Part of my edible forest foliage, these acorns are used on my Chocolate Forest Cake (see p.135) and Tree Trunk Cakes (p.120). They make fantastic presents packed into jars with a collection of biscuit leaves.

Break the dough into 5g balls (you only need to weigh the first one or two, then you'll be able to judge them by eye). Roll each into a round-ended cylinder, 3cm long and 1.5cm thick. Place on a baking tray lined with baking parchment and chill for 15 minutes.

Preheat the oven to 180°C/160°C fan/gas 4 while the biscuits are chilling. Bake for 10–15 minutes or until deep golden. While still warm, cut each cylinder across in half to form two acorn caps, then leave to cool on the tray.

Cut your brazil nuts in half across the middle – these will form the acorns themselves. The nut pieces should be slightly longer than the gingerbread acorn caps, and the cut surfaces need to be as flat as possible to make it easy to join them to the caps. If your nuts still have a lot of dark skin on them, scrape some of it off with a small sharp knife. With the paintbrush, apply a dab of melted chocolate to the cut surface of each gingerbread acorn cap and press to the cut surface of a brazil nut half to form an acorn. Leave to set.

BISCUIT LEAVES

MAKES 15 LARGE (4–5CM),
15 MEDIUM (3CM) AND
15 SMALL (2.5CM) LEAVES

FOR THE LEAVES
About 165g Basic Butter Biscuits
    or Basic Gingerbread dough
    (about ¼ quantity; see
    p.206 and p.238)

EQUIPMENT
Leaf plunger cutters (see
    directory, pp.308–9)

These leaves appear on my Chocolate Forest Cake (see p.135), Tree Trunk Cakes (p.120) and Giant Strawberry Dodger (p.230). They are a great way to use up spare bits of butter biscuit or gingerbread dough.

Roll out the dough between two sheets of baking parchment to the thickness of a 50-pence piece. Peel off the top layer of parchment and and cut out biscuit leaves with the cutters. Pull up the trimmings and re-roll them between more parchment, then cut more leaf shapes. Lift the biscuits, on the parchment, on to baking trays and chill for about 15 minutes.

Preheat the oven to 180°C/160°C fan/gas 4 while the biscuits are chilling. Bake for 5–8 minutes, depending on size and thickness, until golden brown round the edges. Leave the biscuits to firm up on the trays, then lift, still on the parchment, on to a wire rack to cool.

BISCUIT BUTTONS

MAKES 15 LARGE, 15 MEDIUM
AND 15 SMALL BUTTONS

FOR THE BUTTONS

About 330g Basic Butter Biscuits
or Basic Gingerbread dough
(about ½ quantity; see p.206
and p.238)

EQUIPMENT

For large buttons: 5.5cm round,
sharp cutter and 3.5cm
round cutter with blunt top

For medium buttons: 3.5cm
round, sharp cutter and
2.5cm round cutter with
blunt top

For small buttons: 2.5cm round,
sharp cutter

Cocktail stick

You can create a wonderful range of shapes and sizes of button from both
my butter biscuit and gingerbread doughs, as the photograph on pp.304–5
shows. I've given the method to make round buttons here, but be inspired by
your own button collection or sketch out designs from looking on the
internet, in textile-related books or in haberdashery departments.

Roll out the dough between two sheets of baking parchment to the thickness
of a £1 coin or up to 5mm thick, depending on the style of button you'd like.
Peel off the top layer of parchment and use your choice of cutters to cut out
shapes. Pull up and re-roll the trimmings between more parchment to cut more
buttons, or refrigerate or freeze for other designs.

Lift the discs, on the parchment, on to baking trays. If you've made a selection
of sizes, have all the smaller discs on one tray and larger/medium discs on
a separate tray as the smaller ones will take less time to bake.

To make each disc resemble a button, use the rounded, blunt side of the
smaller cutters to indent a circle on the dough's surface.

Create buttonholes with the cocktail stick or a bamboo skewer or the end of
a fine paintbrush handle. More button detail can be added by pressing tools,
such as wooden latte stirrers, rulers and knives, into the buttons. Transfer
the trays of biscuits to the fridge to chill for 15 minutes.

Preheat the oven to 180°C/160°C fan/gas 4 while the biscuits are chilling.

Bake for 5–15 minutes, according to size (see the tables on p.207 and p.239).
If you're using butter biscuit dough, the biscuit buttons should be lightly
golden brown round the edges; gingerbread should be a slightly richer golden
brown. Leave the biscuits to firm up on their trays for a few minutes, then
transfer, still on the parchment, to a wire rack to cool.

GINGERBREAD GIFT TAGS

MAKES 15 TAGS

FOR THE GIFT TAGS

About 220g Basic Gingerbread dough (about ⅓ quantity; see p.238)

About 15g white fondant icing

Honey or melted apricot jam

EQUIPMENT

Gift tag template (see below) or an actual gift tag, about 4.5 × 6.5cm

Plastic drinking straw, 7.5mm in diameter

1.5cm round piping nozzle

Fine paintbrush

Ribbons and/or string, to decorate

These can be attached to my Fruit Cake Parcels (see p.160), but also make a lovely present in a bundle on their own. You can leave them plain or stamp them using letter plunger cutters (see directory, p.308).

Roll out the dough between two sheets of baking parchment to the thickness of a £1 coin. Peel off the top layer of parchment and, using the template or gift tag, cut out your tags with a sharp knife. (You could also use a suitably sized cutter.) Pull up the dough trimmings and re-roll them between more parchment paper to cut more tags.

Lift the tags, on the parchment, on to a baking tray. If necessary, trim off the top corners of each tag with a knife to make the classic tag shape. Create a 7.5mm hole near one end with the end of the drinking straw or a pen lid. If you want to cut out shapes from the tags or stamp them with text, do it now. Chill for about 15 minutes.

Preheat the oven to 180°C/160°C fan/gas 4 while the biscuits are chilling.

Bake for 8–12 minutes or until golden brown around the edges. Leave to firm up on the tray, then lift, still on the parchment, on to a wire rack to cool.

To finish the biscuit tags, roll out the fondant on a sheet of baking parchment to a 2mm thickness. Use the 1.5cm round piping nozzle or a pen lid to cut out 15 circles. Use the paintbrush to apply a tiny bit of honey or jam to each biscuit tag around the cut-out hole, to act as glue, then place a circle of fondant on top. Use the drinking straw or the end of the paintbrush to push the fondant through the hole in the biscuit, leaving just a white border.

Leave to set before threading ribbon or string through the holes. Or leave the biscuit tags as they are and package them up with the ribbon or string.

GIFT TAG
TEMPLATE

GINGERBREAD RIBBON REELS

MAKES ABOUT 15 REELS

FOR THE RIBBON REELS

About 220g Basic Gingerbread
dough (about ⅓ quantity;
see p.238)

250g natural marzipan or
white fondant icing to make
lengths of ribbon, optional

EQUIPMENT

Reel template (see below) or
an actual ribbon reel, about
4.5 × 6.5cm

Ribbons, to decorate

Along with the Gingerbread Gift Tags opposite, these biscuit reels wound
with neutral or colourful ribbon make perfect partners for my Fruit Cake
Parcels (see p.160). Like the tags, they're also just as sweet given as gifts.
To 'reel-y' take the biscuit, you can wrap lengths of marzipan or fondant
around them rather than actual ribbon.

Roll out the dough between two sheets of baking parchment to the thickness
of a £1 coin. Peel off the top layer of parchment and, using the template or
ribbon reel, cut out your reels with a sharp knife. (You could also use a suitably
sized rectangular cutter plus a smaller one to cut out the indents.) Pull up the
dough trimmings and re-roll them between more parchment to cut more reels.

Lift the reels, on the parchment, on to a baking tray. Chill for about 15 minutes.
Preheat the oven to 180°C/160°C fan/gas 4 while the biscuits are chilling.

Bake for 8–12 minutes or until golden brown around the edges. Leave to firm
up on the tray, then lift, still on the parchment, on to a wire rack to cool.

Once cool, carefully wrap lengths of ribbon around your biscuit reels, securing
the end in place by tucking it under the wrapped ribbon.

If you want to use marzipan or fondant ribbons, roll out the marzipan or
fondant on a sheet of baking parchment to about a 1mm thickness. Use a sharp
knife or pizza cutter (a herb chopper with rotating blades also works well)
with a ruler to cut out long, thin, straight strips – 30cm lengths are ideal. Wrap
these around your biscuit reels and secure as above.

REEL
TEMPLATE

DIRECTORY

INGREDIENTS

HEALTHY SUPPLIES

healthysupplies.co.uk | **01273 660316**
Good variety of healthy and natural ingredients, many baking-specific. Stockist of freeze-dried blackberries used in **Edible Confetti** (see p.295)

HOLLAND AND BARRETT

hollandandbarrett.com | **0370 606 6606**
Comprehensive range of natural health products and ingredients, including 'Tropical Wholefoods' chewy dried banana slices used in **Banana Button Bites** (see p.55); the harder, crunchier 'Neal's Yard' banana chips for **Banoffee Tumbler Trifles** (p.52), **Banana-llama** (p.58) and **Edible Confetti** (p.295); and 'Neal's Yard' coconut flakes used in **Sweet Bombay Mix** (p.214)

MERIDIAN FOODS

meridianfoods.co.uk | **01962 761935**
Producer of the barley malt extract used in **Bourbon Brick Brownies** (see p.174) and **Malted Milk & Cookies** (p.182), as well as the natural date syrup used in the **fruit cake** recipes (pp.148–63) and the various nut butters as used in **Painter's Palette** (p.216)

SOUS CHEF

souschef.co.uk | **0800 270 7591**
Stockist of more unusual ingredients, including pistachio paste for **Fish & Chip Cakes** (see p.34) and freeze-dried raspberries and strawberries and slivered pistachios for **Edible Confetti** (p.295). Also stockist of edible gold leaf 'sheets' for **Edible Confetti** (p.295) and **Marzipan Tealights** (p.298)

WAITROSE

waitrose.com | **0800 188 884**
Wide range of baking ingredients, including 'Cooks' Ingredients' dark chocolate chunks for **Fair Isle Fruit Cake** (see p.156); 'Ndali' organic vanilla powder and 'Taylor & Colledge' vanilla bean grinder for **Fish & Chip Cakes** (p.34); 'Heston for Waitrose' popping candy for **Lolli-Popcorn Pops** (p.186); crystallised ginger pieces and 'Snapz' dried apple and pineapple crisps for **Edible Confetti** (p.295); and decorative chocolate and silver stars, balls and shimmer pearls for **See-in-the-dark Cake** (p.70)

WHY NUT

whynut.co.uk | **07879 658041**
Stockist of skinless pistachios that can be ground for **Wimbledon Cupcakes** (see p.31) and **Pistachio Marzipan** (p.287)

EQUIPMENT

ALAN SILVERWOOD

alansilverwood.co.uk | **0121 454 3571**
Family firm that manufactures high-quality essential bakeware, including cake tins, baking trays, moulds and cutters in a range of different sizes (see pp.17–18)

CAKES, COOKIES AND CRAFTS

cakescookiesandcraftsshop.co.uk | **01524 389684**
A wide range of bakeware, including 8 x 4cm 'Easy Bake' mini-loaf cases for **Sandwich & Toast Cakes** (see p.38) and **Hidden Carrot Cake** (p.76). Also cake-decorating supplies, including 'Sugarflair' tangerine/apricot food colour paste for **Sweet Beans or Hoops on Toast** (p.43), **Hidden Carrot Cake** (p.76) and **Terracotta Marzipan** (p.287)

CATER FOR YOU LTD

cater4you.co.uk | **01524 389684**
Wide range of equipment, including cake storage boxes, cupcake and muffin cases and cake-decorating products. Supplier of 1fl oz paper sauce pots for **Fish & Chip Cakes** (see p.34); 4oz rustic insulated (kraft ripple) paper espresso coffee cups for **Coffee Shot 'Cup' Cakes** (p.84); and 4oz hot drink paper espresso coffee cups for **Walnut Whippies** (p.86); also available from Amazon

COOKWARE ESSENTIALS

cookware-essentials.co.uk | **01923 510 193**
Stockist of all kinds of bakeware and cake-decorating supplies, including the mini fish-shaped cutter for **Fish & Chip Cakes** (see p.34)

DIVERTIMENTI

divertimenti.co.uk | **0330 333 0351**
Online stockist, with shops in London, of quality cookware, including springform tins, muffin and cupcake cases, storage boxes and cutters, including 'Kilo' maple leaf 5cm cutters used for **Chocolate Forest Cake** (see p.135) and **Biscuit Leaves** (p.300)

EDDINGTONS

eddingtons.co.uk | **01488 686572**
Fun, innovative and practical kitchen products, including display stands and cutters. Supplier of the squirrel cutter used for **Tree Trunk Cakes** (see p.120) and the 10cm heart cutter for **Giant Strawberry Dodger** (p.230); both also available from Amazon

FRED & FRIENDS

fredandfriends.com | **+1 (855) 739 1500**
American designer of innovative kitchen products. Supplier of the 'Cakewich' mould for **Sandwich & Toast Cakes** (see p.38); also available from Amazon

KITCHENCRAFT

kitchencraft.co.uk | **0121 604 6000**
Large selection of baking, sugarcraft and decorating equipment, including silicone spatulas and excellent cake tins made by 'Master Class'. Supplier of the following equipment used in this book:
- 'Kitchen Craft' 2cm spanner-shaped cutter for **Ginger Nuts & Bolts** (see p.250)
- 'Let's Make 9' numeral cutters and 'Let's Make 26' alphabet cutters for **Cloud Cut-outs** (p.210) and **Ginger Snap Cards** (p.248)
- 'Assorted mini-cutters', including hearts and clubs for **Ginger Snap Cards** (p.248)
- 'Master Class' 20cm loose-based heart-shaped tin for **Heart Beet Cake** (p.142)
- 'Master Class' biscuit and icing set (includes biscuit maker) for **Sweet Bombay Mix** (p.214)
- 'Sweetly Does It' message maker (letter plunger cutters) for stamping text on **Gingerbread Gift Tags** (p.302) and **Seedlings** plant labels (p.184)
- 'Sweetly Does It' curved modelling tool for **White Rabbit Cakes** (p.66)
- 'Sweetly Does It' set of 3 heart fondant cutters for **Heart Beet Cake** (p.142), **Strawberry Hearts** (p.224) and **Beetroot Hearts** (p.292)
- 'Sweetly Does It' set of 3 leaf fondant plunger cutters (2.5cm, 3cm, 4cm) for **Tree Trunk Cakes** (p.120),

Chocolate Forest Cake (p.135), **Giant Strawberry Dodger** (p.230) and **Biscuit Leaves** (p.300)
- 'Sweetly Does It' set of 3 snowflake fondant plunger cutters for **Winter Wonderland Cake** (p.124)
- 'Sweetly Does It' set of 3 star fondant cutters for **Gingerbread Baubles** (p.244)
- 'Sweetly Does It' large closed star icing nozzle for **Midnight Munchies & Hidden Gem Stars** (p.266)

KITCHEN RANGE COOKSHOP

kitchenrangecookshop.com | **01858 433533**
Family-owned company with a shop based in Market Harborough, Leicestershire, renowned for its eye-catching window displays. Online store sells baking products, including plunger cutters, cake pop equipment, piping bags and confectionery bags

LAKELAND

lakeland.co.uk | **01539 488100**
Huge collection of kitchenware, including essential and more creative products

NJ PRODUCTS

njproducts.co.uk | **01924 443763**
Suppliers of disposable cookware, such as 'Easy Bake' tulip muffin cases, brightly coloured muffin cases and black and white and foil mini-muffin cases

NORDIC WARE

nordicware.com | **+1 (952) 920 2888 (ext. 629)**
American kitchenware company known for speciality Scandinavian products. Supplier of the holiday tree bundt tin for the **Winter Wonderland Cake** (see p.124)

PAPERCHASE

paperchase.co.uk
customerservice@paperchase.co.uk
Useful for interesting paper, card, ribbons and general craft items that can be used to customise your bakes

VONSHEF

vonshef.com
Stockist of reasonably priced dehydrator, which is useful for drying out slices of fruit for decoration – see **toppings** recipes (pp.291–5) and **Banana Button Bites** (p.55), **Heart Beet Cake** (p.142) and **Strawberry Hearts** (p.224); also available from Amazon

CAKE STANDS, BOARDS & DISPLAY ITEMS

ABIGAIL BROWN

abigail-brown.co.uk | **07940 497488**
Artist and illustrator based in London, known for her beautiful bird sculptures, including the one photographed for the **Salty & Tweet Nest** (see p.188)

ANTHROPOLOGIE

anthropologie.eu | **00800 0026 8476**
Unique and colourful designer baking products, including aprons, measuring spoons and mixing bowls

BAGEL & GRIFF

bagelandgriff.com | **01858 468764**
Stockist of beautiful wooden stands and bowls, including the tree-trunk cake stands and wooden boards shown in photographs of the **Rustic Showstopper** (see p.106), **Tree Trunk Cakes** (p.120), **Chocolate Forest Cake** (p.135) and **Midsummer Night's Dream** (p.258)

CASSART

cassart.co.uk | **020 7619 2601**
Large range of good-quality art and craft materials

THE HAMBLEDON

thehambledon.com | **01962 890055**
Department store based online and in Winchester and Cowley Manor. Stockists of designer bakeware, including cake stands and moulds

HEALS

heals.co.uk | 020 7896 7451
Designer kitchenware, including the 'Jansen & Co' yellow cake stand photographed for the **Confetti Cupcakes** (see p.104)

HOP & PECK

hop-peck.myshopify.com | 01799 522737
Beautifully designed British handmade gifts made in Saffron Walden, England, including the wooden chopping boards in photographs of **Cheese Biscuits** (see p.240) and **Heart Beet Cake** (p.142)

JOHN LEWIS

johnlewis.com | 0345 604 9049
Wide range of good-quality baking equipment, gadgets, tins and accessories

KILNER JARS

kilnerjar.co.uk | 0151 486 1888
Twist-top and round clip-top jars – useful containers for **Edible Confetti** (see p.295)

LIBERTY

liberty.co.uk | 020 7734 1234
High-end department store based in Regent Street, London, and stockist of handmade tableware and floral stationery

LOOP KNITTING

loopknitting.com | 020 7288 1160
A knitter's heaven, with a shop based in Islington, London. Stockist of yarns, buttons and haberdashery bits and bobs

RAY STITCH

raystitch.co.uk | 020 7704 1060
Haberdashery, sewing patterns, fabric, ribbons and buttons available to purchase online, and from a store in Islington, London. Stockist of the tape measure ribbon shown in photograph around **Knit One, Bake One Cake** (see p.152)

SELFRIDGES

selfridges.com | 0800 123 400
High-quality cookware and speciality ingredients

SKANDIUM

skandium.com | 020 7823 8874
Scandinavian design and furniture company based in London, stockist of the Kay Bojsen wooden monkey shown in photograph of **Banoffee Tumbler Trifles** (see p.52)

VV ROULEAUX

vvrouleaux.com | 020 7224 5179
Ribbon shop based online and in southwest London

WASHI TAPES

washitapes.co.uk | info@washitapes.co.uk
Decorative masking tape, which is a versatile craft item useful for accessorising gift items, cake stands and cups, as photographed for the **Sweet Bombay Mix** (see p.215)

FLOWERS

SHRINKING VIOLET FLOWERS

shrinkingvioletflowers.com | 07802 894538
Creative florists known for unique floral designs, based in Essex. Their beautiful flowers are shown in the photographs of **Rustic Showstopper** (see p.106) and **Midsummer Night's Dream** (p.258)

INDEX

ACKNOWLEDGEMENTS

• •

Like the recipes themselves, this book has been the accumulation of lots of ideas and ingredients that have been brought together thanks to a team of incredible people, and the support and love of so many more.

First and foremost I'd like to thank my family and friends. Mum and Dad, thank you for allowing me the freedom to express myself, both in and out of the kitchen, from those very early flapjack-making days to the late-night baking sessions that followed. And to each of you in your own special way, I love and owe a great deal to Damian, Mary, Oliver and Patrick. Mary, Alex, Tash, Lou and Sinead, you girls are my rock, with or without cake. I've missed you all so much during these last months as my days have been taken up with flour and baking. Roisin, Sarah and Kate, my Market Harborough friends who have been there whenever I needed you and have provided laughter amid the mayhem and Maltesers! Paul, you've known when to pull me away from the kitchen when I badly needed to escape. Bourbon brownies will be for ever yours. Thank you Filipa, Jenny, Emma and Josh for the friendship and faith. Gemma, you truly are, and have been, a star. Bonnie, here's to a life in Technicolor. Janna, Andrea and Mauri, no amount of cinnamon buns will match your company, and Michael, thank you for being the London Canuck I can always call on. Tasha, as my cousin, fellow perfectionist and vanilla enthusiast, your commitment to me and the book has been 5*. And to Joey and Lou, one of whom I have known all my life and the other who has been especially supportive since coming into it, life wouldn't be the same without you. Ben, not only an incredible cousin but chef and confidant too. STP love. Clo, I'm grateful for the words, keys and owls!

Felicity, you are a wise and wonderful agent whose insight and shared love of food has reassured me throughout both our deliveries! And thanks to both Emmas at Curtis Brown, for all your assistance and baking. Bloomsbury, from the moment you sent me those paper-pencil flowers to designing the front cover of my first book around my 'spencil', you have been a publishing house to be proud of. Natalie, you have surpassed your role – not least for allowing me to build upon that coffee and walnut wall idea, and for being involved in more talk of nuts than any editor should have to be subject to. I am eternally grateful. Your clarity and calmness have been the pot of gold from the start of this book right through to the end of the rainbow (cake). Liz, you are a marvel. Not only have you managed the book, but have managed to manage me and my pie charts! Brownie points all round. Ali, from running with me and my ideas, to your meticulous testing, you are the publishing world's equivalent of a hidden gem star. Marina, you truly are a diamond. Sarah, the creative care, time and dedication you have given to my ideas and illustrations has been unbelievable. No amount of coconut milk can thank you enough for being just lovely. Nikki, your dedication to the puns, llamas and spirit of this book has been invaluable, and Norma, you have been a master at bringing together the grids, grams and endless queries regarding bakes and bananas. If I ever need a team member on Mastermind, you are getting that call!

And then there was method to the madness (and madness in the method) in those photoshoot days... that ran into nights! The endless mood boards and the memories created will be cherished and accompany me always – much like all the bags I carried with me to the shoots! Georgia, you are a photographer with not just humour and heart, but inimitable talent and a household to behold. Together with Bobby and Jen's incredible assistance, you have not only given the photographs focus, but injected a lot of fun as well. Tab, where would I be without my kindred giant-jam-sandwich-loving, neon-pink-elephant-spraying prop star? The conversations and crates of jars, paintbrushes and toy animals – not least that monkey – have been the cornerstone of this book. Emily, I have so much respect and spicy slipper love for you and your work, thank you for keeping me sane and smiling amid meringues and marzipan-making train journeys! Lorraine and Nicky, aka 'the girls', your flowers and commitment to the cause of cake has made you part of the team. Thank you for making the bakes and Georgia's house look like a Midsummer Night's Dream in the depths of winter. Abigail, you are not only a friend, but a talented feathered-friend-maker at that. The photograph of the finished Tweet Nest bake is one of my favourites, thanks to you. Kerry, your dedication to engineered baking is beyond brilliant. Susie, you and Cricut have quite simply been a cut above the best. Chloe and Dave, you bring not just bounce, but boundless creative enthusiasm and input to everything you do. Roy, you have not just tested recipes, but talked a lot of sense and taught me so much.

The neighbours who ate, aided and advised, I thank you and your taste buds. Thank you also to the Davis family for their ginger-cake-loving ways, especially Richard for his generosity of time; to the Eddys for taking both bakes and burdens off my hands; to the Pethericks whose style and support have been a constant inspiration; and to Heather and Nike for keeping me up and running throughout the marathon that was this book.

Thank you Jo and team for keeping me company with the music and mix-tapes during the hours in front of the worktop and laptop, amid my own recipe compilations and mix-bakes.

I owe Joules a special acknowledgement for employing me initially to encouraging me to follow both my passions: design and baking. You have provided me with friends, support and the creative spark behind so many of my initial baking creations.

And a big thank you to a certain Baker's Dozen – my *Bake Off* siblings – together with Dean and Claire! Without the baking challenges and the opportunity to work alongside such a brilliant group of people both on and behind the screen, this book might never have happened.

I also owe a heartfelt credit to the Kitchen Range Cookshop for providing me with not just the first secret squirrel cutter, but also a wealth of equipment and expertise. I certainly won't forget all those taste-testing times! I'd like to make a special mention to all the suppliers and producers who have so generously stocked my workspace: Alan Silverwood; Cadbury; California Prunes; Dorset Cereal; Doves Farm; Easy Bake Cases; Elizabeth Shaw; Green & Blacks; Heal's; Hop & Peck; Joe and Seph's; Kitchen Aid; Kitchen Craft; Meridian; Nielsen-Massey; Roberts Radio; Rude Health; Salter; Skandium; The Somerset Cider Brandy Company; Sous Chef; Tate & Lyle and Tiptree.

Finally, I'm sorry I've not been able to mention everyone who has tasted, tested and contributed in some form or another to these pages. I am instead crediting you as the book's secret ingredient (together with a certain secret squirrel). I thank you!

TO CATHERINE

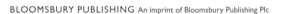

BLOOMSBURY PUBLISHING An imprint of Bloomsbury Publishing Plc

50 Bedford Square London WC1B 3DP UK
1385 Broadway New York NY 10018 USA

www.bloomsbury.com

BLOOMSBURY and the Diana logo are trademarks of Bloomsbury Publishing Plc

First published in Great Britain 2015

Text and illustrations © Frances Quinn, 2015
Photography © Georgia Glynn-Smith, 2015

Frances Quinn has asserted her right under the Copyright, Designs and Patents Act, 1988, to be identified as Author of this work.

British Library Cataloguing-in-Publication Data
A catalogue record for this book is available from the British Library.
Library of Congress Cataloguing-in-Publication data has been applied for.

ISBN: 978-1-4088-6238-4

2 4 6 8 10 9 7 5 3 1

Project editing: Norma MacMillan
Design and art direction: Sarah Greeno www.sarahgreeno.com
Photography: Georgia Glynn-Smith
Food editing: Nikki Duffy
Food styling: Frances Quinn and Emily Kydd
Prop styling: Tabitha Hawkins
Indexing: Hilary Bird

Printed and bound in Spain by Tallers Gràfics Soler

To find out more about our authors and books visit www.bloomsbury.com. Here you will find extracts, author interviews, details of forthcoming events and the option to sign up for our newsletters.

www.francesquinn.co.uk